The Syntax of

SPOKEN BRAZILIAN PORTUGUESE

Earl W. Thomas

Vanderbilt University Press   *Nashville*

© 1969 Vanderbilt University Press
Nashville, Tennessee

Fourth printing, 2000
ISBN 0-8265-1221-6
Library of Congress Catalogue Card Number 69-11280

To my wife,
who decided finally that the Portuguese language
was irresistible and learned it.

INTRODUCTION

PERHAPS the most important contribution of linguistic science to the teaching of foreign languages in the United States in recent years has been its emphasis on the teaching of the spoken language. Certainly in the present age of increased personal contact of Americans with peoples of all parts of the world, the relative importance of speaking ability as contrasted with the ability to read has increased enormously. The student of French or German, and to a lesser extent of Spanish, of fifty years ago was likely to read a great deal and to profit mostly from books written in those languages; but he was not likely to have a great deal of personal contact with the peoples who spoke them. Even when he did, his contact was often restricted largely to the most highly educated groups among those peoples—persons who, if they did not communicate with him in English, used a highly literary form of their native language and found the bookish form the American had learned both intelligible and appropriate.

Today, several factors have changed the situation greatly. Large numbers of Americans are in continual contact with other people of all nations, and with people of all classes within those nations. The reading of books has not decreased: on the contrary, it is much greater than ever before. But great numbers of Americans are involved in innumerable ways with the peoples of many countries, and in particular with the peoples of Latin America. There are so many today who must communicate directly with the people of Latin America that the spoken language must be given first importance.

The rapid leveling of social classes in many countries, or at least the blurring of the lines of separation among them, has eliminated much of the difference of language among the classes. Few parts of the earth have been affected more greatly than Brazil, where persons of considerable education today are unable to read with any facility some of their native authors of the beginning of this century. Different levels of speech do, of course, persist, but the degrees of separation are much smaller than they were even a generation ago.

In Brazil, as elsewhere, the teaching of the native language is carried out largely through the medium of normative grammar, which makes very little attempt to analyze the language as it is habitually spoken by the student but concentrates its attention on teaching him to use what is considered a better form of the language. It is the fashion today among students of linguistics to look with some scorn on normative grammar. Undoubtedly the criticism does have sound bases, particularly concerning the teaching methods of normative grammar. But normative grammar should not be dismissed as valueless; it makes an important contribution to national culture. It functions as a means of establishing a form of the language which is intelligible to all the people who use it as a vehicle of culture, and it prevents the language from breaking up into mutually unintelligible dialects. Normative grammar also allows the people of the present generation to read and understand the literature of the past. In Brazil, even more than in the United States, grammar has concentrated on this second function, to the extent that it has little relevance to the language spoken in Brazil today. However, the situation of the person who is learning the language of a foreign country is very different from that of the native speaker. He does not bring to the study of the language that intimate knowledge of the common spoken forms which, to the native speaker, is second nature. This spoken language holds within itself the most thoroughly national traits of the people who speak it—the ways of thinking, the cultural assumptions that are so universal they need not be expressed separately, the turns of expression, those subjects of conversation which often loom so important in the speech of one people but which another one hardly mentions.

This language that one learns in childhood is the real living tongue. The normative grammarians do not teach it and are often largely unaware of it, for both they and the students knew it to complete perfection long before they began the study of grammar. If he notices it at all, the grammarian observes this language only in those traits which differ from the literary language which he has studied, and he attempts to replace those traits with the more "correct" ones of his accepted norms.

The spoken form of a language is always more complex in its syntax and more difficult for the foreigner to learn than the literary form. The native speaker has learned it through an incredible amount of practice. He makes immediately, and without the slightest hesitation, choices among forms and constructions based on principles so tenuous and difficult of analysis that the most expert linguist never quite succeeds in explaining them clearly. The student of the language who has been exposed in similar fashion to another language, based on other principles, must of necessity analyze the new language. But unless he can acquire the same subconscious understanding of the new language that the native speaker has, he will always speak it more or less woodenly.

The literary form of a language is relatively easy to acquire, at least for the ordinary purposes of reading, after one has learned the spoken form. The student who can use the literary form of his own language with some facility and who is reasonably adept at speaking and understanding the popular spoken form of another needs expend little effort to read the literature of the second language fairly easily. And the increased understanding of that literature which he will gain from knowing the spoken language will more than compensate the relatively small extra effort.

In the Portuguese of Brazil, as in the languages of all countries of large populations, wide areas, and various levels of culture, there are several levels of language, as well as regional varieties. However, in Brazil the variety of types of language is rather limited, for several reasons.

Here, as in other American countries, the European settlements were made by people from all parts of the mother country. The varieties of speech which existed, and which still exist, in Portugal were mixed and combined into a more or less general speech in the colony. There was, of course, in the early colonial period, a speech characteristic of a limited class, which was, or tried to be, similar to that of the Portuguese court. But the speech of the ordinary folk of each region of the colony became more or less uniform. Certain differences developed among the various regions; these still persist to some extent, although within the last generation there has been a strong tendency toward uniformity.

After Brazil became independent, the feeling of nationalism that arose largely destroyed the earlier fashion of imitating the Portuguese way of speaking. The influence of formal education and the continuance of the class system for a long time perpetuated a considerable difference between the speech of the upper levels of culture and the lower ones. But during the present century a new middle class has arisen in considerable numbers and has brought with it a great deal of its own manner of speaking, so that the special language of the former upper classes has generally disappeared.

In this work, the basis for the statements concerning syntax is found in the speech of Brazilians of moderate or higher education. The language they speak is herein called **brasileiro falado**, abbreviated BF. The definition of this speech is necessarily somewhat arbitrary. It is recognized that almost no one uses the same type of language on all occasions. One's language varies with the occasion on which he speaks and with the people who compose his audience. All normal speakers, even those who are completely illiterate, are familiar with expressions more literary in character than those they normally use. Most speakers are also familiar with language of a cultural level lower than their own. Most speakers will on occasion speak on a level higher or lower than their more usual one.

We will, then, define BF as the language spoken habitually by Brazilians of moderate or higher education, on normal conversational occasions, to others of their own social and cultural level. The professors will not often use BF in the classroom or the lecture hall, but most of them will use it at home and with their friends. The priests will not speak thus from the pulpit, but most of them use it elsewhere. It will not be found in pure form on the stage, but the actors and the author use it among themselves. The purest speakers of BF, and the most trustworthy for purposes of checking, are found among the younger children of educated families. Until they have attended school long enough to become conscious of different ways of speaking and to acquire a feeling for the necessity of speaking "correctly" on certain occasions, these children speak BF quite naturally and unconsciously. Although they have heard other types of language and understood them, they have no reason to speak in any way except the one which is most natural to them.

There are among Brazilians, as among people from other nations possessing a higher culture, expressions, syntactic structures, words, etc., which they know directly or indirectly from literature, understand perfectly, even use when writing essays, books, poetry, etc., but never use in conversation. Such elements of the language are included herein at times so that a clear distinction can be made between literary Portuguese and BF. They are labeled literary (Lit).

There are other constructions which are also basically literary, avoided in normal informal conversation but used by speakers on certain occasions, e.g., in an informal talk before a group of people, in lecturing to students, in speaking in public to a person of a prominent position in culture, politics, or religion. Certain persons also seem to feel that their positions in life demand that they speak in a somewhat more literary style than is the custom among other educated persons. For example, a teacher of Portuguese, a writer, or a priest might speak in this fashion. Such expressions and constructions are likely to occur at times in the speech of most educated people. They cannot in all accuracy be labeled BF, but they are sufficiently used to make an acquaintance with them important to a student of the language. Such elements of the language are herein labeled semi-literary (SLit).

There are other expressions and constructions which are well known to all speakers of the language, used on occasion by a very large percentage of them, but always noticed by hearers who are even moderately educated and condemned by them as incorrect. Some such constructions are normal at the lower levels of speech and are noticed as incorrect only among those who speak a more nearly literary form of the language. Constructions of this type are labeled substandard (Subst). If, however, they are used only by uncultured speakers, they are labeled **inculto** (Inc).

In the literature of Brazil many expressions and constructions foreign to the speech of the country are used. Most of these are used in imitation of the Portuguese, among whom they are often normal in the spoken language. They are familiar to the Brazilians from their reading of Portuguese literature, or perhaps even from their contact with Portuguese immigrants in Brazil. At times it is necessary to refer to these in order to clarify the differences between Portuguese and Brazilian usage, or to specify that such expressions are not used in BF. Such expressions are labeled Lusitanian or Lusisms (Lus).

While little attention is given in the pages of the text to regional differences within Brazil, since relatively few of these differences are in the field of syntax, some regional usages have sufficient importance to require mention. They are labeled regional (Reg).

The slang of Rio de Janeiro is extraordinarily rich and varied. It is universal in the speech of the area, to the extent that the boundaries between slang and more formal language have been practically obliterated. Slang long ago penetrated even serious literature. It is heard in the lectures of the university professor and even from the pulpit. There are, of course, many types and levels of slang. Many expressions which were once considered to be slang unacceptable in serious conversation have now entered fully into the everyday language. Other expressions appear and disappear within a few years. Some types are specialized—used by students, the military, certain professions, or by the underworld. Slang does not often affect the structure of the language but is confined largely to unusual use of words, or to phrases which have special meanings in the context in which they are used. Those situations in which slang affects the syntactic structure are labeled herein **gíria** (Gir). If only the vocabulary is slangy, no reference is made to the fact.

It is sometimes necessary to distinguish clearly between current usage and obsolete or archaic constructions. Such constructions are met rather frequently in older books and a few even in the most recent ones. The texts for the study of the language, both in and out of Brazil, often devote a great deal of space to them without clarifying the fact that they are no longer a part of the modern language. Such constructions are labeled obsolete (Obs) or archaic (Arc).

A number of Brazilian scholars have attempted to demarcate speech areas within the country, but so far they have only been able to give some general indications. While certain regional traits are universally recognized, there has not been a great deal of research on regional speech. There are differences which anyone, Brazilian or foreign, who has traveled very widely in Brazil can recognize easily. They consist mostly of certain traits of pronunciation and of a certain amount of regional vocabulary. The boundaries between regions have never been studied in any detail. Such studies as have been made were chiefly concerned with the speech of the lowest levels of culture and tend to exaggerate the differences among regions. It is not known with any accuracy whether some of these regions are more or less uniform, or whether clearly defined subregions exist within them. In any case, the rapidly increasing mobility of the Brazilian population is weakening, if it has not already eradicated or moved, some of the boundaries among regions. Certainly the speech of the educated classes with which this study is concerned differs much less from north to south than the speech of the uneducated persons in those areas.

The variety of speech within the great territory of Brazil is amazingly small. No Brazilian has any difficulty in understanding, on first contact, the speech of any region of the country, if we make exception for the relatively small percentage of regional vocabulary. The Spanish of Argentina differs more from that of Chile, or the Spanish of Mexico City from that of Veracruz, than any two varieties of Brazilian Portuguese from one another. If we compare the regional literature of Rio Grande do Sul to that of Ceará, or of Amazonas, the difference seems to be fairly great. But such regional literature tends to insist on the differences and to make a special effort to include as much as possible of the vocabulary peculiar to its own area. Of course, the southern Brazilian is not familiar with the vocabulary which refers to plants, animals, and geographical peculiarities of the jungle, because those things themselves are almost totally strange to him.

The speech area on which this work is largely based is that one whose linguistic center is the city of Rio de Janeiro. Like all other regions, this one is characterized principally by certain features of pronunciation, some of them peculiar to the city itself, others common to the entire area. The region may be defined roughly as consisting of the states of Guanabara, Rio de Janeiro, Espírito Santo, and most of Minas Gerais. The southwestern part of Minas, roughly the part known as the Zona Sul, shows great similarity of speech to the state of São Paulo.

The most noteworthy characteristics of the pronunciation of this region are the affricate sounds (English *ch* and *j* respectively) which replace the traditional sounds of *t* and *d* whenever they are followed by the sound of Portuguese *i,* and the sound which is given to the *rr* phoneme. This phoneme varies considerably from place to place and from person to person, but throughout this region the point of articulation is in the back part of the mouth. The most usual sound is that of a voiceless velar spirant. It occurs initially in a word, between vowels when it is derived from a double *r*, and very often in final position in a syllable.

The speech of Rio itself is characterized, in addition to the general traits of the region, by frequent palatalization of the sibilants at the end of a syllable and by very frequent development of an *i*-glide between stressed vowels and following sibilants in the same syllable.

One of the most notable developments in the speech of Brazil in the last twenty-five years has been the rapid expansion of the typical speech of Rio de Janeiro through a large part of the country. There are several reasons for this. The cultural prestige of the city is doubtless one of the greatest. The influence of radio and, more recently, television has also been very considerable. Most network programs originate in Rio, and a majority of the well-known personalities of radio and television are either natives of Rio or have lived there and adopted the local speech. In addition, the educational system of the country has adopted the speech of Rio as the standard of language for the schools. While this fact undoubtedly enhances the prestige of **carioca** speech, the influence of other factors is probably much greater.

The greatest influence which leads to the spread of the speech of Rio is probably the mystique of the "Marvelous City" itself. Those who go to Rio almost immediately begin to speak like **cariocas**. Those who leave it (and they include only those who cannot avoid leaving it) never lose the characteristic **linguajar carioca** and even pass it on to children who have never been there. There are cities in the interior of the State of São Paulo which, twenty-five years ago, were strongholds of the **caipira** dialect handed down from early colonial times. Today, most of the people of those cities speak like natives of suburban Rio.

The materials used in the body of this book were collected over a period of more than twenty-five years. At the time that I became interested in the study of Portuguese, there were no textbooks in English on the Portuguese language which accurately analyzed even literary Portuguese, whether of Brazil or Portugal. Even a limited amount of reading made it evident that such books as existed were often at error even in reference to some of the most basic principles of the language. It soon became clear that accurate information on the subject, especially on the spoken language of Brazil, could only be acquired in direct contact with the people of the country.

Since then I have spent about ten years in daily contact with Brazilians; I have spent more than three of those years in Brazil. Of course, I have used the written word a great deal. Works written in the more or less popular vein—folk literature, plays, magazines, comic strips, children's stories, newspaper articles—all kinds of written works have been studied, analyzed, noted down, and compared and contrasted with the spoken word. But no principle of language stated herein is based on any written work, except those considered literary or semi-literary. My main use of the analysis of the written language was to find and classify constructions for the purpose of checking against the spoken language.

The system of syntactical analysis and the terminology used in this work are traditional. Both of them have been subjected to considerable criticism in recent years. There is no doubt that both of them suffer from serious defects. However, there is as yet no new system of syntactical analysis which is familiar to the educated public—in fact, none which is generally accepted by linguists. Until a new system has been created and its terminology has become familiar to most students of language, a work using such new system and terminology would be extremely difficult to use. However inexact and even illogical traditional terminology may be, it is intelligible to almost any student of language, whether his training be in traditional grammar or modern linguistics.

The language of a very large number of individuals was used as the basis of this study. In very many cases, I caught expressions from chance encounters, individuals met or heard in crowds, on the street, in cafés, etc. However, I collected a large part of the material from some thousands of individuals with whom I came in contact, about a third of whom I knew well enough to have some accurate knowledge of their education and background. The great majority of them had completed secondary education, and a very substantial part of them held, or were working on, university degrees. Included in this classification are children from homes in which the parents had completed secondary education or gone beyond it. I met most of the ones I did not know personally in circumstances in which one might confidently expect them to have secondary education: they held

positions in which education would be an almost automatic requirement, or I met them in the company of, or in relation to, other persons of this cultural class. While I took a good many notes from the
speech of chance acquaintances or of persons who were totally unknown to me, I checked such notes again in other circumstances.
No one, however, was ever asked for his opinion on such matters or
whether he himself used a particular construction. In fact, on a
number of occasions Brazilians stated with conviction and evident
sincerity that they never said such and such, although they had said
that very thing only moments earlier in the course of the same conversation.

Of course, I made considerable efforts to meet and listen to persons
of lower cultural levels—servants, unskilled laborers, beggars, etc.
The language of such persons differed considerably in vocabulary
from that of the more cultured classes, but syntactic differences were
relatively few. The speakers were more careless in their pronunciation, less able to use many words correctly, and less likely to use
syntactic constructions of a literary character. But the difference was
mainly a question of less variety of construction, although there are
certain syntactic forms peculiar to uncultured language.

I have made no attempt in this study to count constructions or
to gather any statistical data on them. The decision against this is
not based solely on the difficulty of doing it but on the firm belief
that, even if it were done, it would have little validity. If we were
to take such a feature as the use of the definite article with the
possessive adjective, for example, we could arrive at a figure to show
that the article is used a certain percentage of the time and omitted
a certain percentage of the time. Such information would be of no
value, since its use or omission is of no significance and is purely
optional, except in a few specific cases. If we were to take the use
of the subjunctive and of the infinitive after **dizer** in the meaning
"to order," the statistics would be of no importance. What significance there is lies in the social and literary situation. It is important,
of course, to state whether one construction is used more frequently
than another, if the difference is considerable, and whether one is
more literary, more socially acceptable, or more specific than another.
I have done this whenever there is a clear preference. Beyond this,
I feel that statistics would be no less subjective than the present work,

only more arbitrary. There are Brazilians of all levels of culture, including persons who are totally illiterate, who like to fill their conversation with literary and archaic words, phrases, and even verb tenses. If this were accepted as normal by others, it might very well be included as a part of spoken Brazilian. However, as a matter of fact, the great majority of Brazilians consider such speech absurd and ridicule it. The speech of such persons deserves no consideration as a part of the usual spoken language.

The examples used herein are, except in the relatively few cases that are noted, taken from actual conversation. That is, the part of the example which illustrates the point under discussion is quoted from conversational Portuguese, except where otherwise labeled. However, it has been necessary in a good many cases to add something to the example, in order to give context. In others I preferred to modify names and circumstances in another part of the sentence, in order to avoid mentioning actual persons, events, etc. The names used in the examples are real Brazilian names, although they usually do not refer to actual living persons.

My work on the spoken language of Brazil was begun with the help of an Exchange Fellowship granted under the Convention of Buenos Aires, and under an arrangement between the University of Michigan and the Brazilian government. The final stages were carried out in 1965–1966, through a fellowship granted by the Social Science Research Council, a grant from the Graduate Center for Latin American Studies at Vanderbilt University, and a semester's sabbatical leave granted by Vanderbilt University. The work was continued as possible during the intervening years in three visits to Brazil and with the numerous Brazilian students who have been on the Vanderbilt campus during the last twenty years. I wish to express my warmest gratitude to the institutions which have made possible a large part of my residence in Brazil and to the very large number of Brazilians who have given their time and effort to my work and whose only reward has been to know that an American was interested in their language, their culture, and their country.

CONTENTS

ABBREVIATIONS

Arc	**Arcaico**, archaic.
BF	**Brasileiro falado**, spoken Brazilian.
Gir	**Gíria**, slang.
Inc	**Inculto**, uncultured language.
Lit	**Literário**, literary language.
Lus	**Lusismo**, form or construction used in Portugal, not in Brazil.
Obs	**Obsoleto**, obsolete.
Reg	**Regionalismo**, regional speech.
SLit	**Semi-literário**, semi-literary language.
Subst	Substandard.

The Syntax of SPOKEN BRAZILIAN PORTUGUESE

ORDER OF DECLARATIVE SENTENCES

§1. Standard order. The usual order of a declarative sentence is subject, verb, and direct object or nominative complement, with the indirect object varying in position in relation to the direct object. There is, however, a considerable amount of freedom in varying this order, although less in Portuguese than in Spanish, and less in BF than in the literary language. The same practices are followed in subordinate clauses as in main clauses, with the exception noted in §3b below.

> **Um homem alto e moreno abriu a cancela para mim.**
> A tall, dark man opened the gate for me.

§2. Change of position of the subject. The subject may be placed after the verb in certain situations.

a. To emphasize the subject. The position following the verb gives greater emphasis to the subject. This change is not often necessary, since a considerable amount of emphasis can be given to a subject, whether noun or pronoun, without a change of order.

> **Passaram por ali uns trabalhadores.**
> Some workers passed through there.
> **Já que não vou eu, sigam estas palavras.**
> Since I am not going, let these words be sent.

Very short sentences are particularly liable to shift of order, with added emphasis on the subject.

> **Aqui estou eu.**
> Here I am.
> **Já se foi o tempo das mulheres caseiras.**
> The time of the wives who stayed at home has passed.
> **Chegou a hora.**
> The time has come.
> **Lá vêm êles.**
> There they come.

3

b. With the verb **ser**. With an expression used to identify persons, the subject, whether noun or pronoun, follows the verb **ser**.

Quem esteve aqui esta tarde?   —**Fomos nós.**
Who was here this afternoon?   It was we.
Quem bate na porta?   —**Sou eu.**
Who is knocking at the door?   It is I.
Quem levou a porta?   **Foram os carpinteiros.**
Who took away the door?   It was the carpenters.

c. To avoid opening a sentence with an unmodified noun subject. Such subjects are often placed after the verb, especially if they may be replaced at the beginning by an adverbial phrase.

De vez em quando apareciam casas ao longo da estrada.
From time to time, houses appeared along the road.

However, more often than not, such unmodified subjects open the clause.

Bois passeiam na rua.
Oxen stroll down the street.
Mulheres passavam com crianças no colo.
Women passed with children in their arms.

d. To allow a reflexive verb to precede. The reflexive verbs are especially likely to open a clause. If the verb is singular, the noun is probably felt as an object, rather than a subject. Frequently the noun is not at all emphatic.

No céu só se vê uma nuvem branca.
In the sky only one white cloud is seen.
Deve-se respeito aos enfermos.
One owes respect to the sick.
Aqui se pode tocar uma música alegre.
Here one may play a gay piece of music.

Perhaps by analogy with such sentences as these, reflexive verbs are often followed by nouns which are clearly subjects, as the agreement may demonstrate.

Na Europa fabricam-se móveis antigos.
In Europe, antique furniture is manufactured.

e. With **ao** and the personal infinitive. The subject follows regularly in this construction, which is semi-literary.

Ao chegarmos João e eu, a festa já acabava.   SLit
When John and I arrived, the party was already ending.

f. With a perfect infinitive. The subject may precede or follow the auxiliary without emphasis, but follows if it is emphatic.

Foi ótimo ter seu filho ganho uma bolsa.
It was excellent that your son won a scholarship.

g. With certain verbs. Some verbs are nearly always followed by their subjects. In some cases the verb receives more emphasis than the subject; in others the situation is reversed. Most of the verbs express either an affirmation or a denial of existence. Possibly the order is affected by expressions in which **haver** and **ter** are used impersonally, and in which the noun is the object of the verb, rather than the subject. Some of the common verbs of this type are the following:

Existir	**Existem homens capazes de matar até as aves canoras.** There are men capable of killing even song birds. **Não existe tal ilha.** No such island exists.
Faltar	**Falta aqui uma peça desta máquina.** One part of this machine is missing here. **Faltam dez para as cinco.** It is ten minutes to five.
Sobrar	**Quase acabamos com as panquecas; só sobraram duas.** We almost finished off the pancakes; only two are left. **Tudo está acabado, e sobrou argamassa.** Everything is done, and there is some mortar left.
Ficar (*In the sense of* **restar**)	**Do passado só ficou a lembrança.** Of the past, only the memory remained.
Aparecer	**Já começam a aparecer os palpites sôbre a próxima corrida.** Hunches on the next race are already beginning to show up. **Naquela época já apareciam os primeiros carros.** In that period the first cars were already appearing.
Surgir	**Por tôda parte surgiam boatos acêrca dêle.** From all sides there appeared rumors about him.
Sumir	**Sumiu a bola que eu tinha guardada aqui.** The ball that I had put here has disappeared.

h. In parenthetical expressions identifying the speaker. In quotations of speech, thought, etc., the parenthetical expressions which identify the person concerned usually state the verb before the subject. If the identification follows the quotation, the same order is normal but much less frequent if it precedes the quotation.

—É verdade, diz ela, que não me dou bem com êle.
"It is true," she says, "that I do not get on well with him."
—Você tem que limpar os sapatos, gritou êle para mim.
"You have to clean your shoes," he shouted to me.

§3. Inversion of the direct object. The direct object is inverted—placed before the verb—much less frequently than the subject. Even more rarely are both subject and object inverted. The object is inverted:

a. To give it unusual emphasis.

Langosta eu como, caranguejo não.
Lobster I will eat, but not crab.
Você quer fazer um bolo? Ah, isso eu sei fazer.
Do you want to bake a cake? Ah, that I can do.
Barulho é fácil. Barulho eu faço. (*Or* Barulho faço eu.)
Noise is easy. *I* can make noise.
Nessa região não existem árvores, mas mato rasteiro há.
In that region there are no trees, but there is low scrub.

b. When the object is a relative pronoun. In this case the object must necessarily precede the verb.

Aquêle é o homem que eu vi no bar.
That is the man whom I saw in the bar.

§4. Order of the indirect object. The indirect object is always expressed by a prepositional phrase when it is a noun, and more often than not when it is a pronoun. Like any other prepositional phrase, these expressions can vary their order in the sentence somewhat. They may be placed before or after the direct object, sometimes with another phrase or an adverb between them. They most often follow the direct object. But for special emphasis, the indirect object may precede the verb.

Vai lá e oferece uma bolacha ao tio.
Go over there and offer your uncle a cookie.

Dei a João um bom par de luvas.
I gave John a good pair of gloves.
Aos amigos êle dá um preço especial.
To his friends he offers a special price.
Vendo a fruta barato aos fregueses fiéis.
I sell the fruit cheap to regular customers.

§5. Change in order of the nominative complement. The shift of the nominative complement to a position before the verb is even rarer than the shift of the direct object. It is used in literary or poetic style and in conversation in which there is considerable emotional content.

Inteligente, não digo que o Clóvis seja, mas sabido êle é.
I don't say that Clovis is intelligent, but he is clever.

§6. Change in the order of the complementary infinitive. The infinitive may be placed before the verb upon which it depends, to express unusual emphasis on the infinitive.

Duvido que você possa fazer isso, mas tentar, pode.
I doubt that you can do that, but you can try.

§7. Sentence reconstruction. In order to place strong emphasis on a logical subject, object, or nominative complement, the entire sentence is often reconstructed, with the addition of a short clause when it is needed. This means is employed frequently to emphasize **me** and **nos**, which cannot be stressed.

Você diz que toma a responsabilidade, mas quem vai ficar falado sou eu. (*For* . . . mas eu vou ficar falado.)
You say that you will take the responsibility, but I am the one who will be talked about.
Não pode botar a culpa em mim, foi êle que deixou o copo cair. (*For* . . . êle deixou, etc.)
You can't put the blame on me; it was he who dropped the glass.
Não sou eu que você vai beijar, vai beijar a mãe. (*For* **Não vai me beijar,** etc.)
You are not going to kiss *me*. Go kiss your mother.
Quem fêz todo o serviço fui eu. (*For* **Eu fiz todo o serviço.**)
I'm the one who did all the work.

§8. For the order of interrogative sentences, see §478.
§9. For the order of exclamatory sentences, see §486.

THE NOUN

The forms of the noun

§10. The Portuguese noun expresses number and gender, but never case. Gender is generally inherent in the word itself, fixed by usage, and may or may not be revealed by the form or meaning of the word. Nouns are limited to the masculine and feminine genders. Number is indicated by the form or, in cases in which there is no separate plural form, by the article, possessive adjective, demonstrative adjective, etc. The usage of the noun, revealed in Latin by its case, is indicated only by the syntax of the sentence.

Syntax of number in the noun

§11. Use of the singular for the plural. In several cases BF uses the singular form where the plural might be expected.

a. With indefinite adjectives. Indefinite adjectives of quantity and the accompanying nouns are nearly always kept in the singular, even though logic would demand a plural form. The plural may be used but is comparatively rare.

> **Existe tanto homem neste mundo de Deus.**
> There are so many men in this great world.
> **Êle sabe muita coisa.**
> He knows a great many things.
> **Quanto carro há na rua hoje.**
> How many cars there are on the street today.
> **Que há de novo?**   **—Pouca coisa.**
> What is new?   Very little.

b. Distributive use of the singular. When each person of a group performs an act with or upon one article, part of the body, etc., the singular is usually employed. If each one uses or acts upon two or more, the plural is used.

> **Vão todos lavar a cara.**
> You are all going to wash your faces.

8

Todos os homens deixaram o carro em casa.
All the men left their cars at home.

c. Nouns singular by nature. Certain nouns are regularly used in the singular, except in very limited circumstances. Others, formerly used generally in the plural, are now widely used in the singular.

Há muita gente na rua.
There are many people on the street.

Tenho uma casa feita de tijolo.   *Cf.* **dois tijolos.**
I have a house made of brick.   two bricks.

Todo brasileiro come feijão.   *Cf.* **Plantam vários feijões.**
Every Brazilian eats beans.   They raise several kinds of beans.

Eu comprei uma calça.   *Cf.* **Um terno com duas calças.**
I bought a pair of pants.   A suit with two pants.

A cinza do cigarro caiu no chão.
The ashes of the cigaret fell on the floor.

Bom dia, rapaz.
Good morning, fellow.

d. Singular in proverbial use. In proverbs the singular is often used in a general sense, without an article. In imitation of this, such statements are very frequently used in BF. The plural may also be used, with a definite article.

Pássaro voa, peixe nada.
Birds fly, fish swim.

Eu gosto de cachorro.
I like dogs.

Gato persegue rato.
Cats chase rats.

e. Plural of family names. A family name is usually kept in the singular, but with a plural article, to refer to all members of the family. If the name is such that it is easily pluralized, and there is no probability of confusion, the plural may be used.

O senhor Lemos, os Lemos
Mr. Lemos, the Lemoses

O senhor Carvalho, os Carvalho *or* **os Carvalhos**
Mr. Carvalho, the Carvalhos

f. Loss of plural inflection. In substandard Portuguese, there is a widespread tendency to indicate number only with the article or other determinative, leaving all words following—the noun and any adjectives—in the singular. While persons of even moderate education avoid this, it is found among the uneducated in all parts of the country.

> **Lá tem umas brincadeira interessante.**   Inc
> There are some interesting amusements there.
> **Êle tem quatro filho menor.**   Inc
> He has four smaller children.
> **Eu gosto dêstes dia bonito.**   Inc
> I like these pretty days.
> **Lá vinha um major com dois capitão.**   Inc
> There came a major with two captains.
> **Êle tinha idéias meio comunista.**   Inc
> He had ideas that were somewhat communistic.

Syntax of gender

§12. Gender recognizable by form. In general, nouns which terminate in -u and -o (not including -ão) and -me are masculine, while those which end in -a, -z, -ice, -ise, -ção, and -dade are feminine. There are exceptions in each case. The other endings do not indicate the gender.

§13. Gender determined by meaning. Regardless of ending, nouns which denote a male person are masculine, and those which refer to a female person are feminine, with certain exceptions.

> **O guarda, o profeta, a soprano, a modelo**
> The policeman, the prophet, the soprano, the model

a. Animate nouns of fixed gender. A few nouns denoting persons have fixed gender, regardless of the sex of the person.

> **A criança, o bebê, a criatura, a testemunha, a vítima, o chefe, o individuo**
> The child, the baby, the creature, the witness, the victim, the boss, the individual

b. Names of animals. The names of many animals have only one gender, which includes both sexes. If a distinction of sex is needed, it is made by adding the nouns **macho** or **fêmea** after the name of the animal.

> **Pegamos a onça macho, mas a fêmea escapou.**
> We got the male jaguar, but the female escaped.

O jacaré fêmea é tão feroz como o macho.
The female alligator is as ferocious as the male.

§14. Nouns which may be of either gender. Many nouns referring to persons, which do not end in **-o** in the masculine form, change gender by changing the article only.

O colega, a colega
The colleague
O cliente, a cliente
The client
O mártir, a mártir
The martyr

§15. Gender of nouns ending in **-a**. Although the ending **a** generally indicates that the word is feminine, there are a great many of these words in Portuguese, and especially in Brazilian Portuguese, which are masculine.

a. Words of Greek origin. These words occur in several European languages. If they refer to persons, they vary in gender according to the sex of the person. Most of them end in **-ista**, **-ta**, or **-ma**.

Artista, florista, pirata, jesuita, tema, cinema, mapa
Artist, florist, pirate, Jesuit, theme, movie, map

Perhaps because of **a grama**, "grass," popular speech uses **duzentas gramas** when speaking of the weight. But **o quilograma** is universal.

b. Feminine nouns which become masculine in certain cases. Many nouns which are basically feminine become masculine when they take a special sense referring to a male person.

O corneta, o guarda, o cabeleira, o cabra
The cornet-player, the policeman, the long-hair, the mulatto

c. Words of other origins. Many words ending in **-a**, but masculine, have been added to the vocabulary in Brazil. Some are taken from Tupi, some from African languages, some are slangy deformations of other Portuguese words.

O caçula, o sósia, o pinóia, o anhanguera, o carpina, o portuga, o penetra
The youngest child, the double, the weakling, the devil, the carpenter, the Portuguese, the gate-crasher

d. Words ending in stressed **-a**. These words are normally masculine. The number of such words has been increased very greatly in

Brazil by additions from the Tupi Indian language and from African languages.

> **Xará, vatapá, caroá, guará, cará, carcará, ganzá, maracá, maracajá, cajá, piritá**
> Namesake, a typical dish of Bahia, a plant, a wild dog, a plant, a bird, a musical instrument, a maraca, a wildcat, a fruit, a bird

Many of these words are regional, but others are in common use in all parts of the country.

§16. The masculine plural used to include both genders. If the feminine word is formed on the same root as the masculine form, the masculine plural may be used to include persons of both genders. This is also true in some cases, when the roots are different, but in others it is not. The following may include either all masculine persons, or persons of both genders.

> **Os pais, os tios, os filhos, os compadres, os primos, os meninos, os garotos**
> The parents, the uncle and aunt, the children, the godfather and godmother, the cousins, the children, the boys and girls

But "grandparents" is **os avós**, the feminine plural **as avós**, and some use a masculine plural **os avôs**.

The following plurals include only male persons: **os rapazes** (the boys), **os guris** (the boys) (feminine singular: **a rapariga, a guria**).

The noun used as a modifier

§17. Nouns used as adjectives. As a general rule, a noun may not be used as an adjective to modify another noun directly. In some cases, such as with adjectives of nationality, origin, religion, etc., the same word may be used as either, but it retains its adjectival quality as a modifier of a noun. However, in a number of cases a noun may modify another directly.

a. Nouns ending in **-ista**. Any such noun may be used as an adjective.

> **A viuva florista tem uma loja na Rua do Ouvidor.**
> The widowed florist has a shop on Ouvidor Street.

b. Two nouns which form a compound noun. There are many expressions (and others may be freely invented) in which two nouns occur one after the other. They form a kind of compound noun, but the second describes or modifies the first. The main stress is on the second, as if it were an adjective. Examples include:

O **homem macaco, pedra sabão, bolo mármore, uma mulher dama, pedra ímã**
The ape-man, soapstone, marble cake, a prostitute, loadstone

c. Nouns of direction. The points of the compass may be so used in the singular, after a noun referring to a geographical region.

A zona sul, a região leste
The South Side, the Eastern Region

d. Geographical names. Names of streets, avenues, squares, lakes, rivers, etc., consist of the class-word plus the name directly, when the name is derived from a proper noun. Other nouns used as names usually require a preposition, but there is much variation. Usage of capitals in the class nouns differs.

Avenida Rio Branco, Rua Barão de Jaguaribe, Lagoa Rodrigo de Freitas, Praça Tiradentes, Rio Amazonas, etc.
Rua do Catete, Praça da República, Rio das Mortes.

e. Nouns used as titles. Titles precede names directly.

D. Helder Câmara, Dona Adelaide, Senhor Garcia, Senador Tavares, a Senhora Pires.

f. Epithets used with names. Epithets usually require the preposition **de** before a name or a noun referring to the person. This construction is especially frequent in name-calling. Apposition may also be used in many cases.

O cachorro do Nicolau me fêz uma safadeza.
That dog Nicholas played a dirty trick on me.
A porca da empregada nunca lava o chão.
That pig, the maid, never scrubs the floor.
Aquêle bandido Olavo fugiu com o dinheiro da empresa.
That bandit Olavo ran away with the company's money.

§18. Nouns forming an adjectival phrase. The usual way of expressing the adjectival use of a noun is by means of a phrase formed of a preposition and the noun, with no article. In the great majority of cases, the preposition is **de**. In a few cases, another preposition is used for greater clarity. The phrase follows the modified noun immediately. Any other adjective which modifies the noun must follow the phrase.

> **Uma perna de mesa.**
> A table leg.
> **Uma casa de roceiro branca.**
> A countryman's white house.
> **Um dia de verão.**
> A summer day.
> **Um copo para água.**
> A water glass.

§19. Nouns in apposition. A noun in apposition with another is usually parenthetical, and the intonation is appropriate for parenthetical expressions.

> **O senhor Borges, chefe da repartição, está de férias.**
> Mr. Borges, the office boss, is on vacation.

A few expressions consist of a noun or pronoun followed by the noun in apposition without pause, with stress on the second, as if it were an adjective. This is especially true of names followed by the profession where the article has been lost. The name of the profession is used as if it were a name.

> **Eu menina colhia muitas flores.** (*More often* **em menina . . .**)
> As a girl, I picked many flowers.
> **Pedro barqueiro, João canoeiro.**
> Peter the boatman, John the canoeist.

Use of nouns in the sentence

§20. The noun as subject. In this usage, the noun presents no problem.

§21. The noun as nominative complement. In this situation, if the noun is unmodified, it is treated as an adjective. The indefinite article is omitted regularly in this case, sometimes even if the noun is modified. See §59.

> **A Dra. Sálti é pediatra.**
> Dr. Salti is a pediatrician.

§22. Nouns used as direct objects. As direct object of the verb, the function of the noun is revealed in most cases solely by its position in the sentence. It may be displaced in certain cases to a position preceding the verb, provided the sentence remains clear. In the following example, the fact that the subject also precedes the verb clarifies the first part, but the second part is liable to misunderstanding.

Carlos, João conhece, mas a irmã não.
John knows Charles, but not his sister.

Such sentences are generally avoided, although they may be heard in conversation in which the context clarifies the meaning.

The preposition **a** before direct objects is found to a limited extent in literature. In BF, it is confined to a very limited use with pronoun objects and with nouns referring to God. These are mostly fixed expressions which persist in usage, but they are not felt as establishing a pattern for noun objects. This construction is never used to clarify the function of a noun. For further details, see §63k.

Só posso louvar a Deus.
I can only praise God.
Era tão ruim que desafiava a Deus e ao mundo.
He was so evil that he defied God and the world.

§23. **Nouns used as indirect objects.** As the indirect object of the verb, the noun is always expressed with a preposition, either **a** or **para**. Both are used in BF, with preference for the second.

Li a carta para minha mãe.
I read the letter to my mother.
Mandei o relatório ao juiz. (*Or* **para o juiz.**)
I sent the report to the judge.

§24. **Adverbial use of noun phrases.** A noun phrase without a preposition may be used adverbially in any of three ways.

a. It may express extent of space.

Andamos três quarteirões.
We walked three blocks.
Viajamos várias léguas.
We traveled several leagues.

b. It may indicate the time of an action.

Eu vi você o outro dia.
I saw you the other day.
Estivemos em casa domingo passado.
We were at home last Sunday.

c. It may indicate duration of time.

O passeio durou duas horas.
The trip lasted two hours.
Fiquei quinze dias em São Paulo.
I stayed two weeks in Sao Paulo.

Other parts of speech used as nouns

§25. Several other parts of speech may be used as nouns. In many cases they have developed into pure nouns, and only the identity of forms reveals the origin of the noun.

a. Adjectives used as nouns. Almost any adjective may be used substantively, accompanied by an article or other determinative.

Os grandes, êstes cegos, os intocáveis
The grownups, these blind men, the untouchables

b. The infinitive is essentially a verbal noun and often loses its verbal force completely, becoming a pure noun.

Eu quero ver teu sapatear.
I want to see your tap-dancing.
Eu moro no quarto andar.
I live on the fifth floor.

c. Some adverbs may be used as nouns.

Meu bem, você gosta de mim?
Darling, do you love me?
Dá o fora.
Get out!
Êsse "ai" saiu do coração.
That "oh" came from the heart.

d. Substantivized words and expressions. This phenomenon is very common in conversational language. Any word or phrase may be thought of as an abstract noun.

No "ora, veja," eu não prestava atenção.
When he said "Hey, look," I wasn't paying attention.
Você deve pôr os pontos nos "ii."
You should dot your *i*'s.

THE DEFINITE ARTICLE

The forms of the definite article

§26. Spelling and pronunciation. The forms of the definite article are: **o, a, os, as**, representing the two genders and two numbers. The vowel of the masculine forms is pronounced like final **o**, that of the feminine like stressed **a**. The fact that the singular articles consist of a single vowel, while the plural forms begin with a vowel, is of considerable importance. When these vowels come in contact with like vowels in speech, the two tend to fuse into one, so that there is no longer an audible, separate vowel of the article. In addition, the masculine article, when followed by any other vowel, tends to lose its syllabic value and become a semivocalic **w**. When the article is no longer audible, it tends to be lost as a necessary part of the sentence. Some of the irregularity of the use of the article in Portuguese is probably due to this fact, for there is some tendency for the article to disappear in phrases in which it would be audible, by analogy with those in which it is not. Examples of loss of the article in speech follow.

Written:	*Pronounced:*
Na alma	nalma
In his heart	
Para a avenida	pravenida
To the avenue	
Todo o mundo	todumundo
Everybody	
Vejo o rato	vejurrato
I see the rat.	

§27. Contractions with prepositions. Partly for the reasons given above, and partly for historical reasons, the definite article forms numerous contractions with various prepositions, some of them represented in writing, others not.

a. With **de: do, da, dos, das,** obligatory and written.

b. With **por: pelo, pela, pelos, pelas,** obligatory and written.

c. With **em: no, na, nos, nas,** optional in both writing and speech, but nearly always used in both.

d. With **a: ao, à, aos, às,** obligatory and written. The masculine forms are pronounced with the diphthong **au,** while the feminine forms are indistinguishable from the article alone.

e. With **para: pru, pra, prus, pras,** not indicated in writing, but universal in speech, except that no contraction is made when the expression refers to a future period of time, e.g., **para o ano,** with the meaning **no ano que vem** (Next year).

f. With **com:** No written contractions are used today, although they were frequently written in the past. In speech, this preposition forms combinations with the masculine forms of the article pronounced **cõu, cõus.** The feminine forms may remain intact or may contract in rapid speech to **kwã, kwãs.**

g. In titles of newspapers, books, articles, etc. The article is usually not combined with a preceding preposition in writing, or, if this is done, the article is used twice.

> **Eu li isso no "O Globo."**
> I read this in the *Globe.*

BF disregards this rule entirely, contracting here as elsewhere.

> **Eu li isso no "Globo."**

Use of the definite article

The use of the articles is less fixed and regular in Portuguese than in most European languages. There is considerable variation in usage, both in the literary language and in BF. In addition, it is often idiomatic, used in certain expressions, but omitted in others which would seem to require the same construction. The definite article is used:

§28. With nouns in series. The article is usually placed before each noun, if there is more than one.

> **O pai e a prima do menino são louros.**
> The father and the cousin of the boy are blond.

But there are some cases in which it may be omitted after the first noun.

a. In an enumeration. Especially if there are several items, the article may be omitted before all, or the speaker may desist early in the list.

Quero os sapatos, meias, chapéu, casaco e luvas.
I want the shoes, socks, hat, coat, and gloves.

b. If the nouns are synonyms. If the nouns are different appellations referring to the same person or thing, only the first article is used.

Êle é a glória e orgulho da mãe.
He is the glory and pride of his mother.

c. When clarity does not require repetition. In familiar conversation, where there is no probability of misunderstanding, the second and subsequent articles may be omitted.

Êsses buracos quebram as molas dos carros e caminhões.
Those holes break the springs of the cars and trucks.

§29. With plural nouns modified by singular adjectives. If the noun is accompanied by two or more adjectives, each of which refers to only one individual of the class signified by the noun, the noun is plural, but the adjectives are singular. In this case, the article agrees in number with the word which follows it immediately.

O govêrno quer ajudar a pequena e média indústrias.
The government wishes to help small and medium industries.
O govêrno quer ajudar as indústrias pequena e média.
The government wishes to help small and medium industries.
Êle fala as línguas francesa e portuguêsa.
He speaks the French and Portuguese languages.

§30. To make noun reference specific. The definite article helps to identify the individual of the class named by the noun, concerning which some statement is made. This identification may be clarified in various ways.

a. Reference to a known individual. It may indicate the particular specimen of a class which has some relation to the person or persons concerned, and which they readily recognize.

Eu vou à cidade.
I am going downtown.
Êle assiste à escola.
He attends school.

Exception: Before the word **casa**, when it refers to the residence of the speaker or of another person mentioned, the article is omitted.

Êle está em casa.
He is at home.
Quer ir para casa comigo?
Do you want to go home with me?

b.   Reference to future clarification. The reference may be made specific by a limiting expression to which the article calls attention.

Esta é a casa de meu amigo.
This is my friend's house.

c.   Reference to previous mention. It may make the noun reference specific by referring to previous mention.

Era uma vez uma raposa. A raposa gostava muito de comer coelhos.
Once upon a time there was a fox. The fox liked very much to eat rabbits.

§31.   With nouns referring to the entire class. The definite article is used with nouns which refer to all individuals of a class, including them in a generalization. As the complement of the verb, the noun is often in the plural.

O gato é o inimigo dos ratos. (*Or* **do rato.)**
The cat is the enemy of rats.
Você ajuda as plantas a crescer. (Singular not possible.)
You help the plants to grow.

As the subject, the noun and article are usually in the singular.

O cachorro é o bom amigo do homem.
The dog is the good friend of man.

But note the following exceptions:

a.   Partitive use. If the noun may be interpreted as referring to only some, not all, of the specimens of the class, Portuguese tends to do so and to omit the article. Thus, Portuguese omits the article very frequently in cases in which it would be required in other Romance languages.

O delegado se recusou a permitir jôgo na cidade.
The police chief refused to permit gambling in the city.
Festas são raras por aqui.
Parties are rare around here.

Êle gosta muito de louras.
He likes blondes a lot.

b. Proverbial construction. The traditional form of the proverb expresses the general noun in the singular, without an article. Modern expressions in imitation of this style are in very frequent use in colloquial Portuguese.

Cachorro não gosta de gato.
Dogs don't like cats.
Silêncio segue barulho.
Silence follows noise.
Pássaro voa, peixe nada.
Birds fly, fish swim.

§32. With abstract nouns. Abstract nouns are generally accompanied by the article if they are used in a general sense. But if there is any partitive sense, in that only some of the quality is meant, the article is omitted.

A natureza é cruel na selva.
Nature is cruel in the jungle.
Não há qualidade mais importante que a bondade.
There is no quality more important than kindness.
Os oficiais juraram fidelidade ao presidente.
The officers swore loyalty to the president.
Êle tinha pena de criaturas assim.
He was sorry for such creatures.

§33. With unique nouns. The article is used before many nouns referring to something of which there is only one, including parts of the world or the universe. In some cases, although there may be more than one, the noun deals with the class as if it were one thing.

Certo cearense morreu e foi direto para o céu.
A certain native of Ceará died and went straight to heaven.
O mar está bravio.
The sea is wild.
Que será que os discos voadores querem na terra?
What do you suppose the flying saucers want on earth?
Se êle estivesse no paraíso, queria voltar para o Rio.
If he were in Paradise, he would want to return to Rio.
O tempo está abafado hoje.
The weather is sultry today.

§34. With the names of meals.

Já tomou o café da manhã?
Have you had breakfast?
É a hora da merenda.
It's time for lunch.
Êle saiu depois do jantar.
He went out after dinner.

§35. With the names of languages.

O português é a língua do Brasil.
Portuguese is the language of Brazil.
Não há língua mais bonita que o italiano.
There is no language more beautiful than Italian.

a. Omission in adjectival phrases. It is omitted after such words as **professor, texto,** etc., when used with the preposition **de,** to form an adjectival phrase.

Eusébio se prepara para professor de inglês.
Eusebio is studying to be an English teacher.
Perdi meu livro de alemão.
I lost my German book.
But:
Êste livro foi traduzido do inglês.
This book was translated from English.
A palavra "abajur" vem do francês.
The word "abajur" comes from French.

b. Omission after **falar,** etc. The article is omitted after the verb **falar.** If the name of the language is separated from the verb, the article may be used or omitted.

Você fala português.
You speak Portuguese.
Fala-se inglês na Austrália.
English is spoken in Australia.
Êle fala muito bem (o) português.
He speaks Portuguese very well.

It is also nearly always omitted in BF after several other verbs denoting intellectual or sensory activity: **escrever, entender, compreender, saber, ouvir, aprender, estudar, decorar,** etc.

Êle escreve francês bem.
He writes French well.

Fulano acha que sabe francês.
So-and-so thinks he knows French.
Estou estudando russo.
I am studying Russian.

c. Omission after **em**. The article is omitted after the preposition **em**.

O livro é em português.
The book is in Portuguese.

d. Use and omission if the language is modified. If the name of the language is modified, either after the verbs mentioned in (b) or after **em**, the article may still be omitted, unless we are speaking of the language as spoken or written by a certain person or group of people. In this case, the article is used.

Tivemos que ler português arcaico.
We had to read archaic Portuguese.
Êle fala (o) inglês dos Estados Unidos.
He speaks the English of the United States.
O professor quer que escrevamos o português de Camões.
The teacher wants us to write the Portuguese of Camoëns.
Você compreende o português dos caipiras?
Do you understand the Portuguese of the hillbillies?

§36. With names of beings of a supernatural, mythical, or folkloric nature. Even when these are used as proper names, the article is used.

Que foi que o Saci fêz?
What did the Saci do?
O Quimbundo vem aí.
The Quimbundo is coming.
Acho que êle tem parte com o capeta.
I think he has a pact with the devil.

§37. With names of persons. Either the given name or the surname of a person known to both speaker and hearer, or previously identified by the speaker, is frequently preceded by the definite article. It is always optional.

Onde está o José hoje?
Where is Joe today?
Já viu o Magalhães?
Have you seen Magalhães?

Era um menino chamado José; o José era um garoto muito levado.
There was once a boy named Joe; Joe was a very mischievous boy.

a. Omission with names of unknown persons. If the person is not recognized to be known to the hearer and has not been mentioned previously, no article is used.

Você conhece Eduardo Ribeiro?
Do you know Eduardo Ribeiro?

b. Omission with names from the past. The article does not accompany names of persons from the past, unless the names are modified.

Vamos ler um romance de Alencar.
We are going to read a novel by Alencar.
Temos os contos do velho Machado.
We have the short stories of [the great] old Machado.

c. Use with family names. The article is used in the plural with a family name, to refer to the entire family. The surname may or may not take a plural form.

Devíamos visitar os Macedo(s).
We should visit the Macedos.
Você conhece a casa dos Magalhães?
Have you ever been in the Magalhães's house?

d. Use with names of famous persons. The article is used in the plural form before the name of a famous person with the meaning "people such as." The name itself is kept in the singular.

Não podemos comparar êste autor com os Dante, os Shakespeare. Lit
We cannot compare this author with people like Dante and Shakespeare.

§38. With certain titles. These include the usual social titles and those derived from the professions.

O Sr. Mendes não está em casa.
Mr. Mendes is not at home.
O Dr. Trigueira foi nomeado juiz.
Dr. Trigueira was named judge.
No tempo do Padre Cícero, muita gente ia a Joazeiro.
In the time of Father Cícero, many people went to Joazeiro.

O professor Nascentes leciona na Universidade.
Professor Nascentes teaches at the University.
O coronel Barbosa já saiu do quartel.
Col. Barbosa has already left the barracks.

a. The article is omitted in direct address.

Senhor Pereira, como vai o senhor?
Mr. Pereira, how are you?

b. Sporadic omission. It is occasionally omitted elsewhere, especially with professional titles.

Padre Antônio ontem foi posto em liberdade.
Father Antonio was set free yesterday.
Bispo Câmara fez aos jornais a seguinte declaração.
Bishop Camara made the following statement to the papers.
Senhor Bispo ficou na cabeceira da mesa.
The Bishop sat at the head of the table.
Eu vi Dr. Peres.
I saw Dr. Peres.

c. Omission with certain titles. The article is always omitted with certain titles: **frei, santo, dom, dona.**

Frei Caneca ganhou muita fama.
Friar Caneca won great fame.
Santo Antônio é oficial do exército.
St. Anthony is an officer of the army.
A imprensa falou com D. Hélder Câmara.
The press spoke with D. Helder Camara.
Dona Maria é a esposa do Senhor Tavares.
Maria is the wife of Mr. Tavares.

d. Omission with words of relationship. It is omitted with nouns of relationship used as titles.

Tia Ana foi morar conosco.
Aunt Anne went to live with us.
Mãe-preta contava histórias de assombrações.
Mammy told stories of haunted places.

e. Omission with foreign titles. These do not take the article, when they are used in Portuguese.

Quase todos estavam torcendo por Miss Mato Grosso.
Almost everybody was rooting for Miss Mato Grosso.

Eu queria falar com Madame Paixão.
I should like to speak to Madame Paixão.

f. Use with appellations. It is used with appellations which follow the names of famous persons, nicknames, etc.

Manuel o Afortunado.
Manuel the Fortunate.
Sancho o Maior.
Sancho the Great.

But it is omitted with **magno.**

Alexandre Magno.
Alexander the Great.

Nor is it used with ordinal or cardinal numbers with the names of kings, popes, etc.

D. Pedro Segundo.
Peter the Second.
João Vinte e três.
John the Twenty-third.

§39. With geographical names of countries, regions, etc. It is used with some, but omitted with others.

a. The names of most countries take the article.

Êle mora no Brasil.
He lives in Brazil.
Qual é a população da França?
What is the population of France?

b. The following countries do not take the article: **Portugal, Cuba, Haiti, Guatemala, Honduras, Nicarágua, Costa Rica, Panamá, Israel.**

Êstes melões vieram de Portugal.
These melons came from Portugal.

c. With divisions of a country. The names of provinces, states, and other territorial divisions of a country are subject to no general rule; those of which Brazilians speak constantly have each its own rule, others may vary from one speaker to another. Thus we have, in Brazil: **O Rio Grande do Sul, o Paraná, a Guanabara, o Espírito Santo, a Bahia, a Paraíba, o Rio Grande do Norte, o Ceará, o Piauí, o Maranhão, o Pará, o Amazonas, o Acre, o Rio Branco,** but, without the article, **Santa Catarina, São Paulo, Minas Gerais, Pernam-buco, Alagoas, Sergipe, Goiaz, Rondônia, Fernando de Noronha.**

In Portugal, all provinces except **Trás-os-Montes** ordinarily take the article. In Spain, the following take it: **A Andaluzia, a Catalunha, a Biscáia, a Galiza, as Astúrias.**

In referring to states or provinces of other countries, usage is some-what uncertain, but sometimes attains surprising uniformity.

> **Na Califórnia, na Flórida, no Alaska**
> **Em Tennessee, em Nova Iorque, em Puerto Rico**

d. With names of cities. Names of cities take the article in only a few cases. Most do not, even if the name includes an adjective, or takes an article in the language spoken in the city.

> **Eu já estive em Havana, em Nova Orleans, em Nova Friburgo, em Háia.**
> I have been in Havana, in New Orleans, in Nova Friburgo, in The Hague.

The following are exceptions: **O Rio (de Janeiro), o Cairo, a Corunha, o Crato, o Pôrto.** Usage with Recife varies: **Recife, o Recife.**

e. Modified geographical names. If the name is modified, either by an adjective within the name itself (except in the case of cities), or by an adjective or phrase outside the name, the article is usually employed.

> **Os Estados Unidos, a Cuba colonial, a Lisboa da Idade Média,** (*But* **Lisboa Antiga.**)
> The United States, colonial Cuba, the Lisbon of the Middle Ages, Old Lisbon

§40. With geographical features. These require the article in most situations, excluding enumerations and use on maps.

a. Names of rivers. These are preceded by the masculine article, whether or not the word **rio** is used.

> **O Rio Amazonas, o São Francisco, o Plata, o Mississippi, o Nilo**
> The Amazon River, the São Francisco, the Plata, the Mississippi, the Nile

b. Lakes, seas, bays, gulfs, and mountains. These take the article and generally also retain the classifying word.

O Lago Salgado, a Lagoa Mirim, o Golfo do México, a Serra do Mar
Salt Lake, Lake Mirim, the Gulf of Mexico, the Serra do Mar

c. Names of oceans. These take the article, but often drop **oceano.**

O Oceano Atlântico, o Pacífico
The Atlantic Ocean, the Pacific

d. Cities named for geographical features. When a city is named for a geographical feature, the article may be dropped from the name and the usage may be extended to the feature itself.

Passamos Cabo Frio, onde fica a cidade de Cabo Frio.
We passed Cape Frio, where the city of Cabo Frio is located.

e. Names of streets, avenues, etc. These are accompanied by the article.

A Avenida Rio Branco, a Rua Joana Angélica, o Passeio Público, o Parque do Flamengo
Rio Branco Avenue, Joana Angelica Street, the Public Park, Flamengo Park

f. With names of buildings.

O Catete, o Palácio Mônroe, o capitólio
The Catete Palace, the Monroe Palace, the capitol

§41. With the cardinal points. There is some variation, but in general the article tends to be used with **norte** and **sul,** and the combinations which begin with a form of these words, but not with **este (leste)** and **oeste.** See §513.

Este de Samoa, a leste das montanhas, rumo a oeste, para o norte, ao sul do equador, rumo ao nordeste
East of Samoa, east of the mountains, westward, toward the north, south of the equator, toward the northeast

§42. With many expressions of time. See §504.

§43. In place of possessive adjectives. When the possessor is the subject of the clause, the possessive adjective is almost universally replaced by the article. In the third person there is no possessive adjective in BF, since **seu** is reserved for the modern second person subjects. See §145 ff.

Elas ficaram adormecidas nos quartos.
They remained asleep in their rooms.

O ladrão levantou os braços.
    The thief raised his arms.
Êle trouxe o carro.
    He brought his car.
Êle puxa ao pai.
    He takes after his father.
Você já vendeu a casa?
    Have you sold your house?
O Sr. Pires veio com a esposa.
    Mr. Pires came with his wife.
Vou tirar os sapatos.
    I am going to take off my shoes.

a. Clarification of an article used for possessive. If a third-person possessive does not refer to the subject, or the reference is not otherwise clear, the article is used, but clarified by a phrase which follows the noun.

Eu vou no carro dêle.
    I am going in his car.

b. The article for "one's." The article may refer to an impersonal, unexpressed subject, and is equivalent to "one's." It may also have this meaning when the subject is expressed but is not a person.

É importante proteger a saúde.
    It is important to protect one's health.
O frio entrava pelos ossos adentro.
    The cold penetrated one's bones.

c. With possession expressed by the dative. The article may denote possession by a person expressed as an indirect object pronoun, rather than by the subject. However, this pronoun is used mostly to express "dative of interest," i.e., the person concerned in the action, and is not used solely to identify the possessor.

Eu lhe quebrei uma perna.
    I broke his leg.
Me aperta a mão.
    Shake my hand.

Since a reflexive contributes no added meaning either as a dative of interest nor to identify the possessor, it is not used in such cases.

Eu lavei as mãos.
    I washed my hands.

§44. The article is used in some cases before a noun of quantity. It follows an expression of price or other word implying rate. This use has become rare but survives in a few expressions.

Custam mil cruzeiros o cento.
They cost a thousand cruzeiros a hundred.
Comemos três vezes ao dia. (*Usually* **por dia.**)
We eat three times a day.

§45. With infinitives, in certain cases. See §268c.

§46. With the possessive adjectives and pronouns. See §147.

§47. With nouns or substantivized words in adverbial phrases. These expressions are very numerous, but often the use or omission of the article seems to be arbitrary. Many such expressions with the article are paralleled by others without it.

Outros aderiram ao depois.
Others joined later.
O chapéu tem abas curtas na frente e atrás.
The hat has a narrow brim in front and behind.
Você vai na frente e segue sempre para frente.
You go first and keep going.
Êles têm sete filhos, ao menos. (*Or* **pelo menos.**)
They have seven children, at least.
Êle vai chegar atrasado, na certa.
He is going to get in late, for sure.
Quem está na cama ao lado?
Who is in the bed next to yours?
Há um senador na casa do lado.
There is a senator in the house next door.
Saiu em direção ao curral. (*Or* **na direção do curral.**)
He left toward the corral.
Ouvia música ao longe.
He was hearing music in the distance.
Não quero você aqui. Dá o fora.
I don't want you here. Get out.
Tomaram-lhe a cesta à fôrça.
They took her basket by force.
Vamos progredindo aos trancos e barrancos.
We are progressing by jerks and jolts.
Estamos ganhando aos poucos.
We are gaining little by little.

Omission of the definite article

The article is omitted:

§48. In designating personal physical features. In describing a person, the article is not used before a noun referring to physical features, followed by a descriptive adjective.

> **Êle tem olhos azuis.**
> He has blue eyes.
> **Gonçalves usa barba comprida.**
> Gonçalves wears a long beard.
> **A môça ostentava cabelo ruivo que caia até a cintura.**
> The girl was showing off red hair which came to her waist.

But if it represents the possessive adjective, or if the adjective is predicative, the article is used.

> **Com a barba comprida, êle parece caricatura de santo.**
> With his long beard, he looks like a caricature of a saint.
> **O pé, descalço e ferido, manchava o chão.**
> His foot, bare and hurt, stained the ground.

It is generally used otherwise, with expressions combining a noun of physical features and an adjective, but is omitted idiomatically in many cases.

> **As orelhas grandes do menino chamavam a atenção.**
> The boy's big ears attracted attention.
>
> **Cabelo liso como eu nunca vi, . . .**
> **Lá vai ela e pensa que é mulher.**
> > **—Cançao.**
> The smoothest hair I ever saw, . . .
> There she goes, thinking she is a woman.
>
> **Agora êle deu para usar cabelo pintado.**
> Now he has taken to having his hair dyed.

§49. With a noun in apposition.

> **Eu já estive em Cuiabá, capital de Mato Grosso.**
> I have been in Cuiabá, the capital of Mato Grosso.
> **O capitão, comandante do destacamento, só chegou pela tarde.**
> The captain, the commander of the detachment, arrived only in the afternoon.

But the article may be used if the speaker wishes to specify the noun as the only one of its class, or otherwise define it more specifically.

> **Esta é D. Nair, a filha do coronel.   (=Filha única.)**
> This is Nair, the daughter of the colonel.   (Only daughter.)
> **Carlos, o primo louro do gerente, apareceu na porta.   (Outros primos não são louros.)**
> Charles, the manager's blond cousin, appeared in the doorway. (Other cousins are not blond.)

§50.   After **todo** in the singular. The article is inaudible, of course. As a result, it has been largely abandoned in writing. It is generally used in the plural, although some expressions may omit it.

> **Todo mundo sabe disso.**
> Everybody knows that
> **Êle perdeu tudo que possuia.**
> He lost all he owned.
> **Todos os outros já partiram.**
> All the others have already left.
> **Eu já vi todos (os) dois.**
> I have seen both of them.

§51.   After **tocar, passar, ter, dar,** before many nouns. But if the noun is a specific example of the class, the article is used, according to §30.

> **Ela toca piano, e êle violão.**
> She plays the piano, and he the guitar.
> **É proibido tocar buzina.**
> It is forbidden to blow your horn.
> **Passei pito nêle.**
> I gave him a bawling-out.
> **É preciso passar vassoura neste quarto.**
> It is necessary to run a broom through this room.
> **A caixa tem forma de livro.   (*Or* a forma.)**
> The box has the shape of a book.
> **A expressão dêle dá idéia de um homem amargurado.**
> His expression gives one the idea that he is an embittered man.
> **Ela tocava o piano lá de casa.**
> She played the piano at our house.
> **É proibido tocar a buzina dêste carro.**
> It is forbidden to blow the horn of this car.

§52.   After the verb **jogar,** before the name of a game. It is not used in general before the name of a game, unless it is modified. There are, however, some exceptions.

Você gosta de jogar cartas?
Do you like to play cards?
Basquete é o esporte mais popular naquele estado.
Basketball is the most popular sport in that state.
O jôgo de futebol, o jôgo do bicho, o jôgo da queda de braços
The game of soccer, the animal lottery, Indian wrestling

§53. Before nouns followed by postpositions. The words **acima, abaixo, adentro, afora, adiante, atrás** are classified as adverbs but often act as postpositions, i.e., exactly like prepositions, except that they follow the noun. This usage must be distinguished from the purely adverbial usage in, e.g., **anos atrás**. The postpositional usage is not very frequent in BF and only slightly more so in the literary language.

O bote seguiu rio acima.
The boat went on upstream.
A casebre escorregou ladeira abaixo.
The hut slid down the hill.
Eu voltei caminho atrás.
I backtracked.

THE INDEFINITE ARTICLE

The forms

§54. Pronunciation of the indefinite article. The forms are **um, uma, uns, umas**. The masculine singular is pronounced as a single nasal vowel. This sound is frequently lost in combination with other vowels. Nor is it sufficiently different from the definite article for easy distinction. Both facts undoubtedly affect the syntax of the articles.

The feminine forms have the same vowel as the masculine, in their first syllable. In BF, the consonant **m** is often lost. These forms are quite old, appearing in classical Portuguese as **u'a, u'as**. Some persons today maintain that the consonant should be dropped before a word with initial **m-**, thus avoiding confusion between such pairs as **um mamão** and **uma mão**. Modern newspapers tend to write **u'a** in such cases. However, there is no regularity of usage in BF. One may hear either form before any word, although there is a somewhat greater tendency to drop **m** before a word which begins with it.

To distinguish the article from the number **um**, the article is always unstressed; the number **um** is always stressed.

§55. Contractions with prepositions. The indefinite article forms contractions with certain prepositions, some of them recognized in writing, some not. All such contractions are optional, but they are almost universal in BF, whether written or not.

a. With **de**: it forms written contractions, **dum, duma**, etc. In the speech of Rio this form is quite rare. In its place, one hears another form. The consonant of the preposition becomes an affricate similar to English *j*, and absorbs the following vowel. In other areas of Brazil, where the affricate pronunciation is not used, the traditional contraction is often heard, or the words may be left separate.

b. With **em**: it forms **num, numa**, etc., which are nearly always used, rather than the complete forms.

34

c. With **para**: the contractions are not written, except in attempts to imitate colloquial speech. However, the contractions **prum**, **pruma**, etc., are practically universal in speech. The number **um** does not contract with this preposition, although it may with the preceding ones.

d. With **com**: the contraction is no longer written, although the classic writers often wrote **co'um** or **c'um**. Contrary to the case of the definite article, the indefinite one usually carries the stronger vowel in the combination, so that the contraction usually sounds **kwum**, **kwuma**, etc.

e. With **por**: it does not form contractions, each word maintaining itself entire.

Use of the indefinite article

This article is even less regular in its use than the definite one. It is extremely idiomatic, and often by its use or omission very subtle shades of difference can be transmitted. It is used:

§56. Before a noun not previously referred to. The noun has not been identified by the speaker, is not clearly identified at the moment of first reference, and is not assumed to be identifiable by the hearer.

> **Vi uma môça de bikíni na praia.**
> I saw a girl in a bikini on the beach.

§57. Before each noun in a series.

> **Um homem e uma mulher.**
> A man and a woman.

If two or more nouns are synonyms, or refer to the same person, the article is not repeated.

> **Êle é um comerciante e político natural de Duque de Caxias.**
> He is a merchant and politician, a native of Duque de Caxias.
> **Quero apresentar um meu amigo e camarada.**
> I want to introduce a friend and comrade of mine.

§58. Use of the plural forms. The plurals of the indefinite article are comparatively little used. They express a degree of indefiniteness intermediate between their omission and the use of **alguns**.

> **De uns dias para cá, êle anda macambúzio.**
> For the last few days he has been downcast.

a. They are used to express approximate amount.

Isto deve custar uns vinte contos.
This must cost about twenty thousand cruzeiros.

b. They are usually omitted elsewhere.

Tôdas as noites, mulheres passavam na rua.
Every night, women passed along the street.
Bois passeiam no pasto.
Oxen walk about in the pasture.
Eu vou lhe dar parabéns.
I am going to congratulate him.

Omission of the indefinite article

It is omitted:

§59. Before an unmodified noun used as a nominative complement. With nouns denoting profession, class, religion, nationality,
etc., the omission is regular. With other nouns the article is generally used, but there are many cases of omission. Sometimes the
noun is not actually a nominative complement, but the meaning is
equivalent. E.g., dar para, dizer-se, estudar para, considerar take
objects of verb or preposition, but the basic meaning is equivalent
to "to be," or "to become."

Êle é doutor.
He is a lawyer.
Duas insolações e êle ficou brasileiro.
Two sunstrokes and he became a Brazilian.
A Rosa deu para protestante.
Rose ended up a Protestant.
**Êle insistiu no contrário, considerando cristão só aquêle que obrasse
bem.**
He insisted on the contrary, considering that a Christian was only
one who performed good works.
Meu filho está estudando para médico.
My son is studying to be a doctor.
É lástima que você não ganhasse.
It's a shame you didn't win.

a. Omission before a modified noun. Sometimes, even when the
noun is modified by an adjective or a phrase, the whole expression
is felt as a noun complement and the article is omitted.

Eu queria ser bom fazendeiro.
I'd like to be a good farmer.
Êle era general do exército.
He was a general of the army.
Essa era regra da casa.
That was a rule of the house.

b. Use before a modified noun. The article is more often used when the noun is modified. The sense is at times somewhat more concerned with identification than description, but often there is little or no difference.

Jorge é um conservador empedernido.
George is a dyed-in-the-wool conservative.

§60. After negatives. The article is omitted, although the number **um** may be used.

Não posso viajar sem carro.
I can't travel without a car.
Meu tio não tem filho.
My uncle doesn't have a son.
Êle chorou que nem bebê.
He cried worse than a baby.
Às vezes me sinto sem um amigo. (Número.)
At times I feel I am without a friend.

But if the negation applies only to the subject or the verb, rather than to the noun concerned, the article is used.

Ninguém viu um homem que estava de pé na porta.
Nobody saw a man who was standing in the doorway.
Eu não quis comprar um carro que êle me mostrou.
I refused to buy a car that he showed me.

§61. Before an unmodified noun object in questions. It may be used or omitted here, with little difference in meaning.

Você tem carro?
Do you have a car?
O senhor procura (uma) casa?
Are you looking for a house?

§62. Before nouns denoting an indefinite quantity. This is the partitive construction, which is normally expressed in Portuguese by the omission of all articles.

Eu quero açúcar.
　I want some sugar.
Eu senti pena dela.
　I felt sorry for her.
Ela saiu com roupa de ver a Deus.
　She went out in her go-to-meeting clothes.
Ela deu bolo nêle.
　She stood him up.
Quem casa quer casa.
　When one marries, he wants a home.

§63. With the possessive adjective. The omission gives the meaning of "any," the use of the article is equivalent to "a certain."

Mulher minha não sai sòzinha à noite.
　A wife of mine won't go out alone at night.
Uma amiga minha é professora secundária.
　A friend of mine is a secondary school teacher.

§64. With **cem** and **mil.** It is used with **milhão.** With **outro,** it may be used or omitted, with little or no difference in meaning. With **certo** the article makes the noun less indefinite. It is usually omitted.

O atacadista mandou cem camisas e mil pares de sapatos.
　The wholesaler sent a hundred shirts and a thousand pairs of shoes.
A população da cidade está chegando perto de um milhão.
　The population of the city is approaching one million.
Não fui eu; foi (um) outro.
　It wasn't I; it was somebody else.
Certo caipira foi à cidade.
　A certain hillbilly went to the city.
Eu trouxe isto para uma certa pessoa.
　I brought this for a certain person.

§65. At the beginning of titles of books, etc. It is omitted before such words as **tratado, capítulo, método, sistema,** etc. However, if the first word does not refer to the type of book or treatise, the article may be used.

Novo método de ensinar línguas.
　New Method of Teaching Languages.
Um homem em busca da solidão.
　A man in search of solitude.

§66. Before the name of a means of locomotion, after a preposition. The preposition is **a** before **cavalo, bicicleta,** and **pé**, in other cases **de**. The same situation prevails before the names of vehicles used to transport objects, after **por**.

> **Viajamos de trem, de navio, de carro, de ônibus e de avião.**
> We traveled by train, by ship, by car, by bus, and by plane.
> **Êle montou a cavalo.**
> He rode on horseback.
> **Mandamos o embrulho por avião.**
> We sent the package by plane.

§67. With the second object of a verb of calling. The noun which designates what the person is called is preceded by **de**, but without an article.

> **Chamou o desafeto de ladrão.**
> He called his enemy a thief.
> **Êle me xingou de nome feio.**
> He called me an ugly name.

§68. With a noun in apposition. If the intent is descriptive, no article is used.

> **Dona Lígia, dona de casa.**
> Lygia, a housewife.
> **Gouvéia, homem de negócios e grande patriota.**
> Gouveia, a businessman and a great patriot.

a. If identification is intended, the article is used.

> **Malaquias, um sapateiro da praça.**
> Malachiah, a shoemaker on the square.

b. If limitation is intended. If the speaker wishes to imply that others exist but that he refers to only one, the article is used.

> **Luiz, um filho do delegado.**
> Louis, a son of the police chief.

§69. With **como** in the sense of "in the capacity of."

> **Eu lhe falo como amigo.**
> I speak to you as a friend.
> **Ela ficou como secretária do chefe.**
> She remained as the boss's secretary.

But if comparison is meant, the article is used.

A casa está como um brinco.
  The house is neat as a pin.
Êle falou como um sábio.
  He spoke like a sage.

§70. After the preposition **feito** and the verb **virar**. In the first case it may be used at times.

O menino correu feito (um) gamo.
  The boy ran like a deer.
Êle bebe feito gambá.
  He drinks like a fish (*Lit.* opossum).
Você trepa tanto que vai virar macaco.
  You climb so much that you are going to turn into a monkey.

§71. Idiomatically, in many cases. Such cases are often difficult to define. The difference between using an article or not is very small, but we may say in general that the expression is more vague and indefinite without the article. Some may be used either way; some are never accompanied by the article.

Mamãe tomou freguesia com ela.
  Mother became her customer.
Êle quer empinar papagaio.
  He wants to fly a kite.
A quase trezentos metros, enorme vulto marrom ergueu-se.   **Lit**
  Nearly three hundred meters away an enormous brown bulk arose.
Êle vai lavrar queixa contra mim.
  He is going to file a complaint against me.
Creio que isso vai dar galho.
  I think this is going to give trouble.
A vítima deu parte à polícia.
  The victim reported it to the police.
Recebi uma carta escrita com pena.
  I got a letter written with a pen.
Nesse caso, eu teria companheiro de viagem.
  In that case, I would have a traveling companion.
Eu estou sentindo cheiro de queimado.
  I smell something burning.
O trabalho está em fase de conclusão.
  The work is getting close to the end.
Vou tomar banho.
  I am going to take a bath.
Homem direito, aquêle!
  A good man, that one.

Há grande tendência para a emigração.
There is a strong tendency toward emigration.
Coisa que êle precisa são miolos.
A thing that he needs is brains.

§72. In numerous prepositional phrases.

De janela para janela. (*But* **De um janela em outra.**)
From window to window.
De cidade em cidade.
From city to city.
Isso agora está em pauta.
That is now on the agenda.
Tudo está em regra.
Everything is in order.
Isto é bom para chuchu.   **Gir**
This is mighty good.
O motor encrencou de vez. (*But* **Joga de uma vez.**)
The motor has fouled up for good. (Throw it and have done with it.)
Milho a granel.
Corn in bulk.
Entraram a custo.
They entered with difficulty.

THE ADJECTIVE

The forms

§73. The adjective has from one to four forms. The multiple forms may express agreement in number, in gender, or both. Only a few adjectives are limited to one form. They include those which end in -s preceded by an unstressed vowel, such as **simples** (simple) and **reles** (paltry), and a number of compound adjectives of color: **(côr-de-) laranja** (orange), **côr-de-rosa** (pink), **verde-mar** (sea green), **azul-marinho** (navy blue), **vermelho-sangue** (blood red), **furta-côr** (iridescent), etc.

a. In general, adjectives which end in -a, -e, a consonant or a stressed vowel in the masculine singular, have two forms and indicate number, but not gender.

> **Doce, careca, comum, difícil, maior, cortês, carijó, só, hindu**
> Sweet, bald, common, difficult, larger, courteous, speckled, only, Hindu

b. Adjectives of nationality which end in a consonant add -a for the feminine, and therefore have four forms.

> **Português, f. portuguêsa; espanhol, f. espanhola.**
> Portuguese   Spanish

But **provençal** does not change for the feminine.

c. Adjectives in -or, except comparatives, also indicate the feminine gender by adding -a. They may also form the feminine gender in many cases by changing final -or to -eira. This form usually has a pejorative connotation.

> **Trabalhador, f. trabalhadora, trabalhadeira**
> Hard-working

d. Those adjectives which end in -o in the masculine singular have four forms, indicating agreement in both number and gender.

42

Branco, branca, brancos, brancas
White

e. There are numerous irregularities in the formation of both the feminine gender and the plural number of adjectives. Since they are amply treated in readily available works, they will not be detailed here.

Agreement in gender

§74. Regular agreement. An adjective must agree in gender with the noun or pronoun which it modifies, if it has separate forms for the two genders. A noun modified may be placed before or after the adjective, or it may have been mentioned earlier in the sentence, in a preceding sentence, or even not at all.

Ela traz rosas brancas.
She brings white roses.
A rosa é vermelha.
The rose is red.
Eu não gosto de rosa branca. Eu tenho umas vermelhas em casa.
I don't like white roses. I have some red ones at home.
Você está linda hoje.
You are beautiful today.

§75. Agreement with two nouns of different genders. If an adjective modifies two or more nouns, any one of which is masculine, the adjective is masculine, and of course is plural.

Duas mulheres e um homem portuguêses.
Two Portuguese women and one Portuguese man.
Uma casa e um paiol brancos.
A white house and a white shed.

§76. Agreement with neuters. There is no neuter form of the adjective in Portuguese. Although there are only masculine and feminine nouns, there are neuter pronouns with which the adjectives should agree. At other times an adjective is used in connection with an impersonal, unexpressed subject, which must be considered neuter. The form in such cases is the masculine singular, which also serves as a neuter.

Isso não é bom.
That is not good.

É preciso fazer o possível.
It is necessary to do what is possible.

§77. Irregularities of agreement. Except in relatively few cases of confusion concerning the gender of a noun, BF is remarkably consistent in maintaining the agreement of gender. There are, however, a few cases of departure from this pattern.

a. The participle **feito,** when used with the meaning "like," is felt as a preposition and does not agree.

Saiu a sogra, feito uma fera.
The mother-in-law came out, mad as a hornet.

The word **perto,** which is adverbial whether used alone or as part of the phrase **perto de, junto,** when used with **com** or **de,** and **próximo,** when used with **de,** likewise show no agreement. Only **feito** differs from literary usage.

Passa as cebolas na peneira, junto com o pepino.
Sift the onions, along with the cucumber.
Viu uma pequena casa próximo da cidade.
He saw a small house near the city.

b. The subject **a gente** is a feminine noun, and usually takes a feminine adjective. But when it is used to refer clearly to a certain male being, or beings, the adjective becomes masculine in BF.

Como vai a gente? —A gente está bom, mas fica preguiçoso no calor.
How are you?   I am well, but I get lazy in the heat.

Agreement in number

§78. Regular agreement in number. Adjectives regularly agree in number with the nouns or pronouns they modify, except in those few cases in which the adjective has no separate plural form.

§79. Special cases of agreement in number.

a. Two or more singular nouns, when modified by the same adjective, require it to be in the plural. It will be masculine, unless all nouns modified are feminine.

A porta e a janela azuis.
The blue door and window.
Um homem e uma mulher ambiciosos.
An ambitious man and woman.

b. An adjective which precedes two or more nouns normally modifies, and agrees with, only the first. To modify all, it must follow.

Êle usava bom português e boas expressões.
He used good Portuguese and good expressions.
Contos e histórias bons.
Good tales and stories.

c. When two or more adjectives modify a plural noun, but each one refers to only one individual of the class named by the noun, the adjectives are in the singular.

O govêrno ajuda a financiar a pequena e média indústrias.
The government helps to finance small and medium industries.
Êle conhece bem as línguas espanhola e portuguêsa.
He knows the Spanish and Portuguese languages well.

§80. Loss of agreement in uncultured speech. While Brazilian speakers of moderate education tend to maintain the agreement of the adjective with the noun as regards number, the lower levels of speech often show little regard for it. A very widespread phenomenon of uncultured speech is the expression of number only in the determinant—article, demonstrative, possessive adjective, or a number—leaving the noun and any adjectives other than the preceding in the singular. This feature is found in all parts of Brazil.

Lá tem umas brincadeira interessante.   Inc
There are some interesting amusements there.
Êle tem quatro filho menor.   Inc
He has four smaller children.
Os engenheiro são alemão.   Inc
The engineers are Germans.
Os dia são curto agora.   Inc
The days are short now.
Êstes boi dão trabalho.   Inc
These oxen give trouble.

Use of the adjective

§81. The adjective may be used as a noun. While the noun may be used as an adjective only to a very limited extent, the adjective may nearly always be used with some degree of substantivization. The degree varies with the circumstances and the type of adjective.

a. An adjective may be used with an article or other determinative to modify a noun previously mentioned, but not repeated.

Eu tenho um carro preto, e êle um azul.
I have a black car, and he has a blue one.

b. From this construction it is an easy step to the use of an adjective with a masculine singular article when there is no noun it may modify. The adjective is logically neuter.

Eu faço o seguinte.
I'll do the following.
Êle ficou no escuro.
He was left in the dark.

c. Certain types of adjectives are used so frequently without nouns that they have become accepted as nouns and are frequently modified by adjectives. The most common of these are the adjectives frequently used of persons.

Um velhinho simpático.
A nice old man.
Uma loura magra.
A skinny blonde.
Um português baixo.
A short Portuguese.
Os intocáveis.
The untouchables.
O cego e o careca.
The blind man and the bald man.
Êle fala português.
He speaks Portuguese.
O azul do céu.
The blue of the sky.

§82. The adjective used predicatively. Agreement of number and gender are maintained.

A briga ameaçava tornar-se interessante.
The fight was threatening to become interesting.
Não sei se esta acusação é verdadeira.
I don't know whether this accusation is true.
Os macaquinhos pareciam tão engraçadinhos.
The little monkeys looked so cute.

§83. The adjective in absolute construction. Participles are especially frequent in this construction, in which a noun and an adjective are used in a phrase not directly connected with the clause. It may be considered semi-literary.

Terminada a guerra, voltei ao Brasil.　　**SLit**
　　When the war was over, I returned to Brazil.
Várias crianças brincavam na rua, os pés nus.　　**SLit**
　　Several children were playing on the street, with their feet bare.

§84. The adjective used as an adverb. The adjective is found in many cases which would logically require an adverb. BF vacillates between agreement and nonagreement, i.e., whether to consider such words adjectives or adverbs.

A esposa se queixava chorosa.
　　The wife complained, crying.
Eu [uma mulher] cheguei primeira. (*Usually* primeiro.)
　　I [a woman] arrived first.
Os pássaros voavam tão rápido.
　　The birds flew so fast.
Elas corriam ligeiras como o vento. (*Or* ligeiro.)
　　They ran swift as the wind.

a. A number of words may be used indifferently as adjectives or adverbs.

Nem todo gato é preto. Vi uma gata todo coberta de lama.
　　Not all cats are black. I saw a pussycat all covered with mud.
Muitos brasileiros são muito louros.
　　Many Brazilians are very blond.
Acha que isso é pouca coisa? A equipe estava pouco treinada.
　　Do you think that is a little thing? The team was little trained.
Estamos a meio caminho. Ela está meio maluca.
　　We are midway. She is half cracked.
Havia tanta gente na rua. Ela está um tanto cansada.
　　There were so many people on the street. She is a bit tired.
O mesmo homem apareceu hoje. O João foi mesmo?
　　The same man appeared today. John really went?

b. There is a fairly strong tendency to make some of these agree with the noun, even when used to modify an adjective. **Todo** and **meio** are often heard expressing agreement in such cases.

§85. The adjective may be used with a preposition, to form an adverbial phrase.

A onça veio vindo de mansinho.
　　The jaguar kept coming softly.
Foi chegando aos poucos.
　　It approached little by little.

Eram vinte e três pessoas ao todo.
They were twenty-three people in all.

A great many such phrases are formed with the preposition **a**, the feminine plural of the definite article, and the adjective. Presumably the feminine plural form originated in some noun, but often it is impossible to guess which one.

Às ocultas, às cegas, às escuras
Secretly, blindly, in the dark

§86. Other prepositional phrases. Certain prepositions may be used before an adjective without forming with it an adverbial phrase. The expressions are elliptical, each assuming the verb **ser** between the preposition and the adjective. The following prepositions are so used:

a. With **de**. The preposition explains, by means of the following adjective, the reason why the subject does certain actions specified in the verb.

O pobre vive de teimoso.
The poor man lives through stubbornness.
Êle fêz isso só de ruim.
He did that just from malice.
Eu dormi de puro cansado.
I slept because I was so tired.
O govêrno caiu de podre.
The government fell from its own rottenness.
O vento roncava, de tão forte.
The wind moaned, it was so strong.
Ela chorou, de envergonhada.
She cried from shame.

b. With **por**. The adjective explains why something was done to the subject.

Êle foi demitido por burro.
He was fired for stupidity.
Ela foi rejeitada por velha.
She was rejected because she was too old.

c. With **para**. In similar situations, the adjective with **para** tells what the subject becomes.

Os meninos deram para preguiçosos.
The boys became lazy.

§87. The adjective with partitive **de**. The superlative form of the adjective in particular is rather frequent after partitive **de**.

Nós somos dos bons.
  We belong to the good people.
Eu queria um canivete dos melhores.
  I would like a pocket knife of the best quality.
Êle é um gerente dos mais eficientes.
  He is one of the most efficient managers.

§88. Adjectives followed by **de** before the noun. Certain adjectives of high emotional content are often followed by **de** before the noun. Of these, **coitado** always takes **de**. With others it is optional, but it is practically universal before pronouns.

Coitado de meu pai!
  My poor father!
Pobre de meu filhinho!   **Pobre menino!**
  My poor little son!   Poor boy!
Triste dela!
  Poor girl!

Position of the adjectives

§89. Significance of position. The question of the position of adjectives with relation to the noun is extremely complex. While BF has less reason to vary the position than the literary language, which is often preoccupied with style, all the reasons which cause shift of position in literature also operate in speech. They are, of course, applied less frequently.

It should be remembered that the last word of a noun phrase regularly receives the stress. Therefore the adjective is unstressed if it precedes the noun, but stressed if it follows. For this reason also, the attention of the listener is called mainly to the last word of the phrase. When placed in this position, the adjective limits or defines the meaning of the noun to one individual or group within the class named by the noun. The meaning of the adjective is therefore generally objective, in that it simply defines that limited part of the class to which the speaker wishes to refer.

If the adjective precedes, it describes or modifies the noun largely in subjective terms. It may indicate the opinion or the impression of the speaker, or his emotional attitude, or it may merely call attention to a quality that is obvious to all.

Certain adjectives are likely, by their very nature, to follow the noun; others are equally likely to precede. However, very few are so firmly fixed that they do not permit change of position.

§90. The following types of adjectives normally follow:

a. Those which denote specific and easily observable characteristics. Subjectivity plays little part in these.

> **Hoje eu vi um homem feio.**
> Today I saw an ugly man.
> **Ela tem cabelo fino.** (*Cf.* **Seu fino cabelo brilhava ao sol.**)
> She has fine hair. (Her fine hair shone in the sun.)
> **Êste é um vinho azedo.**
> This is a sour wine.
> **Olha aquela menina loura.**
> Look at that blonde girl.

b. Adjectives derived from proper nouns. These include adjectives of origin, religion, language, political party, etc.

> **A universidade coimbrã.**   Lit
> The University of Coimbra.
> **Os reis católicos.**
> The Catholic Monarchs.
> **O candidato pessedista.**
> The candidate of the Social Democratic Party.

In such cases it is often possible to distinguish which word is the noun and which the adjective only from the fact that the adjective is second.

> **Muitos estudiosos estrangeiros vão para lá.**
> Many foreign scholars go there.
> **Êle é um protestante português.**
> He is a Portuguese Protestant.

c. Participles used as adjectives. Only when the verbal force has been completely lost and the adjective is felt as a different word (sometimes with another meaning), may it precede.

> **Os raios do sol parecem fibras douradas.**
> The rays of the sun look like gilded fibers.
> **O chalet dá para o sol nascente.**
> The cottage faces the rising sun.
> **Magoadas pombas cinzentas cantavam.**   Lit
> Mournful gray doves were singing.

d. When the adjective is modified. It tends to follow the noun even if it is used subjectively. While a few frequently used short adverbs are not too likely to affect the position, most adverbs and all prepositional phrases carry the adjective to the stressed position.

Êle é um sujeito bem bom.
He is quite a good fellow.
Era um homem magro como um poste.
He was a man skinny as a post.
Que moça incrìvelmente bonita!
What an incredibly pretty girl!
É um homem grande na prática do bem.
He is a great man in the performance of good deeds.

§91. Adjectives which either precede or follow. A great many adjectives precede or follow with equal ease. The meaning or connotation varies with the position.

a. Subjective and objective use. Many adjectives have meaning which make them normally subjective. In this case they precede. But if they are used objectively, they will follow.

Êste é ótimo pão.
This is excellent bread.
O café bom está caro.
Good coffee is expensive.
Aquêle é um mau sujeito.
That is a bad fellow.
Oh, seu Nicolau! Você é um homem mau!
Oh, Nicholas, you are an evil man.
Põe uma pequena quantidade de sal.
Put in a small quantity of salt.
Você ainda é um menino pequeno.
You are still a little boy.
Pelé é o mais famoso jogador de futebol que temos.
Pelé is the most famous soccer player we have.
Eu gosto der ler as vidas de homens famosos.
I like to read the lives of famous men.

b. Subjective adjective following for emphasis. Even when the adjective is subjective, and especially when it is of a type that is frequently subjective, the speaker may give it greater emphasis by placing it after the noun. It does not thus lose its subjective force.

Roxinha boa aquela que vai ali!
That's an attractive Negro girl over there.

Rapaz bonito!
A good-looking fellow!
Que café bom!
What good coffee!

The word **ruim** follows the noun in all cases.

Êsse homem ruim me estragou a festa.
That bad man ruined the party for me.

c. Change of meaning with change of position. There is, of course, always some change of meaning with any shift of position. However, in some cases the difference is much greater than in others. The following cases illustrate some clearly defined differences.

A onça verdadeira.
The true jaguar. (A species of jaguar.)
Êle virou uma verdadeira onça.
He turned into a real jaguar.
O mar danado quer engulir êle.
The wild sea is trying to swallow him up.
Danado ladrão!
Damned thief!
As oficinas novas.
The newly-built shops.
Tenho uma nova casa.
I have a newly-acquired house.
O Carlos é uma criança grande.
Charles is a big child.
Rui foi um grande orador.
Rui was a great orator.
Auxiliamos uma família pobre.
We help a poor family.
Pobre criança!
Poor child!
Lisboa antiga.
Old Lisbon.
Um antigo patrão meu.
A former boss of mine.

d. An adjective used objectively, if repeated, precedes. There is, of course, no need to repeat the adjective for the purposes of giving information, limiting the noun, etc. Therefore, if the adjective is used again, it is likely to be for subjective, i.e., emotional reasons, and it is likely to precede.

Garcia era um homem alto e calvo. . . . Êste calvo Garcia era um bom sujeito.

Garcia was a tall, bald man. . . . This bald Garcia was a good fellow.

Syntax of two or more adjectives modifying the same noun

§92. Position of two adjectives. If there are two or more adjectives which modify the same noun, each one is likely to take its normal position, unaffected by the other.

Meu velho amigo português vem me visitar.
My old Portuguese friend is coming to visit me.
A casa tem um bonito jardim rústico.
The house has a pretty rustic garden.

a. If two precede. If the first is a possessive, a demonstrative, or an indefinite, the two adjectives are used one after the other.

Meu bom amigo.
My good friend.
Quanta bela flor!
How many beautiful flowers!
Aquêle grande patriota.
That great patriot.

In such cases, we may consider that the first adjective modifies, not the simple noun, but the phrase formed by the noun and the second adjective.

Otherwise, the two are separated by the conjunction **e**, often replaced by a simple pause.

A boa e gaiata viuva do Tênser.
Tenser's good merry widow.
A bela, impressionante obra do pintor.
The beautiful, impressive work of the painter.

b. If one precedes and one follows. This is a frequent situation and requires no comment. However, the noun may be followed by **e**, with the adjective following. We may assume that the adjective is used with reference to an understood repetition of the noun.

Um bom sujeito e inteligente.
A good fellow, and an intelligent one.

c. Two adjectives following the noun. They are generally separated by the conjunction **e**.

Uma casa grande e lúgubre.
A large, gloomy house.
Uma cidade antiga, bela e interessante.
An old, beautiful, and interesting city.

Again, if the noun and one adjective are felt as forming a unit with its own meaning, the conjunction may be omitted.

Uma casa-grande lúgubre.
A gloomy plantation house.
Uma môça morena bonita. (=Uma morena bonita.)
A pretty brunette girl.

§93. Position of an adjective phrase. If the noun is modified both by an adjective which follows and by an adjectival phrase, the latter follows immediately after the noun.

Uma casa de verão bonita.
A pretty summer house.

§94. For possessive adjectives, see §143 ff.
For demonstrative adjectives, see §96 ff.
For adjectives of quantity, see § 108 ff.
§95. For comparison of adjectives, see §494–501.

DEMONSTRATIVE ADJECTIVES AND PRONOUNS

The forms and pronunciation

§96. The forms. The demonstratives are not a very clearcut class, since they border on the article (a demonstrative in origin) on one side and may be considered to include several borderline words on the other. They include most certainly **êste**, **êsse**, and **aquêle**, which may be either adjectives or pronouns, and the pronoun **o. Mesmo** and **tal** should probably be considered demonstratives also. They are treated with the indefinites, in §125 and §136, because of other usages.

a. Use of **um** with demonstratives. While the three forms cited above are used freely as pronouns, in uncultured speech they are sometimes used with the pronoun **um**, as adjectives. This usage is not frequent, and is unacceptable in BF.

> **Olha êsse um.**   **Inc**
> Look at that one.

b. Singular for the plural. When used after the partitive **de**, the singular form is often heard for the plural. This is doubtless the same phenomenon treated in §80, but here there is no other plural to call attention to the loss of final **-s**.

> **Eu também queria um carro dêsse.**   **Inc**
> I, too, would like a car like that.

§97. The pronunciation. It is worthy of note that in these three demonstratives, the variation of gender is marked by the change of two vowels, rather than the usual one. Both the stressed and the final vowel are different for each gender. In the masculine forms, the stressed vowel is **ê**, the final one **e**; in the feminine the stressed vowel is **é** and the final one **a**; and in the neuter forms (pronouns only) the stressed vowel is **i** and the final one **o**. This greater clarity of distinction is, of course, helpful in words of such frequent use.

55

§98. The contractions. The demonstratives combine with various prepositions to form contractions, some represented in writing, others not.

a. With the preposition **a**. Only **aquêle** and **o**, with their respective feminine, neuter, and plural forms, may contract. They give **àquele, àquela, àquilo**, etc., and **ao, à**, etc., forms which are obligatory and written. All except **ao** and **aos** are pronounced exactly like the forms which do not include the preposition.

b. The preposition **de** loses its vowel before all these words, and the consonant is prefixed to the demonstrative. These forms are universal in BF, and generally written.

Disso, daquele, dessa, do, etc.

c. The preposition **em** becomes **n-**, which is prefixed to the demonstratives both in speech and writing. While it is not obligatory, the full preposition is very rarely heard.

Nesse, nisto, naquela, no, etc.

d. The preposition **para** forms no contractions in writing, but it loses its vowels in speech before the forms of **aquêle** and **o**, and the consonants are prefixed to the demonstrative. This does not occur before **êste** and **êsse**.

P'r'aquêle, p'r'aquelas, pru, *but* **p'ra essa, p'ra isto.**

Use of the demonstratives

Êste, êsse, and **aquêle** are used to refer to:

§99. Position in space. Basically, the positions indicated by these three words correspond to the three persons of the personal pronoun —near the speaker, near the person addressed, and more or less distant from both. However, all are interpreted with some latitude, and there is especially some overlapping of **êsse** with both of the others.

> **A casa fica nesta rua. (=A em que eu estou.)**
> The house is on this street. (The one I am on.)
> **Que dinheiro é êsse? (=O que você tem.)**
> What money is that? (The money you have.)
> **Olha aquela terra cinzenta lá em baixo.**
> Look at that gray land down there.
> **Você está vendo essa môça? (A que, embora não esteja com você, não está muito longe.)**

Do you see that girl? (The one who, although she is not beside you, is not far away.)

§100. Position in time.

a. **Êste** generally indicates something just mentioned by the speaker, or about to be mentioned.

Esta idéia é digna de consideração.
This idea (which I am going to present) is worthy of consideration.

b. **Êsse** is used of something mentioned recently by the person addressed, or by the speaker, or otherwise thought of as not very far in the past.

Eu queria um cachorro como êsse.
I would like a dog like that (like the one in the story you told).
Êle carregava um saco. Dêsse saco despejou três gatinhos.
He was carrying a sack. From that sack he spilled out three kittens.

c. **Aquêle** refers to the more distant past.

Naquela época eu era ainda môço.
At that period I was still young.
Desde aquêle dia ficou estabelecida a ditadura.
From that day on, the dictatorship was established.

§101. Position in the sentence. **Aquêle** and **êste** are used respectively to express "the former" and "the latter." Since **êsse** must refer to the nearer antecedent, it precedes **aquêle** in the sentence.

Almir trabalha na mesma loja que Neusa; esta é caixeira, aquêle é vendedor.
Almir works in the same store as Neusa; the latter is a cashier, the former is a salesman.

BF is more likely to use the personal pronouns **êle** and **ela** in this case. If both nouns were of the same gender and number, they would likely be repeated in the second part of the sentence.

§102. Demonstratives used for the personal pronoun. Any of these three demonstratives may be used to refer to a noun previously mentioned. **Êste** is especially common to refer to the last person mentioned.

Fui à repartição falar com o chefe. Êste me disse que não ia haver aumento.
I went to the office to speak to the boss. He told me that there would be no raise.

§103. Demonstratives used for the definite article. This usage is not frequent, but is well established both in literary Portuguese and BF.

O que é isto? —É aquêle ovo de vidro que se coloca no ninho das galinhas.
What is this? It is the glass egg which is placed in hens' nests.

§104. The feminine singular forms are used in many expressions of vague reference. In some cases, at least, there was undoubtedly a feminine noun used. Often we can guess its identity. In other cases, it is difficult to guess.

Ora essa! [idéia].
What an idea!
Essa [piada] é boa.
That's a good one [joke].
Tem mais esta [coisa(?)].
Here's another one [thing?].

§105. Use of the neuter forms. The neuter forms can only be used as pronouns, and are invariable. They are used:

a. To refer to ideas. Since no noun is identified, no gender can be assigned, other than neuter.

Isso que você diz é verdade.
What you say is true.

b. To refer to nouns not yet identified. Since the noun is not known, its gender cannot be determined.

O que é isto que encontrei na mesa?
What is this that I found on the table?

c. Disparagingly, of persons. The implied meaning is **aquela coisa**.

Aquilo (=aquêle homem) é nojento.
That (that man) is disgusting.

d. As subjects of verbs. Since no neuter personal pronouns exist, the neuter demonstratives replace them. In this usage, they have no demonstrative force. Isso is the most frequently used, followed by **isto**. In **aquilo**, the demonstrative force is too great for this usage.

Isso é. (=o que eu já disse quer dizer.)
That is.

e. As objects of verbs. **Isso** is the usual neuter object, when it is stressed, since the neuter personal pronoun **o** has disappeared from usage.

> **Me dá isso.**
>> Give it to me.
> **Joga isso no chão.**
>> Throw it (that) on the ground.

f. To denote cause. With the preposition **por isto**, etc., mean **por esta razão**, etc. (for this reason, etc.)

> **Por isso não comprei o carro.**
>> For that reason I didn't buy the car.
> **Êle não quer se meter na política, por aquilo mesmo.**
>> He doesn't want to get into politics, for that very reason.
> **Henrique não veio por isto que rasgou o terno.**
>> Henry didn't come because he tore his shirt.

g. With other neuters, which modify them.

> **Êle não pôde convencer-se de tudo isso.**
>> He couldn't convince himself of all that.
> **Já fiz aquilo tudo.**
>> I have already done all that.
> **É isto mesmo.**
>> That is exactly right.

§106. Use of the pronoun **o**. In order to avoid the repetition of a noun, the definite article is often used alone, serving as a pronoun which is demonstrative in that it refers to a noun previously mentioned. It is nearly always followed by **de** or **que**, the latter frequently preceded by a preposition.

> **Você viu essa môça—a que estava com Luiz?**
>> Did you see that lady—the one who was with Louis?
> **Vão minha mulher e a do Neves.**
>> My wife and Neves' are going.
> **Vou ver aquela casa, a de que você falou.**
> **(BF=Vou ver aquela casa que você falou.)**
>> I am going to see that house which you spoke of.

a. **Aquêle** may replace the demonstrative **o** in any situation, and usually does before any preposition except **de**.

> **O convite foi aceito por aquêles que eram amigos de peito.**
>> The invitation was accepted by those who were bosom friends.

Prefiro aquêle com quem fui ao cinema ontem.
I prefer the one I went to the movies with yesterday.

b. The neuter forms combine with **que** to form a compound relative pronoun.

Eu sei o que você está pensando.
I know what you are thinking.
Isso que você diz é muito interessante.
What you say is very interesting.

Position of demonstrative adjectives

§107. The demonstrative adjective is placed before the noun. In BF this position is invariable. In literary usage, it occasionally follows when it modifies a noun repeated from a previous statement.

Foram momentos de elevada inspiração, momentos êsses que nos deixaram empolgados. Lit
They were moments of high inspiration, moments which left us thrilled.

INDEFINITES

§108. The class of indefinites. There is a group of words of widely varying uses and of several parts of speech, which are generally termed indefinites for want of better nomenclature. Here they are considered as nouns, pronouns, or adjectives. Somes of them may also be adverbs. As such, they are treated with the other adverbs, in §341 ff. The words dealt with here are listed in alphabetical order.

§109. **Al** is a neuter pronoun, invariable in form. It is now largely archaic in BF, usually replaced by **outra coisa**.

> **Nunca pensei em al. —Canção de Dorival Caymmi.**　　　**Arc**
> I never thought of anything else.

§110. **Algo** is a neuter pronoun, invariable in form. It is now largely archaic in BF, usually replaced by **alguma coisa**. Its one surviving use which is frequent in BF has probably contributed to its disuse otherwise. It is used to mean "an alcoholic drink." The similarity of sounds between **algo** and **álcool** is sufficient to suggest this meaning when one hears **Vamos tomar algo.** (Let's drink something.)

§111. **Alguém** is a pronoun referring to persons, invariable in form. It is considered feminine if it definitely refers to a female person.

> **Alguém esqueceu o chapéu.**
> Someone forgot his hat.
> **Estou ouvindo os passos de alguém.**
> I hear somebody's footsteps.
> **Alguém está cansada.**
> Somebody (that girl) is tired.

If a plural is needed, **alguns** is used.

§112. **Algum** may be an adjective or a pronoun. It has forms for both genders and both numbers.

a. Meaning of selection at random. It is very often similar in meaning to the indefinite article, with some suggestion of selection at random.

Quero achar algum pedaço de pão.
I want to find a piece of bread.
Algum dia vou à capital.
Some day I am going to the capital.

b. Meaning of quantity. At times it signifies "a small quantity of."

Êste estado produz algum gado.
This state produces some cattle.

c. Use in the plural. In the plural, it is equivalent to **uns poucos.**

Eu queria alguns livros, poucos, mas bons.
I would like some books, few, but good ones.

d. Use as a pronoun. It refers to one or more individuals from a group previously mentioned.

Entre tantos homens, deve haver algum que me ajude.
Among so many men, there must be someone who will help me.
Examinei muitas camisas, e comprei algumas.
I examined a lot of shirts, and bought a few.

e. Use of **alguma coisa.** This phrase has replaced the archaic **algo** and acts as an indefinite pronoun.

O senhor deseja alguma coisa?
Do you wish something?

The phrase sometimes takes **de** and an adjective.

Aconteceu alguma coisa de extraordinário.
Something extraordinary happened.

f. **Algum** as a negative. When the adjective **algum** follows a noun, it becomes a vigorous negative. Only the singular can be so used.

Não tomo bebida alguma.
I won't drink anything at all.

§113. **Alheio** is a possessive adjective, and as such is treated in §157b.

§114. **Ambos** is either an adjective or a pronoun, dual in number, with a feminine form **ambas.** As an adjective, it may either precede the noun directly or it may be followed by the definite article. In BF, **ambos** is not common, being replaced usually by **os dois.**

Fiquei ferido em ambas mãos. (*Or* ambas as mãos.)   SLit
  I got hurt on both hands.
Qual está ferida?   —Ambas.
  Which one is hurt?   Both of them.
Teremos que levar os dois carros, e pôr os embrulhos em ambos.
  We'll have to take both cars, and put the packages in both of them.

§115. **Bastante** is usually an adjective. The meaning extends from
suficiente, through **muito**, to **demais**. The shade of meaning is transmitted by the situation and the tone of the voice.

Não tenho bastante açúcar. (Suficiente.)
  I don't have enough sugar.
Põe bastante açúcar. (Muito.)
  Put quite a bit of sugar.
Você botou basta-a-nte água na panela. (Demais.)
  You put plenty of water in the pan.

It may be used as a substantive, with the definite article.

É o bastante para desanimar a gente. (*More often* É bastante . . .)
  It is enough to discourage a person.

§116. **Bocado** is a noun. The expressions **um bocado, um bocadinho** are used alone or (with **de**) before a noun, denoting quantities
ranging from a little to a great deal. The clue to the exact meaning
is given by the tone of voice.

Você tem mato na horta. —Tenho um bocado. (Um pouco.)
  You have weeds in your garden. I have a few.
Põe só um bocadinho. (Muito pouco.)
  Put in just a little bit.
Êle tem um bocado de filhos. (Muitos.)
  He has a lot of children.

§117. **Cada** is a distributive adjective. It is invariable in form,
used only in the singular.

Cada passageiro carrega a própria mala.
  Each passenger carries his own suitcase.

a.   Without a noun. If the noun is not expressed, **cada** is normally
followed by **um** (uma) or by **qual**.

Há um presente para cada um.
  There is a present for each one.
Êle exigia de cada qual um esfôrço maior.
  He demanded a greater effort from each of them.

b. Use with prices. In speaking of prices, BF frequently omits these words, using **cada** as a pronoun.

Comprei êstes livros a cem cruzeiros cada.
I bought these books for 100 cruzeiros each.

c. With expressions of time. **Cada** is used to indicate regular intervals of time.

Cada dez dias. (=De dez em dez dias.)
Every ten days.

d. Use in exclamations. In exclamatory sentences, **cada** indicates surprising numbers of things.

Você tem cada coisa!
You have the wildest ideas!
Êste lago tem cada peixe grandão!
This lake has lots of big fish.

§118. **Certo.** This adjective is an indefinite only when it precedes the noun. It denotes an individual of whom the speaker is thinking, and is less vague than the indefinite article. It is frequent in narration.

Certo homem chegou em casa e encontrou que a mulher tinha fugido.
A certain man came home and discovered that his wife had run away.

a. With the indefinite article. With the article it becomes more specific. The reference is likely to be so obvious that it is immediately clear to the hearers.

Eu trouxe isto para uma certa pessoa. (Você sabe que é para você.)
I brought this for a certain person. (You know it is for you.)
Êle tem uma certa inclinação para o furto. (=Muita inclinação.)
He has a certain inclination for theft.

b. **Certo** after the noun. When placed after the noun, **certo** is no longer an indefinite.

A resposta certa é a seguinte.
The correct answer is the following.
Você está certo disso?
Are you sure of that?

§119. **Os demais** is used as a pronoun or an adjective, always in the plural. If a singular is required, one can use **o resto.** The feminine is formed by changing the article.

> **Alguns tomaram a maior parte do sorvete, deixando pouco para os demais.**
> Some people took most of the ice cream, leaving little for the rest.
> **Eu vou tomar o resto.**
> I am going to take the rest.

§120. **Diferentes,** in the plural, and preceding the noun, is an indefinite adjective, equivalent to **vários.**

> **Os moleques andam pelo montão de lixo, apanhando diferentes coisas.**
> The kids are going through the trash pile, picking up various things.

§121. **Diversos** has the same meaning and usage as the preceding. It is an indefinite adjective only preceding the noun. It varies for gender.

> **Lemos diversos livros na semana passada.**
> We read several books last week.

§122. **Espécie** is a noun used in the indefinite expression **uma espécie de.** It loses its first and its last two vowels in this expression, in BF, becoming in pronunciation **umaspésde.**

> **Os meninos cavaram uma espécie de túnel embaixo do muro.**
> The boys dug a kind of tunnel under the wall.

§123. **Mais,** the comparative of **muito,** may be either adjective or pronoun. As an adjective, it precedes the noun and is invariable.

> **Há mais homens aqui que mulheres.**
> There are more men here than women.

a. Without an article. It is used without an article, with meaning equivalent to **outro** or **outra coisa.**

> **Êle não fêz mais do que trabalhar.**
> He didn't do anything else but work.
> **Quero mais dois.**
> I want two more.

b. As a substantive. It is often substantivized with the masculine singular definite article, occurring in certain expressions whose total effect is adverbial.

Além do mais, êle é rico. (Além disso.)
Besides, he is rich.
No mais, estou atrasado. (Pelo resto.)
Besides, I am late.

c.   In the plural, **os mais** (or the feminine form) is equivalent to
a maior parte, to **os outros**, or to **os demais**.

As mais das vezes. (=A maior parte das vezes.)
Most times.
Luiz, Carlos, José, e os mais.
Louis, Charles, Joe, and the others.

§124.   **Menos** is an adjective or pronoun of quantity. It is invariable.

a.   As an adjective, it does not take an article.

Êle devia comer menos arroz.
He should eat less rice.

b.   As a substantive. It is used with the masculine singular definite
article, forming phrases of adverbial force.

Rendeu-se sem ao menos protestar.
He surrendered without even protesting.
Êle deve ganhar dez mil cruzeiros, pelo menos.
He must make ten thousand cruzeiros, at least.

§125.   **Mesmo** is used as an adjective preceding the noun, or in
the predicate. When used without a noun, it is usually classified as
a pronoun. **Mesmo** could, with some logic, be considered a demonstrative.

a.   As an adjective. It and its article agree with the noun modified.

O mesmo homem passou aqui ontem.
The same man went through here yesterday.

b.   As a pronoun. It agrees with its antecedent. It may also be
used as a neuter, accompanied by the definite article.

Essa môça é a mesma que vi ontem.
That girl is the same one I saw yesterday.
Vou dormir, e aconselho você a fazer o mesmo.
I am going to sleep, and I advise you to do the same.

c.   After a noun or pronoun. When **mesmo** follows immediately,
it is an intensive pronoun, strengthening its antecedent, with which
it agrees.

Você mesma tem que fazer isso.
You yourself have to do that.
Rio-me de mim mesmo.
I laugh at myself.
É isso mesmo.
That's it exactly.

d. For **mesmo** as an adverb, see §353d.

§126. **Muito** is either an adjective or a pronoun, expressing indefinite quantity. It varies to indicate number and gender, and may be used as a neuter pronoun.

Era de tarde, e passava muita gente.
It was afternoon, and many people were passing.

a. As an adjective. When **muito** is an adjective, both it and the accompanying noun are often in the singular, even when the meaning is plural.

Muito soldado que foi à Europa não voltou.
Many a soldier who went to Europe did not come back.

b. As a pronoun. It normally does not take an article.

Muito fica para fazer.
Much remains to be done.
Muitos gostam de subir ao morro para apreciar a paisagem.
Many like to climb the hill to enjoy the scenery.

c. As a substantivized adjective. This usage is found in the plural, with a definite article.

Os poucos governam e os muitos obedecem.
The few rule and the many obey.

d. With a partitive expression. **Muito** may be followed by a partitive **de** and a noun. It agrees with this noun in gender and number.

Muitas das mulheres mais bem vestidas do Brasil compram aqui.
Many of the best-dressed women in Brazil buy here.

e. For **muito** as an adverb, see §349.

§127. **Nada, nenhum, ninguém.** See negatives, §447–467.

§128. **Outrém** is a pronoun, invariable in form, singular only, referring to persons. It is obsolescent, found rarely in modern literature, in certain proverbs, and used occasionally in speech in humorous fashion. In BF it is replaced by **outro** and **outra pessoa.**

Estou vendo alguém falando com outrém. **Obs**
I see someone talking to someone else.

§129. **Outro** may be either an adjective or a pronoun and is declined in both genders and numbers.

a. As an adjective. It precedes the noun and may take the definite article.

O outro carro é mais bonito.
The other car is prettier.

b. Without an article. When the expression is indefinite, the indefinite article is usually omitted.

Luiz veio acompanhado por outro rapaz.
Louis came accompanied by another boy.

c. With the indefinite article. The indefinite article is heard at times, with no definable difference in meaning.

Eu vi uma outra menina lá na sua casa.
I saw another girl there in your house.

d. Adjectives which precede **outro**. It may be preceded by any of the determinatives—possessives, demonstratives, articles—or by the other indefinite adjectives. Numbers usually follow it.

Meu outro irmão está aqui.
My other brother is here.
Come um pouco dêste outro prato.
Eat a little from this other dish.
Conheço muitos outros iguais.
I know many other similar ones.
Êle veio anteontem com outros dois.
He came day before yesterday with two others.

e. Adjectives which follow **outro**. Other adjectives follow **outro**, preceding or following the noun.

Atravessamos outra grande ponte.
We crossed another big bridge.
Conhecemos uma outra môça bonita.
We know another pretty girl.

f. **Outro** as a predicative adjective. Here, **outro** is usually a distinguishing adjective, but it may also have the meaning usual in other circumstances.

O meu carro é outro.
My car is a different one. (*Or* My car is different.)
O meu carro é um outro. (=Não é êste.)
My car is another one, not this one.

g. Preceding the noun as a distinguishing adjective. This meaning is also expressed in certain phrases in which **outro** precedes the noun, although these phrases are often ambiguous.

Quero outra cerveja.
I want another (different) beer.
Cf. **Quero mais uma cerveja.**
I want one more beer.

h. **Outro** referring to neuter ideas. This pronoun has no neuter form, and can refer only to masculine or feminine nouns. Instead, one says **outra coisa.**

§130. **Porção** is a noun which is much used in the indefinite expression **uma porção de** with the meaning **uma grande quantidade de.**

Você tem uma porção de selos.
You have a lot of stamps.

§131. **Pouco** is either an adjective or a pronoun, and is declined in both genders and numbers.

a. As an adjective. It expresses the limitation of the noun to a small quantity or a small number. Usually no article is used.

Põe pouco açúcar.
Put in very little sugar.
Há pouca gente aqui.
There are few people here.
Êle tem cara de poucos amigos.
He has a face of one who has few friends.

b. Use of the definite article. The definite article is used if a modifying clause follows the noun or is implied.

Eu vou gozar dos poucos anos de vida que me restam.
I am going to enjoy the few years which I have left.
Vamos passar o tempo com os poucos bons amigos [que temos].
Let's spend the time with the few good friends we have.

c. Position with relation to the noun. In BF, **pouco** always precedes the noun, although it may occasionally follow in literary style.

d. As a pronoun. The pronoun **pouco** is used without an article, and may be of any gender, including neuter.

> **Êle trabalha como poucos.**
> He works as few do.
> **Eu fico feliz com pouco.**
> I am happy with little.

e. As a substantivized adjective. Although usually considered a pronoun, **pouco** is often merely a substantivized adjective, and as such takes the definite article.

> **Os poucos que ficaram depois da meia-noite saíram à uma.**
> The few who remained after midnight left at one.
> **Êle perdeu o pouco que tinha.**
> He lost the little he had.

f. **Um pouco.** Followed by a partitive **de** and a noun, **um pouco** insists on the existence of a small quantity, rather than on the limitation.

> **Tenho um pouco de açúcar.**
> I have a little bit of sugar.
> **Quer um pouco de pão?**
> Do you want a little bread?

g. **Uns poucos.** The plural limits the number to a small, indefinite quantity. It does not take **de**.

> **Colhemos uns poucos morangos.**
> We picked a few strawberries.

h. Diminutives of **pouco**. Various diminutives are used, to limit the quantity even more.

> **Tenho um pouquinho.**
> I have a little bit.
> **Êle achou só um pouquitinho de sabonete.**
> He found only a tiny bit of soap.

The Lusitanian diminutive **poucochinho** is unknown in Brazil.

i. For **pouco** used adverbially, see §349.

§132. **Próprio.** This word is usually an adjective, although some consider it to be a pronoun when used as an intensive following a personal pronoun.

a. As a possessive adjective. **Próprio** states emphatically that the subject is the possessor. It precedes the thing possessed, when the definite article is used.

> **Êle mordeu o próprio dedo.**
> He bit his own finger.

b. As an indefinite possessive adjective. The adjective follows the thing possessed, with or without an indefinite article.

> **Êle tem casa própria.** (*Or* **uma casa própria.**)
> He has a house of his own.

c. As an intensive. **Próprio** may be used as an intensive, following a personal pronoun. It is relatively rare in BF, the usual word being **mesmo**.

> **Eu próprio não gosto do café.**   Lit
> I myself don't like coffee.

d. As an intensive adjective, with nouns. **Próprio** precedes the noun. This usage is much more frequent than the preceding.

> **O próprio Sr. Soares disse isso.**
> Mr. Soares himself said that.

§133. **Qual . . . tal.** These are adjectives used to join correlative clauses. They are purely literary, and archaic even in literature.

> **Qual pergunta farás, tal resposta terás.—Proverb**
> A silly question deserves a silly answer.

For **qual** as an interrogative, see §477d. For its use as a relative pronoun, see §476.

§134. **Qualquer.** This word is usually an adjective. It has a plural form **quaisquer.** The meaning is equivalent to **não importa qual.** It is not used as a neuter, for which meaning **qualquer coisa** must be used.

> **Quero vender meu carro a qualquer preço.**
> I want to sell my car at any price.
> **Você quer tomar qualquer coisa?**
> Will you drink something (whatever you wish)?

a. Without a noun. When not followed by a noun, **qualquer** is usually followed by the pronoun **um.**

> **Qualquer um fazia o mesmo que eu.**
> Anyone would do the same as I.

b. **As a pronoun.** Only rarely is **um** omitted, leaving **qualquer** in the rôle of a pronoun.

Você é capaz de andar na rua e falar com qualquer.
You are capable of walking down the street and talking to any·
one at all.

c. **Qualquer** placed after word modified. When placed after the word modified, **qualquer** emphasizes a random choice.

Pode perguntar isso ao Sr. Gomes, ou a um homem qualquer. (=A esmo.)
You may ask this of Mr. Gomes, or of anyone.

d. For **qualquer** with relative clauses, see §244b.

§135. **Quanto** may be an indefinite adjective or pronoun.

a. **Quanto . . . tanto.** These are correlatives, and may be used in either order. They are semi-literary today in this usage.

Quantas línguas falas, tantos homens vales.—Proverb
Cf. **BF A gente vale tantos homens como fala línguas.**
You are worth as many men as you speak languages.

b. **As a pronoun.** It is equivalent to **todo o que** and is used regularly in BF. It may be used as a neuter.

Podem ir quantos quiserem.
As many as wish to may go.
Você pode comer quanto quiser.
You may eat as much as you wish.

c. With **todo.** Sometimes **todo** is used before **quanto** although the expression is redundant.

Ela terá tudo quanto possa precisar.
She will have everything she may need.

d. For use as an interrogative, see §477.

§136. **Tal** is either an adjective or a pronoun. It does not vary to indicate gender, but has a plural form **tais.**

a. **As an adjective.** The adjective **tal** is often equivalent to **certo.** The indefinite article is used before it.

Um tal General Morais esteve presente.
A certain General Morais was present.

b. With the definite article. **O tal** is equivalent to **o já mencionado.**

A tal mulher entrou na venda do Silva.
The aforesaid woman entered Silva's store.

c. Without an article. The adjective **tal** without any article may be equivalent to **semelhante**.

Tal mulher podia fàcilmente conquistar-lhe o coração.
Such a woman could easily win his heart.
Tal pai, tal filho.
Like father, like son.

d. **Tal que.** Without an article, the adjective **tal** is often equivalent to **tanto**. The noun is followed by **que** and a clause. At other times **tal**, with or without an indefinite article, is a vague word which calls attention to a kind or class of thing explained later on in the sentence. Usually it precedes the noun, but it may also follow.

Êle falou com tal orgulho que caimos na risada.
He spoke with such pride that we burst into laughter.
Êle falou de tal maneira que convenceu todo mundo.
He spoke in such a way that he convinced everybody.
Tal era a resposta que acabou a oposição.
The reply was such that the opposition ceased.
Era um bicho tal que meteu medo nos garotos.
It was a kind of animal that filled the boys with fear.

e. As a predicate adjective. In the predicate **tal** often conveys the same sense as above.

O frio era tal que sofremos muito.
The cold was so great that we suffered a great deal.

f. **Tal** used to cite examples. **Tal** often follows the noun and is followed in turn by **como** and examples cited.

Coisas tais como pratos, copos, etc.
Things such as plates, glasses, etc.

g. **O tal** as a pronoun. This expression is somewhat slangy. The meaning is often depreciatory, equivalent to **sujeito** or **freguês**.

Quem é o tal que não usa lifebuoy?   **Gir**
Who is the guy who doesn't use lifebuoy?
O tal que mexer nas minhas coisas apanha.   **Gir**
The fellow who gets into my stuff will catch it.

At other times it indicates high praise.

Ganhou o jôgo, hein? Você é o tal.   **Gir**
You won the game, did you? You're hot stuff.
Branca é branca, preta é preta,
Mas a mulata é a tal. —Canção.   **Gir**
The white girl is white, the black one is black,
But the mulatto girl is the one.

§137. **Tamanho,** as an adjective of quantity, is not used in BF. It is replaced by **tão grande.**

§138. **Tanto.** This word, declined in both numbers and genders, is either an adjective or a pronoun.

a. As an adjective. It precedes the noun, and both are usually in the singular.

Meu tio tinha me batido tantas vezes que acabei fugindo.
My uncle had beaten me so many times that I finally ran away.
Há tanta coisa bela neste mundo.
There are so many beautiful things in this world.

b. As a correlative. BF prefers **tanto . . . como** to the more literary **tanto . . . quanto.**

Há tanto homem como mulher neste bairro.
There are as many men as women in this district.

c. As a pronoun. Referring to persons, it is generally plural. There is also a singular form used as a neuter.

Ainda existem tantos que não têm oportunidade de estudar.
There are still so many who don't have a chance to study.
Esta terra produz tanto que sempre há alguma coisa para exportar.
This land produces so much that there is always something to export.

d. **Um tanto** is equivalent to **um bocado.** It is most often used adverbially.

Eu já trabalhei um tanto.
I have already worked a bit.

§139. **Todo** is either an adjective or a pronoun. It varies for number and gender, including a special neuter form **tudo.**

a. Position of **todo.** If it precedes a noun, **todo** is always the first word of the noun phrase. Articles, demonstratives, possessives, etc., follow it.

Todos os meus amigos estão aqui.
All my friends are here.

Tôdas aquelas casas vêm abaixo.
All those houses are coming down.

b. Omission of article in the singular. In the singular, the former distinction of meaning between **todo** with and without the definite article has been lost, since there is no difference in sound. Both forms are still written, but the choice is largely random. If the sense is ambiguous, the speaker resorts to an expression which permits clarity.

Tôda a casa = a casa tôda, a casa inteira.
The whole house.
Tôda casa = tôdas as casas.
Every house.

c. Use of the article in the plural. Since phonetic differences remain in the plural, the use of the article is maintained.

Todos os dias = todo dia.
Every day.

d. Omission of the article in the plural. The plural without the article is heard in a few expressions—before a number, with a pronoun, and in various adverbial expressions.

Todos dois, todos três. (*Also* **todos os dois, todos os três.**)
Both, all three.
Êle trouxe presentes para todos nós. (*Also* **nós todos.**)
He brought presents for us all.
De todos modos, de tôdas maneiras.
In any case (both expressions.)

e. The article replaced by other words. **Todo** may be followed by a possessive adjective, a demonstrative, or an indefinite adjective, instead of the definite article.

Todo (o) meu desejo é de fazer um bom trabalho.
My whole desire is to do a good job.
Tôda essa terra é sêca.
All that land is dry.
Tudo quanto você diz é verdade.
Everything you say is true.
Todos êstes meus grandes amigos se lembraram de mim.
All these great friends of mine remembered me.

f. With the indefinite article. **Todo** may be followed by the indefinite article and a noun, with the meanings **inteiro** or **verdadeiro**.

> **Minas é todo um império.**
> Minas is a real empire.
> **Êle é todo um homem.**
> He is every bit a man.

g. **Todo** after the noun. When it follows the noun, **todo** is equivalent to **inteiro**. The article precedes the noun.

> **Revistamos a casa tôda.**
> We searched the whole house.

h. **Todos** after the noun. In the plural, the meaning of **todos** is the same whether preceding or following. The article precedes the noun.

> **Os homens todos já foram. (=Todos os homens.)**
> All the men have already gone.

i. Pronominal forms in the singular. **Todo** is used only rarely as a pronoun in the singular, but the neuter form **tudo** is used very frequently.

> **Tudo leva a crer que haverá lutas políticas.**
> Everything leads one to believe that there will be political struggles.
> **Eu já perdi tudo.**
> I have already lost everything.
> **Êle tem tudo (o) que quer.**
> He has everything he wants.

j. **Todo** as a substantivized adjective. Used substantively, with the definite article, the form is **todo**.

> **São oito ao todo.**
> There are eight all told.
> **O todo é difícil de compreender.**
> The whole is difficult to understand.

k. Plural form used as a pronoun. As pronouns, the plural forms are used to refer to nouns previously mentioned.

> **Os homens e as môças, todos gostam de dançar.**
> The men and the girls all like to dance.

Or, in the masculine form only, it may refer to people in general.

Todos gostam de ouvir música.
  Everybody likes to listen to music.

The same meaning may be expressed by the phrase **todo (o) mundo**, with agreement in the singular.

Todo mundo veio ver a feira.
  Everybody came to see the market.

l. With a personal pronoun. **Todo** may be used with a personal pronoun in the plural, placed before or after the pronoun or separated from it by other words.

Espera! Daqui a pouco nós vamos todos.
  Wait! in a little while we are all going.

m. With a pronoun implicit in the verb. **Todo** may be used, agreeing with the pronoun implicit in the verb form, even though no personal pronoun is expressed.

Êle quer que todos percamos o trem.
  He wants us all to miss the train.

n. Adverbial use of the adjective. **Todo** is sometimes treated as an adjective, with agreement, when the use is adverbial.

Uma mulher tôda vestida de branco.   Subst
  A woman all dressed in white.

§140. The pronoun **um**. The numeral **um**, and its feminine form, may be used as a pronoun. They are distinguishable from the indefinite article by the fact that they are always stressed, whereas the article is unstressed. But **um** is never used as an indefinite general subject, as in English and Spanish.

Um faz o que quer.
  One (of them) does what he wishes.

a. **Um** not used after adjectives. Since adjectives in general may be used as nouns in Portuguese, it is not necessary to add the pronoun **um** following them, as in English. But **cada** and **qualquer** generally require its use. In uncultured speech, it is also heard with the demonstratives at times.

Tenho uma coisa para cada um.
  I have one thing for each.
Qualquer um é capaz de fazer o que eu fiz.
  Anyone at all is capable of doing what I did.

Eu não gosto dêsse um.   **Inc**
I don't like that one.

b. Use of the plural. The plural forms may also be used, although **alguns** is far more frequent.

Banana ouro é rara nesta época, mas consegui achar umas.
The golden banana is rare at this season, but I managed to find a few.

Uns, umas are usually unstressed as adjectives, and are thus the plural forms of the indefinite article.

§141. **Unico** is an adjective, variable for gender and number.

a. Preceding the noun. The meaning here is **só, excluindo os outros.**

O único homem que veio foi o João.
The only man who came was John.

b. Following the noun. The meaning is **o só que existe.**

Êle é filho único.
He is an only son.

c. Following the noun. The meaning may also be **diferente de todos os outros** or **superior a todos os outros.**

Êle é um artista único no mundo.
He is an artist unique in the world.

§142. **Vários** is an adjective used only in the plural, but in both genders.

a. Preceding the noun. It always precedes as an indefinite adjective of quantity.

Eu tenho vários livros sôbre Rondon.
I have several books about Rondon.

b. Following the noun. The meaning here is **de diferentes tipos.** This usage is purely literary.

Temos um estoque de livros vários.   **Lit**
We have a stock of different types of books.

POSSESSIVE ADJECTIVES AND PRONOUNS

The forms

§143. Forms of the first person. The first person singular forms are **meu, minha, meus, minhas**. Those of the plural are **nosso, nossa, nossos, nossas**.

§144. Forms of the second person.

a. Old second person singular. The forms corresponding to the subject **tu** are **teu, tua, teus, tuas**. While the use of the old second person subject and the corresponding form of the verb has largely disappeared in Brazil, except in certain areas, the possessive forms are still used elsewhere to a limited extent. **Teu** is more intimate than **seu** and is heard frequently in familiar conversation when the usual subject pronoun is **você**, although not usually when this subject is expressed. Even in the literary language, **teu** is now limited mostly to situations in which archaic forms are appropriate.

b. Old second person plural. The forms corresponding to the subject **vós** are **vosso, vossa, vossos, vossas**. They are now totally obsolete, along with all other forms of the old second person plural. They are remembered in such expressions as **Vossa Majestade** and **Vossa Excelência** (which persists in use among high officials on formal occasions), in poetry, and in the services of the Catholic church. This last use is now being abandoned.

c. New second person. The possessive adjective referring to the person or persons addressed is now regularly **seu, sua, seus, suas**, whether the subject be the new familiar forms **você, vocês**, or the formal **o senhor**, etc.

§145. Forms of the third person. The third person does not have possessive adjectives in BF. The adjective **seu**, third person in its origin, has now passed completely to the new second person in BF. **Seu** is still used as a third person form in the literary language, although mixed with other constructions. It is used a great deal in dramatic writing, frequently in popular songs, in formal addresses, and even in informal speeches. However, if introduced into colloquial speech, it is nearly always understood to mean **de você**, even when the logical situation would seem to indicate the meaning **dêle**. Thus, in BF there is no possessive adjective of the third person. The definite article is used, clarified when necessary by a prepositional phrase.

§146. Possessive of the impersonal subject. This subject has no special possessive form and uses either the article or **da gente**.

> **Muitas vezes não há no corpo da gente alguma coisa que dá esta dôr?**
> Is there not often in one's body something which causes this pain?

§147. The definite article with the possessive adjective. The definite article may be used with the possessive adjective or omitted at the will of the speaker, with the exceptions noted below. There is no consistency of usage; all speakers use both constructions at different times, in exactly the same circumstances.

> **Êle mora em nossa casa,** *or* **na nossa casa.**
> He lives in our house.

a. Article omitted in direct address. The article is never used in direct address, i.e., when the possessive modifies the person addressed.

> **Meus amigos, que é que se pode fazer?**
> My friends, what can be done?

b. Omission before relationship. The article is not usually used before nouns of relationship.

> **Minha irmã chegou de táxi.**
> My sister arrived by taxi.
> **Êste é meu compadre.**
> This is my godchild's father.

The article may, however, be used *instead* of the possessive, as long as the reference is clear. See §151.

> **O senhor vai visitar a sogra?**
> Are you going to visit your mother-in-law?
> **Eu estou morando com a tia.**
> I am living with my aunt.

Use of the possessive adjective

§148. Agreement. The words **meu, nosso, teu,** and **seu** agree in number and gender with the thing possessed.

Perdi minhas economias.
I lost my savings.
Glória, teu livro está no chão.
Gloria, your book is on the ground.

§149. Repetition of the possessive adjective. In theory, the adjective is repeated before each noun it modifies, unless they refer to the same thing.

Minha mãe e minha irmã.
My mother and my sister.

In practice, they are not repeated unless different forms are required or the sentence would not be clear without the repetition.

Meu tio e primo vieram hoje.
My uncle and cousin came today.
Meu irmão e minha prima estão aqui.
My brother and my cousin are here.

§150. Position of the possessive adjective. In general, it precedes the word it modifies.

Esta é minha casa.
This is my house.

a. It precedes in direct address.

Meus amigos!
My friends!
Escuta, meu bem.
Listen, my darling.

b. Position with the indefinite article. It may precede or follow.

Eu vou falar sôbre isso com um meu amigo.
I am going to speak about this to a friend of mine.
Um meu amigo de infância está morando lá.
A childhood friend of mine is living there.
Quero que você conheça um amigo meu.
I want you to meet a friend of mine.

c. With an adjective preceding the noun. If another adjective precedes the same noun, the possessive is likely to follow.

Êste velho amigo meu.
   This old friend of mine.
O Borba é um acirrado inimigo seu.
   Borba is a bitter enemy of yours.

d. When the possessive is emphasized. It is somewhat more likely to follow, although it is normal to stress a possessive before the noun also.

Você não pode guiar um carro meu.
   You can't drive a car of mine.

e. With the indefinite article omitted. The possessive follows the noun regularly.

Ela parece irmã sua.
   She looks as if she might be your sister.
Coisa nossa não se deve desperdiçar.
   A thing belonging to us should not be wasted.

§151. Use of the definite article as a possessive. The definite article is used instead of the possessive adjective.

a. When the subject is the possessor. This is nearly always the case when the thing possessed is a part of the body, an article of clothing, or other object of personal use. It is true almost as often with other things possessed, persons, etc.

O ladrão levantou os braços.
   The thief raised his arms.
A môça torceu o nariz.
   The girl made a grimace.
Perdi o lápis.
   I have lost my pencil.
Êle puxa ao pai.
   He takes after his father.
Eu vou me meter no carro. (=meu carro.)
   I am going to get into the car.

The possessive adjectives may be used in such cases, in the first and second persons, but such usage is much rarer than the use of the article.

b. When the possessor is of the third person. Since no possessive adjective exists in BF for third person pronouns, there is no alternative to the article.

c. When the reference is clear. Although the subject is not the possessor, the reference of the article can be understood readily from the context.

> **Um rapaz está falando com a môça aí da vizinha.**
> A fellow is talking to the daughter of our neighbor.
> **Uma coisa dessas dá frio no coração. (=o coração da gente.)**
> A thing like that makes your blood run cold.

§152. Usage when the subject is possessed.

a. First and second persons. If the possessor is of the first or second person, the possessive is used.

> **Meu pai morava aqui.**
> My father lived here.
> **Sua casa é bonita.**
> Your house is pretty.

b. In the third person. If the possessor is of the third person, the article is used and generally requires an explanatory phrase after the noun.

> **A irmã dêle vai chegar hoje.**
> His sister is going to arrive today.
> **A mãe dela também é assim.**
> Her mother is like that too.
> **O carro dêle encrencou.**
> His car went bad.
> *But* **A irmã veio com você?**
> Did your sister come with you?

§153. Clarification of a possessive. At times a phrase, consisting of de and a pronoun, is needed to clarify an article used for a possessive.

a. Not used in first and old second persons. Such phrases are not used in these persons, since the possessive adjective may always be used for clarity. Nor is there any reason to use a phrase for special emphasis, since a possessive adjective may be stressed, even when it precedes its noun.

b. New second person. In the new second person there is sometimes need to be more explicit, since **seu** is used for singular and plural, both genders, and for both the familiar and polite forms. In such cases the article (not the possessive) precedes the noun, and the appropriate phrase follows. These phrases may be used at will, whether for clarity, for added emphasis, for added formality, or for no reason at all.

>   **Vocês vão no carro de você? (O outro também tem carro.)**
>   Are you going in your car?
>   **Êste é o chapéu do senhor?**
>   Is this your hat?

c. In the third person. Since there is no possessive adjective in BF in this person, it is often necessary to add a phrase to clarify the reference. It may be required with the subject of the clause, or later in the sentence when the possessor is not the subject.

>   **O pai dêle é médico.**
>   His father is a doctor.
>   **Você levou o carro dela?**
>   Did you take her car?
>   **José e Maria foram com a tia dela.**
>   Joe and Mary went with her aunt.

d. After **ser.** Such phrases maybe used after **ser,** alternating with **seu** in the second person, and must be used in the third person.

>   **Êste livro é seu** *or* **de você.**
>   This book is yours.
>   **O carro vermelho é dêle.**
>   The red car is his.

§154. The possessor indicated by the dative. The construction in which an article indicates possession by a person mentioned in the form of a dative personal pronoun is not very frequent in BF. The dative is not used for the purpose of identifying the possessor, but to indicate the person concerned in the action. However, once it is used, it may also serve to identify the owner.

>   **A queda lhe quebrou a perna.**
>   The fall broke his leg.
>   **Me aperta a mão.**
>   Shake my hand.

The reflexive pronoun in the dative is very rarely so used. Since it refers to the subject, this last would always be sufficient to identify the owner.

Eu lavei as mãos.   *Cf.* **Eu me lavei.**
I washed my hands.   I washed (myself).
É de se tirar o chapéu.
It is enough to make you take off your hat.

Note that in this example the reflexive pronoun serves to indicate the impersonal nature of the verb.

§155. The possessive adjective used for a phrase. As a prepositional phrase may replace a possessive, so the reverse is true also. The possessive adjective is sometimes equivalent to a phrase following the noun, or even another word which may replace the noun.

Êle passou na minha frente. (=em frente de mim.)
He passed in front of me.
O carro toma a minha dianteira. (=passa para diante de mim.)
The car gets ahead of me.
Olho ao meu redor. (=ao redor de mim.)
I look around me.

§156. The expression **Nossa Senhora**. This expression has come to be treated as a name, so that one says:

Eu gosto daquela Nossa Senhora.
I like that Our Lady.
Minha Nossa Senhora!
My goodness gracious!

Other possessive adjectives

§157. The possessives **cujo, alheio,** and **próprio**.

a. **Cujo** is purely literary. It is a relative possessive adjective. BF uses **de quem** and, colloquially, other expressions.

Hoje eu vi o homem cuja casa comprei.   Lit
Vi o homem de quem eu comprei a casa.   BF
Vi o homem que comprei a casa dêle.   Subst
Today I saw the man whose house I bought.

b. **Alheio**, as a possessive, is equivalent to **de outra pessoa** and regularly follows its noun. It is in common use in BF.

Não gosto de estar em casa alheia.
I don't like to be in another person's house.

c. **Próprio** expresses emphatically the ownership of the subject of the sentence.

Êle maltratou a própria mãe.
He mistreated his own mother.
Meus pais me dão tudo, mas eu queria dinheiro próprio.
My parents give me everything, but I would like money of my own.

Próprio normally precedes the noun when used with the definite article but follows without an article when the expression is indefinite.

The possessive pronouns

§158. The possessive pronouns, when used as pronouns, **meu**, **nosso**, **teu**, and **seu** require the definite article.

Vamos apanhar seu casaco e os nossos.
Let's get your coat and ours.
Não posso distinguir o meu do seu.
I can't tell mine from yours.

a. The pronoun may be replaced by the demonstrative pronoun **o** and a prepositional phrase in the new second person.

Êste chapéu é maior que o de você.
This hat is bigger than yours.
Amanhã vou mudar desta casa para a do senhor.
Tomorrow I am going to move from this house to yours.

b. In the third person, only the demonstrative **o** and the prepositional phrases are used in BF.

Aqui está meu copo. Cadê o dêle?
Here is my glass. Where is his?

§159. Usage after **ser**. After the verb **ser** either the adjective or the pronoun may be used, with a slight difference in meaning. The adjective denotes possession only; the pronoun identifies as well.

Êste chapéu é meu. (Êste me pertence.)
This hat is mine. (This one belongs to me.)
Êste chapéu é o meu. (Há outros, mas êste é que é meu.)
This hat is mine. (There are others, but this is the one that belongs to me.)

For the third person, the difference is indicated by the use or omission of the demonstrative **o**.

Êste lápis é dêle.
This pencil is his.
Êste lápis é o dêle.
This is *his* pencil.

NUMBERS

§160. Agreement of cardinal numbers.

a. **Um** and **dois**. These two numbers take feminine forms to agree with a feminine noun, whether they are used alone or as part of a larger number.

> **Vinte e uma casas.**
> Twenty-one houses.
> **Quarenta e duas mulheres.**
> Forty-two women.
> **Duas mil casas.**
> Two thousand houses.

b. The multiples of **cem** also agree in gender.

> **Quinhentas árvores.**
> Five hundred trees.

Cem does not vary for gender, but it becomes **cento** when a number smaller than 100 is added to it. **Um** never precedes it.

> **Cento e duas aldeias.**
> One hundred two villages.

c. **Mil** is treated as an invariable adjective. **Um** is not used with it, but **dois** becomes **duas** if the noun after it is feminine.

> **Duas mil flores.**
> Two thousand flowers.

d. **Milhão** is a masculine noun. It takes the indefinite article, and is followed by **de** before a noun, if no additional number intervenes.

> **Um milhão de pessoas.**
> One million people.
> **Dois milhões de mulheres.**
> Two million women.
> **Dois milhões e duzentas mil mulheres.**
> Two million, two hundred thousand women.

88

§161. Collective numbers. In addition to **milhão,** there are several nouns designating either exact or appropriate numerical groups.

a. **Par** indicates a group of two. For living beings, the usual term is **casal.**

b. Forms in **-ena.** Several commonly used numbers have derivatives which indicate a group of that number: **dezena, vintena, centena.** But a group of twelve is **dúzia.**

c. **Cento** is used of a group whose exact count is one hundred. It is used in commerce, etc., where the exact number is important. **Centena** is often approximate.

> **Vendem-se a mil cruzeiros o cento.**
> They are sold for one thousand cruzeiros a hundred.
> **Centenas de pessoas foram à praia.**
> Hundreds of people went to the beach.

d. **Milhar** is used in giving prices, etc. In the plural, **milhares** is used for approximate numbers.

> **Custam dois contos o milhar.**
> They cost two thousand cruzeiros a thousand.
> **Vimos milhares de refugiados.**
> We saw thousands of refugees.
> **As vacas morriam aos milhares.**
> The cows died by the thousand.

e. **Conto.** Originally this word meant one million, and was applied only to the coin **real.** With first the reduction of the coin to **milréis** and then its replacement by the **cruzeiro,** it came to mean **mil cruzeiros.** The new **cruzeiro** has now replaced the old, at the rate of one to one thousand, so that the word **conto** is likely to disappear from usage.

§162. Use of **e** in numbers. The conjunction **e** is used:

a. Before tens and units, and the words **cem** and **cento.**

> **Vinte e seis**
> Twenty-six
> **Cento e dez**
> One hundred ten
> **Duzentos e vinte e oito**
> Two hundred twenty-eight
> **Mil e cem**
> One thousand one hundred

Mil e cento e dez
One thousand one hundred ten

b. After **milhão** or **mil,** before a multiple of **cem,** if no smaller number follows the latter.

Dois milhões e trezentos
Two million three hundred
Mil e quatrocentos
One thousand four hundred

c. Otherwise, it is generally omitted.

Um milhão, duzentos mil, quatrocentos e cinco
One million, two hundred thousand, four hundred five

§163. The ordinal numbers. The ordinals are avoided a great deal in BF. In fact, only a few are familiar enough to all to be used with any facility. Those up to tenth are in common use, along with **vigésimo** and **centésimo.** The ordinal forms of the tens from thirtieth to ninetieth are used infrequently, along with those formed by adding the ordinal forms of the units to them.

A quarta casa.
The fourth house.
A vigésima vez.
The twentieth time.
A trigésima quinta pessoa.   **Rare**
The thirty-fifth person.

a. Use with days of the month. Only **primeiro** is used. The cardinal numbers are used for the other dates.

O primeiro de junho.
The first of June.
O dois de maio.
The second of May.

b. With names of kings, etc. With the names of personages such as kings, emperors, popes, etc., as well as in most other uses, the ordinals are used only as far as tenth. The cardinal numbers are used thereafter.

Pio Nono.
Pius the Ninth.
Carlos Quinto.
Charles the Fifth.

No sexto dia.
On the sixth day.

c. With chapters, pages, etc. In speaking of things which occur in long series, such as chapters, pages, streets, etc., cardinal numbers are used. One sometimes hears the ordinals up to tenth, but seldom after that. The cardinal numbers **um** and **dois** do not agree in gender when used for ordinals. The cardinal number follows the noun in this usage.

Capítulo três.
Chapter three.
Página vinte e um.
Page twenty-one.

§164. Fractions. In fractions, the ordinals are used to designate the denominator from thirds through tenths, for the multiples of tenths through hundredths, and for thousandths and millionths.

Dois terços
Two thirds
Vinte e quatro trigésimos
Twenty-four thirtieths
Dezenove milésimos
Nineteen thousandths

a. "Half" is expressed by **a metade de** or by the adjective **meio.** The latter may be preceded by an indefinite article, but not followed by it.

Sobra a metade do espaço.
Half of the space is left over.
Eu esperei meia hora.
I waited half an hour.
Uma meia hora passa depressa.
A half hour passes quickly.

b. Higher fractions. From eleventh on up, with the exceptions noted above, the denominator is indicated by adding the word **avos** to the cardinal number.

Um onze avos
One eleventh
Vinte e dois quarenta e três avos
Twenty-two forty-thirds

c. Use of **parte**. Although they are cumbersome, the expressions **a quarta parte, a décima parte**, etc., are sometimes used instead of the shorter forms, i.e., the masculine form of the ordinal.

§165. The multiplying numbers. These numbers, nouns or adjectives, are used as equivalents of **duas (três, quatro) vezes mais**, etc. But the frequency of such usage decreases as the numbers increase.

> **Eu queria o dôbro.**
> I would like twice as much.
> **Me dá um chope duplo.**
> Give me a double draft.
> **O Brasil daria para o triplo da população atual.**
> Brazil could hold three times its present population.
> **Vamos montar uma campanha tríplice.**
> Let's start a three-pronged campaign.

§166. Approximate numbers. To express approximate numbers, in addition to adverbs such as **mais ou menos**, one may use:

a. The plural of the indefinite article.

> **Vimos umas trinta pessoas.**
> We saw about twenty persons.

b. A preposition.

> **Há cêrca de (*or* perto de) trinta pessoas.**
> There are about thirty persons.

§167. Distribution by numbers.

a. To express intervals, the construction is as follows:

> **Vamos lá de dois em dois dias.**
> We go there every other day.
> **Paramos de três em três quilômetros.**
> We stop every three kilometers.

b. To express grouping by numbers, one may say:

> **Os convidados partiam dois a dois e três a três.**
> The guests left by twos and threes.

§168. Use of **meia**. It should be noted that in telephone conversations, in reading numbers aloud for copying or memorization, etc., when difficult conditions for understanding prevail, **seis** is replaced by **meia** or **meia dúzia**.

THE PERSONAL PRONOUN

Pronouns used as subjects

§169. The forms. The personal pronouns used as subjects in BF are the following:

First person	eu	nós
Second person (familiar)	você	vocês
Second person (formal, masc.)	o senhor	os senhores
Second person (formal, fem.)	a senhora	as senhoras
Third person (masc.)	êle	êles
Third person (fem.)	ela	elas

a. Old second person forms. The subject pronoun **tu** is no longer in common use in most of Brazil. It is retained in some regions of the far South, the North, and the Northeast, for limited use within the family and among close friends—usually childhood friends. Speaking to others, even people from these regions tend to use **você**, and even in the circumstances mentioned above use it frequently. Elsewhere, **você** is the universal form, although everyone is acquainted with **tu** and its verb forms.

In the plural, **vós** is completely obsolete, replaced entirely by **vocês**. Very few Brazilians would be able to use the corresponding verb forms correctly.

b. The new second person forms. All new second person subjects require the use of the same form of the verb as the third person. The new familiar forms, **você**, and **vocês**, are used with much more latitude than the familiar forms of most European languages, and their application is constantly being extended. A quarter-century ago, most children addressed their parents as **o senhor** and **a senhora**; today, most children address them as **você**. Younger people who meet for the first time usually use the more familiar form immediately, unless they meet in a formal situation. Masters of ceremonies on television address a guest as **você**, unless he is noticeably

93

older or particularly distinguished. A member of the public is addressed in advertising as **você**. There is a marked tendency for this form to become universal.

The more formal subjects, **o senhor, a senhora**, and their plurals, are largely reserved for persons considerably older than the speaker, persons who are distinguished by their achievements or their position in society, and to one's equals when first met on a formal occasion. It should be noted that a lady whose title is **senhorita** is addressed as **a senhora** when it is used as a pronoun, although one may hear **a senhorita** on rare occasions.

> **Senhorita Lopes, a senhora não quer entrar?**
> Miss Lopes, won't you come in?

In reprimands, the formal subjects are sometimes used to persons whom one addresses regularly with the more familiar forms. Thus, a mother may speak to her child:

> **Se o senhor entornar o café na mesa, vai ter comigo.**
> If you spill your coffee on the table, you'll have trouble with me.

c. Other, even more formal modes of address still exist but are used mostly in set circumstances. Thus, the members of Congress address each other formally as **Vossa Excelência.** One addresses a letter to **Excelentíssimo Senhor Fulano.** In business letters, some still use **Sua Senhoria** in the body of the letter.

d. Third person forms. **Êle** and **êles** may be used to refer to any masculine nouns, animate or inanimate, and the feminine forms to any feminine nouns. Most often, they are omitted when the noun is inanimate.

> **Não quero êste apartamento. Êle é tão ruim.**
> I don't want this apartment. It is so bad.

The subject **êles** cannot be used to mean "people in general" or "vague, indefinite people." The third person plural of the verb may be used, but without an expressed subject.

> **Dizem que Carlos já voltou.**
> They say that Charles has returned.

When a neuter subject is needed, to refer to another neuter pronoun, to a situation, or to an unidentified noun, the neuter forms of the demonstratives are used. The most frequently used of these is **isso**. Such a subject is required only if it is to be stressed and in certain fixed expressions, such as the explanatory **isso é**.

§170. Use of the subject pronouns. The subject pronoun is expressed:

a. For emphasis. If the subject is to be stressed, for any reason, it must be expressed. But if the pronouns are used, they may be stressed or unstressed.

> **João vai à festa, mas eu não vou.**
> John is going to the party, but I am not going.

b. For clarity. The loss of the old second person forms of the verb reduces the forms of each tense to four, and in some tenses, e.g., the imperfect, to three. In addition, the third person plural is not very different in sound from the singular. As a result, the verb used without an expressed subject is often not at all clear.

> **Eu falava, você falava, êle falava, êles falavam, etc.**
> I spoke, you spoke, he spoke, they spoke.

c. To avoid opening the clause with an object pronoun. Normative grammar does not permit a personal pronoun object to open a clause. But in many cases it would be unnatural for the Brazilian speaker to place it after the verb. In order to avoid this dilemma, he uses a subject pronoun, even in cases in which neither emphasis nor clarity requires it. This solution is both natural to the speaker and acceptable in literary Portuguese; therefore it is widely used.

> **Nós nos despedimos.** (*Unnatural*: **Despedimo-nos.**)
> We took leave.

§171. Omission of the subject pronouns. Although the subject pronouns are expressed much more often today than formerly, and considerably more often in BF than in the literary form of the language, they are still expressed considerably less often than in English or French. They are generally omitted:

a. With a second verb whose subject is the same as the first.

> **Eu já disse que queria ir com vocês.**
> I have already said that I wanted to go with you.
> **Eu vi seu pai quando passei.**
> I saw your father when I passed by.

b. When the verb agrees with a noun recently mentioned.

Eu vi seu pai quando passei. Estava sentado na varanda, lendo.
I saw your father when I passed by. He was seated on the porch, reading.

c. When the verb form is so distinctive that the subject is clear without a pronoun. For this reason, the subject **nós** is expressed less frequently than any other.

Vou fumar um cigarro.
I am going to smoke a cigaret.
Já acabaram a tarefa.
They have already finished their homework.
Vamos embora.
Let's go away.

Pronouns used as direct objects

§172. The forms. The personal pronouns used as direct objects of the verb are the following:

First person	me	nos
Old second person	te	
Second person (familiar)	você (o, a)	vocês (os, as)
Second person (formal)	o senhor (o)	os senhores (os)
	a senhora (a)	as senhoras (as)
Third person	êle (o)	êles (os)
	ela (a)	elas (as)
Reflexive (second and third persons)	se	se

§173. Use of personal pronouns as direct objects. This usage varies somewhat among the three persons of the pronouns and requires separate treatment in each person.

a. The first person. The forms **me** and **nos** may not be stressed. In fact, no stressed forms exist in the first person. While prepositional forms are found on rare occasions in literature, their use in BF is quite unusual. The rare person who employs this construction is likely to be a Portuguese or someone highly trained in the literary language. In BF, the unstressed form is generally used. If stress seems necessary, the sentence is reconstructed so that the pronoun occurs in a form which can be stressed. Thus, if one wished to express in BF the equivalent of the sentence, "*I* saw *him,* but he didn't see *me,*" he might say

Eu vi êle, mas êle não me viu.

To emphasize the pronoun object in

Isso me pertence.
That belongs to me.

he might say

Isso é meu. *Or* **O dono disso sou eu.**
That is mine. I am the owner of that.

b. The second person. The object form **te** is in somewhat wider use than the corresponding subject form or the verb form. It, like the possessive adjective, is used in speaking to family and close friends, alternating freely with **você**, even in regions where the subject is always **você**.

Eu te vi quando [você] namorava com aquela menina.
I saw you when you were flirting with that girl.

The forms of the new second person used as subject pronouns—**você, o senhor, a senhora**, and their respective plurals—are also used as direct objects of the verb. For their position with respect to the verb, see § 179.

Eu vi você na cidade hoje.
I saw you downtown today.
Ela encontrou o senhor ontem?
Did she find you yesterday?
Não conheço a senhora.
I don't know you.

For the use of **o, os, a,** and **as,** see (c), below.

c. Use of the third person forms. The textbooks from which the student studies Portuguese in Brazil contain extensive sections which treat the object pronoun **o**, the transformations which it undergoes when used with certain verb forms, its contractions when used in combination with the various indirect object forms, etc. However, most of this is so far removed from the language of the present day that he would not be able to understand these forms if they were used in speaking to him.

Whether used to refer to the new second person subjects or to those of the third person, these object pronouns are used only in the following situations, and even in those are the exception rather than the rule.

In a few traditional fixed formulas following the infinitive:

Muito prazer em conhecê-lo.
Delighted to meet you.

After infinitives in general, but rather infrequently:

Comecei o trabalho, mas não posso acabá-lo.
I began the work, but I can't finish it.
Êle não está aqui; vamos procurá-lo.
He isn't here; let's look for him.

After the adverb **eis**. This word itself is somewhat archaic and is now used mostly with humorous intent.

Falávamos no Jorge, e ei-lo aqui.
We were speaking of George, and here he is.

If there is no reason to stress a third person object pronoun, it is not expressed at all. To the speaker of a language such as English (to say nothing of Spanish), in which many object pronouns are used, it would seem that their omission would cause great ambiguity and confusion. Actually, no such difficulty is met in BF. An object pronoun has little clarity in itself; it refers to a noun which makes it specific. The noun is sufficient, and little or nothing is added by its repetition in the form of a pronoun. Without context, as in the translation of isolated sentences, the ambiguity is considerable. But the spoken language does not exist out of context.

Quem foi que entrou na loja? —Eu não vi.
Who was it that came into the store? I didn't see him.
Tenho uma coisa na mão. —Me dá.
I have something in my hand. Give it to me.
Não te dou esta laranja. —Eu não quero.
I won't give you this orange. I don't want it.
Comecei o trabalho, mas não posso acabar.
I began the work, but I can't finish it.

If an object pronoun of the third person requires stress, for any reason, the forms used as subjects—**êle, ela, êles, elas**—are used. They are treated like demonstratives or nouns, i.e., placed immediately after the verb. The stress may be used to emphasize the object, rather than the subject or the verb; it may be required to insist on one individual as the object, rather than another, e.g., **êle** rather than **ela**; or the stressed form may be used with weak stress for no special reason except that the speaker wishes to use an object.

> **Dá êle para os ciganos.**
> Give him to the gypsies.
> **Conheço êle, mas não conheço ela.**
> I know him, but I don't know her.
> **Meu pai está lá na sala. —Chama êle.**
> My father is there in the living room. Call him.

Pronouns used as indirect objects

§174. The forms. The forms used as indirect (dative) object pronouns in the three persons are as follows:

First person	me	nos
Old second person	te	
New second person	lhe	lhes
Third person	lhe	lhes
Reflexive (second and third persons)	se	se

§175. Use of the indirect object pronouns. The dative personal pronouns are used:

a. To express the indirect object, i.e., the person to whom or for whom something is done.

> **A Joana me deu um presente.**
> Joann gave me a present.
> **Êle me contou uma piada.**
> He told me a joke.
> **Você quer que eu lhe preste dinheiro?**
> Do you want me to lend you some money?
> **Êle chegou perto do ministro e pediu-lhe uma esmola.**
> He came up to the minister and asked for alms.

b. As the ethical dative, i.e., to refer to a person who has some more or less vague concern in the action.

> **Êle me roubou a carteira.**
> He stole my billfold.
> **Eu lhe quebro êsse galho.**
> I'll remove that difficulty for you.

c. To explain the reference of articles used for possessive. This usage is not frequent, and practically always secondary to use as ethical dative.

A queda lhe quebrou a perna.
The fall broke his leg.
Me roubaram o carro.
They stole my car.

d. **Lhe** and **lhes** (pronounced **li** and **lis** in Brazil) are sometimes used as direct objects. This usage is felt as substandard, and is not a regular practice in any circles, but it is heard sporadically at most levels. It may be a result of confusion between direct and indirect objects, or it may be an attempt to find a direct object acceptable to literary Portuguese.

Eu não lhe vi. (=Eu não vi você.)   Subst
I didn't see you.

Personal pronouns as objects of prepositions

§176. The forms. There are only a few special forms for use following prepositions. For the most part, the subject forms are used.

First person	**a mim**	**a nós**
Old second person	**a ti**	
Second person	**a você, etc.**	**a vocês, etc.**
Third person	**a êle, a ela**	**a êles, a elas**
Reflexive, second and third persons	**a si**	**a si**

With the preposition **com**, the special forms **comigo, conosco,** and **consigo** exist, along with the old second person **contigo.**

§177. The prepositional forms are used:

a. As the indirect object of the verb. The simple dative forms given above may be replaced at any time as indirect objects by a phrase consisting of **a** or **para** and the prepositional form of the personal pronoun. This construction is an alternative to the dative pronoun and is not used in addition to it. It may be used at any time, for emphasis, for clarity, or simply at the will of the speaker. **Para** is used more often than **a** to form the indirect object.

Me dá isso.
Give me that.
Dá isso para mim. (*Less used* **a mim.**)
Give that to me.
Eu lhe comprei êstes bombons.
I bought you these chocolates.

Comprei êstes bombons para você. (*Not* **a você.**)
I bought these chocolates for you.

b. After most prepositions.

Perto de mim, longe de nós, nêle, por mim, etc.
Near me, far from us, on him, by me, etc.

c. The preposition **com** is not followed by **mim, nós, ti,** or **si.** Instead, the forms **comigo, conosco, contigo,** and **consigo** are used.

d. Non reflexive use of **si.** Among the Portuguese, the prepositional form **si** and the special form **consigo** are sometimes used as formal second forms. This usage is considered affected in Brazil, and is seldom heard.

Apanhei o correio e trouxe uma carta para si. (=**para o senhor.**) Lus
I got the mail and brought a letter for you.

e. Prepositions followed by the nominative case. For these, see §361.

Position of object pronouns with the verb

§178. Confusion and variation in usage. The question of the placing of the personal pronoun object is one of the most complex and confusing in both literary Portuguese and BF. Much of the confusion has arisen as a result of the insistence of the Brazilian schools on the rules as they existed, or were thought to exist, in the literary language of Portugal. Usage in that country, both in speech and in writing, is quite different from that of Brazil. Brazilian usage was therefore considered to be erroneous and unacceptable. However, the numerous differences between the forms of the language spoken in the two countries make it impossible for the Brazilian to follow the usages of Portugal without often sounding absurd to his fellow-countrymen, and at times even unintelligible.

After several years of study during which the schools insist on a foreign speech pattern, the Brazilian is often completely confused. He feels some obligation to speak, and especially to write, "correctly," even though it is often unnatural. As a result, he sometimes attempts to "improve" his language by speaking in an unnatural way, sometimes with a construction that is abnormal in either country. Thus, many constructions one encounters in Brazilian books are completely artificial. However, the weight of public opinion has veered much more toward the natural speech of the country in recent years. One can speak more naturally in almost any social situation than he could a generation ago. And even the literary language has been closing a great deal of the gap between it and the normal spoken language. The schools are still conservative, but they have felt considerable influence from recent literature. It seems that Brazilian patterns are becoming more accepted. As for the people, they no longer make much effort to change their way of speaking.

The usual patterns of verb and personal pronoun object in BF are extremely complicated and leave room for considerable variation, even without considering the still important effects of grammatical training. The position of the pronoun may be affected by the choice of the pronoun itself, by several types of words which may precede the verb, by the tense form of the verb which is used, or by the fact that a second verb form follows the first. Sometimes these influences work against one another, usually producing more or less free variation. The effects of these different factors are discussed below.

§179. Object pronouns of fixed position. The very system of object pronouns has been transformed by the development of the new second person and the use of the subject pronouns of the third person as objects. These words have escaped from the patterns which developed in the Romance languages, and are treated syntactically like nouns or demonstrative pronouns. They follow the verb of which they are objects, without regard to the form of the verb nor to the words which may precede it. Like nouns, they may be separated from the verb by an adverb or a phrase.

Eu vejo o senhor amanhã.
I'll see you tomorrow.
Êle tinha visto, lá em casa, você e seu irmão.
He had seen you and your brother, back home.
Êle reconheceria ela, e talvez você também.
He would recognize her, and perhaps you, too.
Não conheço êle.
I don't know him.
Aquela é a moça que levou você à feira.
That is the girl who took you to the market.
Vou retirar dinheiro do banco para pagar você.
I am going to withdraw money from the bank to pay you.

§180. Vestigial use of **o, a, os, as.** These words are rarely, if ever, used by a large part of the population. The only usage which can be considered as BF is heard following an infinitive. Even here it is omitted much more often than used. In this situation, the infinitive loses its final **-r**, and the object pronoun receives an initial **l-**. These forms do not precede the infinitive in BF.

Muito prazer em conhecê-lo.
  Delighted to meet you.
Dá gosto vê-la restabelecida.
  It's good to see you are recovered.
É um bom cavalo; não quero perdê-lo.
  It is a good horse; I don't want to lose it.

§181. Objects whose position is variable. The remaining forms, whose position with respect to the verb must be determined, are **me, nos, lhe, lhes, te,** and **se.** The various situations which affect their positions are discussed in the following paragraphs.

§182. Pronouns with a one-word verb at head of a clause. Traditional rules categorically forbid that the first word of a clause (including a clause following a co-ordinating conjunction) should be a personal pronoun object. The tendency of BF is to place the pronoun first in a great many cases. This construction is in wide and increasing use but is still considered somewhat substandard.

a. Object placed after the verb. To avoid substandard speech, many speakers, especially the more educated ones, place the object after the verb. This satisfies the rules which are taught, and the construction is used with sufficient frequency to be acceptable and intelligible to everyone. It should be classed as semi-literary.

Disseram-me que houve um desastre de trem.   SLit
  They told me that there was a train wreck.
Diga-me como foi.   SLit
  Tell me how it went.
Sentava-se à cabeceira da mesa.   SLit
  He sat at the head of the table.

b. Subject pronoun used. A compromise solution, more common than the preceding, is to express the subject pronoun, even though the meaning does not require it, or even if it is somewhat redundant. The object pronoun then precedes the verb in a construction which is both accepted and natural.

Êles me disseram que houve um desastre de trem.
They told me that there was a train wreck.
Ela se sentava à cabeceira da mesa.
She sat at the head of the table.

c. Reflexive **se** at head of clause. The reflexive pronoun **se** rarely begins a clause, probably because it could easily be confused with the conjunction **se**. Whenever possible, it is omitted. A personal pronoun subject may be expressed in other cases. However, there are numerous expressions in common use in which this pronoun follows the verb, so that it sounds less stilted when placed after than do the other pronoun objects.

Está vendo aquêle homem? Chama-se Pires.
Do you see that man? His name is Pires.
Não vou ao cinema, e acabou-se.
I am not going to the movies, that's all.

d. The verb is first person plural. This form of any tense or mood of the verb is never followed by an object pronoun in BF. One must place it before the verb and decide whether to use a subject pronoun or not. The problem arises almost solely with reflexive verbs, since other objects are rare with this form. Whenever it is possible to do so without changing the meaning, BF omits the reflexive object.

Até logo; nos vemos.
So long; we'll see each other.
Nós nos divertimos muito.
We enjoyed ourselves a lot.
Levantamos cedo.
We got up early.
Sentamos no chão.
We sat down on the ground.

e. The verb is imperative. The object pronoun generally precedes the imperative in BF, unless it is reflexive. Since the imperative does not have an expressed subject in most cases, the reflexive **se** follows.

Me diz a verdade.
Tell me the truth.
Me dá isso.
Give me that.

Lhe ajuda a mudar a geladeira. (*Also* **ajuda êle.**)
Help him to move the refrigerator.
Diverte-se na praia hoje.
Enjoy yourself at the beach today.

f. The verb is future or conditional. These tenses were formed from the infinitive followed by forms of the verb **haver**. Formerly the object pronouns were placed between the infinitive and the ending. This practice has long since been abandoned.

Conhecer-me-á, pedir-lhe-ei.   **Obs**
He will know me. I shall ask him.

These forms cannot, however, take object pronouns after them. The subject pronoun may be used to authorize placing it before.

Me verão de novo no outono.
You will see me again in the fall.
Êle me pagará.
He will pay me.

g. The expression **ir-se embora.** In this expression, the reflexive pronoun never precedes the verb in BF. In the first person plural, it may not follow. Consequently, the reflexive pronoun is not used at all in this form. It may, of course, be omitted in other forms as well.

Eu vou-me embora.
I am going away.
Não vai-se embora.
Don't go away.
Vamos embora.
Let's go.

In the literary language, the pronoun sometimes precedes the verb if it is negative or in a subordinate clause, etc.

O homem que se vai embora é meu tio.
The man who is going away is my uncle.

§183. Objects of one-word verbs, preceded by other words. The object is usually placed before a one-word verb, if it does not become the first word of the clause. The strictness of this rule varies somewhat with the type of word or words which open the clause. However, BF rather consistently places the object first.

a. The word is a negative.

João não me deu isso.
 John didn't give me that.
Nem se apercebem da situação.
 They don't even realize the situation.
Ninguém lhe levava a palma nisso.
 Nobody got ahead of him in this.
Nunca te vi mais gordo.
 I never saw you in my life.
Nada me faz esquecer o que passou.
 Nothing will make me forget what happened.

b. The word is interrogative.

Quem me mandou êste embrulho?
 Who sent me this package?
Onde nos viu?
 Where did you see us?

c. The word is a relative pronoun. The object is never placed before a negative in a relative clause, as is done in Portugal.

Recebi um telefonema do capitão, que nos deu ordem de irmos.
 I got a call from the captain, who ordered us to go.
Faço a primeira coisa que me entra na cabeça.
 I'll do the first thing which comes into my head.
Passou um guarda, que não me viu. (. . . que me não viu. Lus)
 A policeman passed, who didn't see me.

d. The word is the conjunction **que**.

Não compreendo que se demore tanto na rua.
 I don't understand his staying so long on the street.
Não quero que me tragam queixas.
 I don't want you to bring complaints to me.

e. The word is an adverbial conjunction.

Não sei o que fará quando lhe disser o que me contaram.
 I don't know what he will do when I tell him what they told me.
Me escondi das crianças antes que me vissem.
 I hid from the children before they saw me.

f. The word is an adverb.

Êle faz das suas, e depois se queixa quando o povo fala.
 He does what comes naturally, and then complains when people talk.

Só se vê ao longe uma mancha verde.
One sees only a green spot in the distance.
Sempre te dizia que não podia ganhar a vida vendendo jornais.
I always told you that you couldn't earn a living selling papers.
Assim se conseguem as coisas.
That's how one gets things.

g. After a prepositional phrase. The most natural tendency is to place the object before the verb, as it is when the object and verb open the clause. But SLit speech often prefers to place it after.

Neste momento me vi em perigo de cair.
At this moment I saw myself in danger of falling.
De repente, lembro-me do forno aceso.
Suddenly I remember the lighted oven.
Na hora do aperto, dá-se um jeito a tudo.
In a tight squeeze, you find a way out of everything.

h. After a noun subject. Literary Portuguese permits the object pronoun to precede or follow, but it always precedes in BF.

O menino se machucou.
The boy hurt himself.
O médico me fêz um exame completo.
The doctor gave me a complete examination.
Dora contou-me esta história.   **Lit**
Dora told me this story.

i. After a pronoun subject. This subject is frequently used when not required for clarity, in order to permit the object to precede the verb. Again, literary Portuguese permits the object to precede or follow, but BF regularly places it before.

Êle me disse que Carlos estava na sala.
He told me that Charles was in the living room.
João não ficou muito tempo. Êle se despediu às nove horas.
John didn't remain long. He took leave at nine o'clock.

§184. Position of objects with the infinitive.
a. With the infinitive used alone. In the relatively few situations in which the infinitive is not dependent upon another verb nor on a preposition, the object pronoun follows.

Olhar-te? Para quê?
Look at you? Why?
Ver-nos foi amar-nos.
To see each other was to love each other.

b. After a preposition. An object pronoun may either precede or follow with equal propriety, entirely at the will of the speaker. However, it precedes much more often than it follows. The position of the objects in the following examples may all be reversed, but the first would become ambiguous in meaning.

Para se entender o mar, é preciso tempo.
In order to understand the sea, time is necessary.
Êle não gostava de mim, já antes de me conhecer.
He didn't like me, even before he knew me.
Nunca tivemos a oportunidade de ver-nos.
We never had the opportunity to see each other.
A sabiduria consiste em conhecer-se.
Wisdom consists of knowing oneself.

After the preposition **a**, the tendency of the object to follow is increased somewhat. After **ao**, confined mostly to literary usage, the object usually follows.

O barco está prestes a fazer-se ao mar. (*Or . . . a se fazer.*)
The boat is ready to put to sea.
O ladrão fugiu ao ver-me.   Lit
The thief fled when he saw me.

c. After a verb form. The object pronoun is placed in relation to the verb whose object it is. If it is the object of the infinitive, it usually precedes but may follow.

Vim te dar um abraço.
I came to give you a hug.
Você vai se arrepender. (arrepender-se.)
You are going to be sorry.
Não posso me casar tão cedo. (casar-me.)
I can't get married very soon.
Lamento ter que me retirar. (retirar-me.)
I am sorry to have to leave.
Ela não quis me ver. (ver-me.)
She wouldn't see me.
Me deixa sair. (deixa-me.)
Let me leave.
Não me deixa sair.
Don't let me leave.

d. The infinitive is personal. The plural forms of the personal infinitive, which have personal endings, are rarely, if ever, followed by a pronoun object.

Para nos encontrarmos, é preciso que saiamos sem os pais nos verem.

In order for us to meet, it is necessary for us to get out without our parents' seeing us.

§185. Objects used with the present participle.

a. Participle used without an auxiliary verb. The object pronoun precedes the participle in the negative, follows in the affirmative.

Não nos vendo, o guarda acabou indo-se embora.

Not seeing us, the policeman finished by going away.

Apertando-lhe a mão, me despedi.

Shaking his hand, I took leave.

b. Participle is part of a progressive form. The various auxiliaries of the progressive are intransitive verbs. The object pronoun is the object of the participle, and therefore normally precedes it. It is also possible to place the object after the participle. If the verb phrase is preceded by a negative, an interrogative, a relative pronoun, or an expressed subject, it is also possible to place the object before the auxiliary. However, these last two positions are rare.

Progressive with **estar.**

Escuta o que estou lhe dizendo.

Listen to what I am telling you.

Não estou te conhecendo hoje.

I don't recognize you today.

Disseram que Rosa estava se preparando para os exames.

They said that Rose was getting ready for the examinations.

Que é que te está machucando?

What is hurting you?

Progressive with **andar.**

Andaram me falando dessa môça muito tempo.

They kept talking to me about that girl for a long time.

O bem-te-vi anda nos espiando.

The flycatcher keeps spying on us.

O Berto nunca andou me rondando.

Berto never was after me.

Progressive with **ir.**

Êle foi se servindo um pouco de cada prato.

He went around serving himself a little from each dish.

Êle vai se despedindo de todos os parentes.

He is taking leave of all his relatives.

Não vou me dando bem com ela.
I haven't been getting along well with her.
Olha para o céu, que se vai tornando claro.
Look at the sky; it's starting to clear up.

c. The participle is used with a verb not an auxiliary of the progressive. The object pronoun is placed in relation to the verb form whose object it is.

Não me viram correndo pelo parque.
They didn't see me running through the park.
Surpreendemos o Menezes no quintal, espreguiçando-se.
We caught Menezes in the back yard, stretching.
Ouvimos você nos chamando lá de cima.
We heard you calling us from up there.

§186. Pronoun objects with the perfect tenses. These include all the compound tenses formed with the auxiliary **ter**, including the future and conditional perfect and the compound subjunctives.

a. The tense form opens the clause. The object pronoun follows the auxiliary.

Tinha me batido tantas vezes.
He had beaten me so many times.
Tenho me preocupado muito com você.
I have been worrying a lot about you.
Teria me resignado a perder mais duas horas.
I would have resigned myself to losing two more hours.

b. The verb is negative. The object usually precedes the auxiliary, although exceptions are heard.

Êles não me têm visto.
They haven't been seeing me.
Ela não te teria deixado, se você fôsse rico.
She wouldn't have left you, if you were rich.
Não tinha me esquecido de você.
I had not forgotten you.

c. The verb is preceded by an interrogative. BF places the object indifferently before or after the auxiliary, following an interrogative pronoun or adverb.

Quem nos terá feito essa malvadeza?
Who do you suppose did that wicked deed to us?
Onde tinha se encontrado com o Sr. Amado a primeira vez?
Where had you met Mr. Amado the first time?

d. The verb is preceded by a relative pronoun. The object usually precedes the auxiliary.

Tenho uma tia que me tem tratado muito bem.
I have an aunt who has treated me very well.

e. The verb is preceded by the conjunction **que**. The object pronoun nearly always precedes the auxiliary. Occasional exceptions occur.

Êle esperava que nos tivessem encontrado em casa.
He hoped that they had found us at home.
Êle disse que já tinha me pago.
He said that he had already paid me.

f. The verb is preceded by an adverb or adverbial phrase. These words seem to have little effect on the position of the object. While the speaker may put the object before the auxiliary if he wishes, it more often follows.

Além disso, tinham me dito que não havia lugar no hotel.
Besides that, they had told me that there was no room in the hotel.

g. The verb is preceded by an expressed subject. These words have little effect on the position of the object. They increase somewhat the probability that the object will precede the auxiliary, but it usually follows.

Júlio terá se arrependido dessa decisão.
Julius has probably regretted that decision.
Meu pai me tinha dado uma bicicleta de presente.
My father had given me a bicycle as a present.

h. The object pronoun never follows the participle in the perfect tenses.

§187. Use of two personal pronoun objects. Two pronoun objects of this type used with one verb are extraordinarily rare in BF. Such usage by the Portuguese is ridiculed in Brazil. A rare Brazilian example follows.

Dário não protestou; pouco se lhe dava que eu fôsse embora.
Darius did not protest; it mattered little to him that I was going.

Such combinations of objects are avoided by the following methods:

a. Avoidance by omission of the direct object. Since unstressed objects of the third person are not expressed, in most cases only the indirect object is left.

Essa bolsa é minha; me dá.
That purse is mine; give it to me.

b. Avoidance by expressing the indirect object in a prepositional phrase.

Os turistas não conhecem o valor das coisas; êstes objetos se vendem a êles.
The tourists don't know the value of things; these objects are sold to them.
Não se deve dar a elas o que se pode precisar mais tarde.
One should not give them what one may need later.
Me apresentaram a ela.
They introduced me to her.
Creio que o guia nos traiu a êles.
I think the guide betrayed us to them.
Se você não quer esta criança, dá para mim.
If you don't want this child, give it to me.

THE VERB: TENSES OF THE INDICATIVE

The indicative mood is the normal form for making statements, asking questions, or exclaiming. It will be assumed as the usual mood of the verb, with departures from it studied in detail under the subjunctive and the imperative.

The forms of the indicative

§188. Forms peculiar to Brazil. The conjugation of the Portuguese verb is readily available and will not be included here. There are, however, a number of departures from the standard forms of the literary language which are used in BF, even though they are not normally recognized in writing. The forms in which differences exist are the following:

a. The first person plural preterite of the first conjugation. This form is theoretically distinguishable from the same form in the present tense. In Luso-Portuguese, the present tense has a close **a**, the preterite an open **a**. In Brazil, there is no difference whatever. The vowel in both cases is close and nasalized. Thus all verbs in all three conjugations whose preterites are regular have the same form in the first person plural of the present and the preterite.

Present and preterite: **Falamos, aprendemos, partimos.**

b. Third person plural preterite, all conjugations. While Brazilians write the standard forms ending in **-am**, the spoken form is universally derived directly from the Latin, and is pronounced **-om**. In other tenses the ending **-am** is etymological, and is maintained in BF.

Falarom, aprenderom, disserom. (*pronunciation only.*)

c. Reduction of radical changes. The nasalization, and consequent closing, of vowels in open syllables before a nasal consonant has reduced considerably the number of radical changing verbs.

Such verbs as **tomar, comer,** etc., maintain the same vowel throughout the conjugation. On the other hand, a verb such as **amar,** with stem vowel **a** followed by a nasal consonant, tends to have the open vowel when it is unstressed but the close one when it is stressed.

    Âmo, âma, *but* **àmava, àmei.**

    d. Lack of variation in unstressed vowels. Preceding the stressed syllable, the Portuguese of Rio de Janeiro tends to pronounce only close **e** and **o** and only open **a,** unless it is nasal. This eliminates a great many of the complexities of conjugation in Portugal, where the pretonic vowels vary, not only according to rather complex patterns, but irregularly in the cases of certain individual verbs.

    e. Loss of nasalization. In many rural districts of Brazil, the nasalization of the final vowel of verb endings is lost. As a result, the third person singular and plural are indistinguishable, both in the indicative and the subjunctive. The lack of distinguishable verb forms is supplied by a personal pronoun.

    Êles fala, os menino come, dois home chega, etc.   **Inc**
      They speak, the children eat, two men arrive, etc.

    f. Loss of final **-s.** In even wider areas, the final **-s** of verb endings is lost, along with those of nouns and adjectives. This does not affect one's ability to understand the first person plural but has doubtless contributed to the loss of the second person singular form.

    Nós vamo, tu fala, etc.   **Inc**
      We go, you speak, etc.

§189. Loss of traditional verb forms. The loss of forms has affected the language much more than the rather slight differences in some of those still in use. The historical second person has, for all practical purposes, been lost in Brazil. As a result, there are in general use only four forms of each tense, and in many cases only three.

    a. The second person singular survives in some areas of the far South and in parts of the North and Northeast, for use within the family and among close friends. But the pronouns have often been retained when the verb forms have completely disappeared, replaced by the third person forms. In general, the informal pronouns are **você** and **vocês,** with the third person forms of the verb.

    b. The second person plural is completely obsolete. Very few, even of the most highly educated people, can use it correctly. It is universally replaced by the third person plural with the subject **vocês.**

§190. Tenses used in BF. The following tenses are in use in the indicative mood: present, imperfect, future (plus several periphrastic forms), conditional (plus periphrastic forms), present perfect, pluperfect, future perfect, conditional perfect.

The verb has an active voice and two passives formed with auxiliaries.

In addition, all tenses have progressive forms along with the simple ones. The progressive and the simple forms must be distinguished in all tenses except the imperfect, where the simple form may always be used.

The classifications listed above are traditional labels which serve as convenient and understandable terms of reference. They are often inaccurate as descriptions of the functions of these forms. In the paragraphs which follow, an attempt will be made to clarify the principal uses to which each is put in BF, and the distinctions of meaning, time, aspect, etc., expressed by choice of forms.

The present tense

§191. Use of the present tense. In the present, even more than in the other tenses, it is necessary to keep in mind the differences between the simple and progressive forms of the verb. The progressive will be treated separately. See §294. Its existence and firm establishment in usage have caused certain shifts in the usage of other forms, especially the simple present. We cannot, then, use the simple present to describe what is happening at the moment. This form is used:

a. To express habitual action or condition. The time of the habitual action or conditions includes the present, a certain amount of the past, and presumably also of the future.

> **Eu assisto à Escola Beija-flor.**
> I attend the Beija-flor School.
> **Êle é médico.**
> He is a doctor.

b. To express condition at the present moment. No statement as to duration is made. Present action would require the progressive.

Você parece triste.
  You look sad.
A porta está aberta.
  The door is open.

c. Instead of the future tense, to express future action. The simple present may be used whenever the time of action is made clear by an adverb of time, by any other expression of time, or by the context.

Eu venho amanhã.
  I am coming tomorrow.
Eu faço isso quando puder.
  I'll do this when I can.
Cuidado! Êle te dá um tabefe.
  Look out! He'll hit you.

d. To express a threat. These are regularly in the simple present, although the meaning clearly implies futurity.

Eu te quebro a cabeça.
  I'll break your head.

e. To express a promise. The present may be used, but the future is also possible.

Se você me ajudar, eu lhe pago bem.
  If you help me, I'll pay you well.
Seja bonzinho, e eu te compro umas balas.
  Be good, and I'll buy you some candy.

f. As an imperative. In the singular, it is often difficult to distinguish between the indicative and the imperative, since the form is the same. In the few cases in which they differ, neither is used. But the indicative is likely to be accompanied by a pronoun subject; the imperative is not. In the singular, the indicative is likely to be used if the speaker wishes to avoid informality.

O senhor vai até a segunda esquina e dobra à esquerda.
  You go to the second corner and turn left.

In the plural, since the imperative is now entirely lost, the indicative is used a great deal. In certain verbs which have a short form in the third person plural, the indicative is frequently used as if it were an imperative form, without a subject.

Lêem o primeiro capítulo.
Read the first chapter.
Vêm para a mesa.
Come to the table.
Têm cuidado.
Be careful.
Vão depressa.
Go quick.

g. Instead of a past tense, in narration. It may replace either the preterite or the imperfect in narration, more often the former. Probably it is somewhat less frequent in speech than in writing, but it is far from rare in spoken narration.

O João vai até a Praça da Penha e lá pergunta onde fica a barbearia São Caetano.
John goes to Penha Square and there he inquires where the São Caetano barber shop is located.

h. To express past action continuing into the present. As in the other Romance languages, an action or state which began in the past but is still continuing in present time is expressed in the present tense. Various verbal and adverbial expressions of time accompany and define this situation.

Há and an expression of time. In this construction, **há** is an unstressed word. The order of the two parts of the sentence is of no importance.

Há quanto tempo você está aqui?
How long have you been here?
Êle trabalha lá há muitos anos.
He has been working there for many years.

Faz and an expression of time. If **Faz** is in the first clause of the sentence, **que** opens the second clause. If **faz** follows, **que** is not used.

Já faz três dias que estamos aqui.
We have already been here three days.
Estamos aqui já faz três dias.
We have already been here three days.

Note: This verb is often heard in the plural when a plural noun follows, but this practice is not to be recommended.
Desde and an expression designating a point in past time.

Êle mora ali desde o ano passado.
He has been living here since last year.
Desde então, não vamos mais a êsse restaurante.
Since then we haven't been going to that restaurant.

Desde que and a clause designating a point in past time.

Desde que teve o desastre, êle não guia mais carro.
Since he had the accident, he hasn't been driving a car.

Depois de and an expression designating a point in past time.

Depois do Natal não vejo mais êle.
Since Christmas I haven't seen him again.

Depois que and a clause designating a point in past time.

Êle não anda mais em farras, depois que se casou.
He hasn't been going to wild parties since he got married.

i. After **a primeira vez que**. This expression, which counts all past time in making the exclusion of previous action, is followed by the present if the action is occurring at the moment.

É a primeira vez que vejo metodista fazer pelo sinal.
It is the first time I ever saw a Methodist make the sign of the cross.

The preterite tense

§192. Use of the preterite. This form (called in Portuguese **préterito perfeito simples**) has retained in Portuguese, contrary to the situation in the other principal Romance languages, both of the two main uses of the Latin perfect tense. It combines most of the uses of the past definite and those of the compound perfect tense in other languages. In the latter case, an exception must be made for the rather limited scope of the Portuguese compound perfect tense, which expresses certain types of situations in the perfect. The preterite is used:

a. In narration in the past, to narrate single acts.

Eu caí, mas levantei logo.
I fell down but got up immediately.
Levantou a espingarda e puxou o gatilho, mas a arma negou fogo.
He raised the shotgun and pulled the trigger, but the gun missed fire.

b. To express an action repeated a limited number of times. This number may be definite or indefinite.

Ontem choveu três vezes.
Yesterday it rained three times.
Falei com o promotor várias vezes no escritório.
I spoke to the prosecutor several times in his office.
Cada vez que almocei lá, vi êsse sujeito gordo.
Every time I had lunch there I saw that fat fellow.

c. To express action repeated within a limited period. The action may have been performed an indefinite or unknown number of times. The limitation required for the use of this tense is expressed in terms of time elapsed.

Estive muito com êle enquanto éramos estudantes.
I spent a lot of time with him while we were students.
Andamos juntos com freqüência em certa época.
We went out together frequently during a certain period.

d. To express a state or condition which lasted for a limited period. This condition is now regarded as belonging completely to the past, with no connection with the present.

Êle foi presidente da República cinco anos.
He was president of the Republic for five years.
Meu pai foi sócio dêle numa camisaria que tiveram.
My father was his partner in a haberdashery they had.

e. To express continuing action which lasted within time limits.

Eu trabalhei duro muitos anos.
I worked hard for many years.

f. To express activity or condition which ended in the past. The duration is not important.

Do Carmo ficou naquela casa até a volta de Henrique.
Do Carmo remained in that house until Henry's return.

g. To express action or condition complete at the present. The distinction between this use and the preceding ones, in which the action ended in past time, is often not strongly felt, nor important. But in many cases it is clearly distinguished. One common way of clarifying the use of the preterite as a perfect tense is the use of the adverb **já**. This word is often used with its full adverbial meaning, but when used with the preterite it frequently amounts only to a tense-forming particle.

Você já foi à Bahia?
Have you ever been to Bahia?
Eu já viajei à Europa três vezes.
I have been to Europe three times.
Êle já acabou o trabalho.
He has finished his work.

This tense has this meaning without *já*, of course, but it is not usually possible to distinguish whether or not it expresses the idea of action concluded at the present moment. In a great many cases, this distinction is not of any importance.

h. In place of the pluperfect. When one action occurred before another which also occurred in the past, logic would require that the former should be expressed in the pluperfect. Even in literary style this action is often expressed in the preterite when no confusion of meaning results, and its use in BF is even more frequent.

Eraldo me contou o que você disse. (*For* tinha dito.)
Eraldo told me what you said.

The imperfect tense

§193. Use of the imperfect indicative. The imperfect tense represents the past from a point of view within the past. One might say it is the present tense transferred into the past. Very often the same events or situations may be expressed in either the preterite or the imperfect, according as the speaker looks back from the present or transfers his point of view into the past. The imperfect is used:

a. To describe a condition in past time. The point of view of the speaker is contemporaneous with the condition, which also existed for some vague amount of time before and after this point.

O céu estava nublado.
The sky was cloudy.
O dono da fazenda era um velho sovina.
The owner of the farm was a miserly old man.

The condition may be mental or emotional.

Naquela época, eu queria ir à Europa.
At that period, I wanted to go to Europe.

Eu não sabia que você era artista.
I didn't know that you were an artist.
Êle não apreciava a arte abstrata, porque não compreendia.
He didn't like abstract art, because he didn't understand it.

b. Of habitual action in past time. There is no reference to the duration of this action, and especially no limitation on its duration.

Em criança, eu ia todos os domingos à casa dos avós.
As a child, I went every Sunday to my grandparents' house.

c. Of an action which was in progress at the time of another action. This latter action may be one act, represented by the preterite, or it may be another action in progress, expressed in the imperfect. This is the situation which the progressive form expresses, but in the imperfect, and in this tense only, the simple verb may be used for the progressive.

Êle ainda dormia quando eu bati na porta.
He was still asleep when I knocked on the door.
Janir lia, enquanto Afrânio e eu jogávamos.
Janir read while Afranio and I were playing.

d. To express an action or condition in being previous to a point in past time, continuing at that point. This corresponds to the use of the present given in §191h. The verbs used in the expressions of duration of time are also in the imperfect.

Havia quanto tempo você estava ali? (*Often* **há quanto tempo . . .**)
How long had you been there?
Fazia três dias que estávamos aqui.
We had been here for three days.
Estávamos aqui fazia três dias.
We had been here for three days.
Êle trabalhava ali desde o dia anterior.
He had been working there since the day before.
Era a primeira vez que eu via uma coisa dessas.
It was the first time I had ever seen such a thing.

But if the speaker merely wishes to locate his past viewpoint in relation to the present, he may use **haver** or **fazer** in the present. The activity or condition related from that viewpoint is still thought of as extending before and after that viewpoint, without the consideration of limits.

Há um ano, eu estava ainda no Brasil.
A year ago, I was still in Brazil.
Faz um mês, tudo estava sêco por aqui.
A month ago, everything was dry around here.

Note that in this last case, **que** is not used.

e. To express the indefinite continuation of action. This usage is often not very specific in the imperfect tense alone. It can be made more so by the use of the verbs **seguir** or **continuar**, as auxiliaries.

E o vilão ainda a perseguia.
And the villain still pursued her.
O rio corria sempre para o mar.
The river still ran to the sea.
Os meninos continuavam fazendo progresso.
The boys kept making progress.

f. To replace the conditional. For the details of this usage see §209.

g. The imperfect never replaces the imperfect subjunctive, in conditional sentences or elsewhere.

The future tense

§194. Forms which express futurity. In the indicative, futurity may be expressed by any of several different form of the verb—the traditional simple future, **falarei**; by the simple present, **falo**; or by periphrastic expressions, **hei de falar, vou falar, irei falar.**

§195. Indivisibility of the simple future. The traditional form, which once separated the ending from the infinitive in order to insert personal pronoun objects, has become firmly welded together. The separated forms are now not only obsolete but unintelligible as well. The object must precede the future verb. See §182f.

§196. Use of the simple future. This form may express several shades of meaning, but they overlap and shade into one another so that no clear distinctions can be maintained among them. It may express:

a. Simple future time, without additional connotations.

Sairemos amanhã para São Paulo.
We will leave tomorrow for São Paulo.
Choverá qualquer dia.
It will rain any day now.

b. Promise of future action.

Se você quiser, eu ajudarei.
If you wish, I'll help you.
Serei sempre seu amigo.
I will always be your friend.

c. Determination to perform an action, or that it shall be performed.

Hoje mesmo acabarei com essa loucura.
This very day I'll put a stop to that madness.
Irei, nem que tenha que ir a pé.
I'll go, even if I have to walk.
Isso lhe custará caro.
That will cost you dear.

d. Probability, supposition, conjecture, or the like. Although the time expressed is future, the meaning applies to present time. In BF, this usage is somewhat limited. It is used more often in interrogative sentences than in declarative ones. For the most part, it is limited to verbs whose future stems are monosyllabic (including 'starei). The auxiliaries, **ser, estar,** and **ter** are used most frequently in this way. In questions, if the verb is not one of those mentioned above, BF uses **será que,** followed by the rest of the sentence in declarative order.

Onde estará Maria Clara?
Where can Maria Clara be?
A pessoa à porta será o médico.
The person at the door is probably the doctor.
Êle terá lá consigo as razões dêle.
He doubtless has his own reasons.
Será que seu amigo ainda mora lá?
Do you suppose your friend still lives there?

e. Limited use of the simple future. The simple future is comparatively little used in BF, except in those verbs whose future stems are monosyllabic. These are **ser, (es)tar, ter, dar, ver, vir, pôr, ir,** plus a few others somewhat used, and those whose infinitive is shortened before the future endings—**trazer, dizer,** and **fazer.** Even in these cases the simple present is very common. The use of the future in other verbs is not so unusual as to call attention, and it is more frequent among people of the higher levels of culture, but the percentage of occurrences in the speech of all classes is rather low.

§197. Use of the form **hei de falar**. This form is heard with considerable frequency in BF, more often than the simple future. It is more used in BF than in the literary language. It may express any of several connotations, the lines of separation among which are very vague. It is often stated that this form always has some connotation beyond simple futurity—duty or obligation, promise, previous arrangement, etc. This is not the case. The form is very frequently used as a pure future. However, it is very difficult to separate such ideas from pure futurity, in this form of the verb, or any of the other forms used to express futurity. This periphrastic form may express:

a. Simple futurity, with no further intent.

> **Sou datilógrafa e hei de arranjar algum emprego.**
> I am a typist and I'll get some job.
> **O senhor há de ir longe na sua profissão.**
> You will go far in your profession.
> **Esta lei há de acabar com os abusos no comércio do leite.**
> This law will end the abuses in the milk business.

b. Determination or a threat of future action. The threat is not of immediate action, as when the present is used.

> **Hei de contar tudo às autoridades.**
> I'll report everything to the authorities.
> **Meninos! Êsse barulho há de parar!**
> Boys! That noise must stop!

c. Obligation, duty, or previous arrangement.

> **Amanhã você há de estar na escola.**
> Tomorrow you are to be in school.
> **O que hei de pensar de tudo isso?**
> What am I to think of all that?
> **O senador há de falar amanhã sôbre Marcel Proust.**
> The senator is to speak tomorrow about Marcel Proust.

d. Probability, conjecture, or supposition.

> **Êle acha que vai ficar rico, mas não há de ser assim tão fácil.**
> He thinks he is going to get rich, but it probably won't be so easy.
> **Alguém está batendo na porta; há de ser algum jornalista.**
> Someone is knocking on the door; it is probably some newspaperman.

e. Prohibition, if the verb is negative.

Por que é que não hei de ter um gato?
Why can't I have a cat?

§198. Use of the form **vou falar.** This is of very frequent use in BF, as in English and several Romance languages. While it may have the meaning of movement toward another place in order to perform an action, in most cases this original meaning of the verb **ir** is completely gone, so that the phrase is essentially a future form of the verb represented by the infinitive. In many cases it is impossible to determine whether the speaker has in mind an idea of movement or only futurity. However, even when movement is clearly implied, the time indicated is still future.

Eu vou trabalhar agora.
I am going to work now.

This form may express:

a. Decision, determination, or promise.

Vou desistir desta empresa.
I am going to give up this project.
Vou ver se posso ajudá-la.
I am going to see if I can help her.

b. Futurity, with no further connotation. Usually the futurity is relatively immediate.

Vou fazer trinta anos amanhã.
I'll be thirty years old tomorrow.
Vai chover.
It is going to rain.

c. This form is not used to express probability.

d. The verbs **ir** and **vir** are seldom heard in this form, although some cases occur.

§199. Use of **irei falar.** This construction is not of very frequent usage, but it is heard in speech sufficiently for it to be considered an established form. It is used in less formal writing, such as newspapers, but is rather rare in more artistic literature. It is not a redundancy which may be used instead of the present of **ir** and the infinitive but has other connotations. It is used to express:

a. Somewhat doubtful future action.

Não sei como nem onde iremos arranjar uma casa.
I don't know how nor where we will be able to get a house.

b. Probability applied to future time.

Menino! Não faz isso. Irá se machucar.
Boy! Don't do that. You will (probably) get hurt.
O Veloso irá ter um faniquito quando souber disso.
Veloso will have a fit when he finds that out.

c. Attribution to unnamed parties. Brazilians sometimes state that the press invented this form to avoid responsibility for its statements. The matter then becomes a rumor or an expectation, rather than a factual statement. In any case, the form is rather popular with the press.

O senador irá votar contra o projeto.
The senator will probably vote against the bill.
O senhor ministro irá proferir um discurso no Rio amanhã.
The minister is to make a speech in Rio tomorrow.

§200. Use of the present for the future. The most common of all forms used to express future time in BF is the simple present. The development of the progressive form in Brazil to the point where its differentiation from the simple present is obligatory reduces materially the possibility of confusion when the present is used for the future. When the present is used, the application to futurity may be revealed by any one of several means:

a. By an adverb of time.

Amanhã é tarde.
Tomorrow is too late.
Quando é que você volta?
When will you come back?
Já vou.
I am going right away.

b. By the future subjunctive in another clause.

Eu vejo você se voltar a tempo.
I'll see you if I get back in time.
Saimos de aqui logo que êle chegar.
We'll leave as soon as he comes.

c. By the context. The situation, known to both speaker and hearer, may reveal the meaning, even though no word in the sentence indicates it.

Finalmente, Celeste, você sai ou não sai?
     Make up your mind, Celeste. Are you leaving or not?
Nos vemos.
     We'll see each other.
Eu como em casa e venho encontrar com você aqui.
     I'll eat at home and come back to meet you here.

d. By the type of statement. Threats, for example, are regularly put in the simple present. Several auxiliaries are regularly used in the present with a future meaning.

Sai, ou eu te quebro a cabeça.
     Go, or I'll break your head.
Eu vou à cidade.
     I am going downtown.
Eu acho que êle vem.
     I think he is coming.
Você deve ir lá em casa.
     You should go out home.

The conditional tense

§201. Meaning of the conditional. The conditional in Portuguese as in other Romance languages, represents two basic usages, between which there is no logical connection. It is first a tense, representing futurity in relation to past time, as the future does in relation to present time. Second, it has modal force in conditional sentences of various types in which it expresses the conclusion. The condition itself may be expressed or only implied.

§202. The forms of the conditional. The forms existing in BF are as varied as in the case of the future. They include the simple, or synthetic, form **falaria**, and several periphrastic forms—**havia de falar, haveria de falar, ia falar**, and **iria falar**. The usages of the conditional may also be expressed by the imperfect indicative.

§203. Indivisibility of the simple conditional. Like the future, the conditional can no longer be broken up and separated by a personal pronoun object in BF. The object must always precede the entire word.

§204. Use of the simple conditional. The synthetic form **falaria** may be used in all cases, in either of the two basic uses of the conditional noted above, as well as in some others. It is used:

a. To express futurity in relation to past time. It is usually in a subordinate clause, with the verb of the main clause expressed in a past tense.

> **João irá? —Êle disse que iria.**
> Will John go? He said he would.
> **Eu resolvi que daí em diante eu faria só o absolutamente necessário.**
> I decided that from then on I would do only what was absolutely necessary.

b. In the conclusion to a contrary-to-fact condition.

> **Se eu pudesse, eu faria o que êle quer.**
> If I could, I would do what he wishes.

The condition may be suggested by a phrase without a verb, or it may be only understood or assumed.

> **Nesse caso, eu faria o mesmo.**
> In that case, I would do the same.
> **Eu gostaria de ir à Europa.**
> I would like to go to Europe.

c. To express probability, supposition, or conjecture in past time. In BF, this usage is limited almost entirely to the verbs **estar**, **ser**, and **ter**, and even then is not much used.

> **O cachorro já estaria em casa.**
> The dog was probably already at home.
> **O homem estaria pedindo esmola?**
> Could the man be asking for alms?
> **Estavam batendo na porta. Seria o João?**
> They were knocking on the door. Could it be John?
> **Seriam quatro horas quando êle chegou.**
> It was about four o'clock when he arrived.
> **O empregado parecia estar pensando se eu teria o dinheiro.**
> The clerk seemed to be wondering whether I had the money.

Note 1. In questions, for the most part, this type of conjecture is expressed by **seria que**, followed by the basic question in the imperfect or the pluperfect.

> **Seria que o trem chegava?**
> Was the train really arriving?
> **Que seria que o guri tinha feito?**
> What do you suppose the kid had done?

Note 2. In statements, the verb **dever** is more often used to express probability.

Êle devia estar em casa. (=provàvelmente estava.)
He was probably at home.

§205. Use of the form **havia de falar**. This form often replaces the simple conditional. For the most part it is unnecessary, since the imperfect is simpler and generally serves. In some cases it aids clarity.

Êle me trouxe umas uvas, dizendo que eu havia de gostar.
He brought me some grapes, saying that I would like them.

Here, **gostava** would be understood as a real imperfect.

a. This form frequently expresses a certain obligation, prior arrangement, or suggestion of promise.

Disseram que eu havia de estar em casa às dez.
They said that I was to be at home by ten.
Ela havia de dar de comer às crianças.
She was supposed to feed the children.

b. This construction is used with modal force, i.e., in the conclusion of a conditional sentence, although with relative infrequency.

Se eu fôsse você, havia de fazer o mesmo.
If I were you, I would do the same.

§206. Use of **haveria de falar**. This form is heard occasionally, but it is infrequent both in speech and writing. It serves on occasion to express both the conditional form and some other additional meaning, such as weak obligation, previous arrangement, or probability. It can always be replaced by **havia de falar**, and usually by other forms as well.

Êle não sabia o que essa mulher haveria de fazer, caso fôsse descoberta.
He did not know what in the world that woman would do, if she were found out.

§207. The form **ia falar**. This construction may be used to express simple futurity in relation to past time.

a. In secondary sequence (following a verb in a past tense), it is an equivalent of the simple conditional, for all practical purposes.

Todo mundo já sabia o que ia acontecer.
Everybody knew what was going to happen.

b. It is used in cases in which it does not follow a verb or other expression which would place it in perspective in relation to past time. In such cases the simple conditional could not be used. Equivalents would be **estava para** and **estava a ponto de**.

> **Clarice ia falar, mas mudou de idéia.**
> Clarice was going to speak, but changed her mind.

§208. The construction **iria falar**. This construction parallels the construction formed of the future of **ir** and the infinitive, and has similar uses.

a. It may indicate probability, supposition, etc. Also, like the future form, it may suggest attribution to unnamed sources.

> **Segundo o boato, a revolta iria estourar no dia seguinte.**
> According to rumor, the revolt would break out the next day.

b. Often it amounts to no more than an alternate form of the conditional.

> **Se você fôsse para as terras do norte, então iria saber o que é frio.**
> If you went to the northern countries, then you would really know what cold is.

§209. Use of the imperfect indicative for the conditional. In BF the simple conditional is very little used. It is limited mostly to the verbs **ser**, **ter**, and **estar**, and to some use in other verbs whose future stems are monosyllabic. The imperfect replaces it in general in other verbs, and even in these it is used about as often as the conditional. The imperfect is not used to express probability or conjecture, but may be used instead of the conditional:

a. To express futurity in relation to past time.

> **João irá? —Êle disse que ia.**
> Will John go? He said he was going.
> **Eu resolvi que daí em diante eu fazia só o absolutamente necessário.**
> I decided that from then on I would do only what was absolutely necessary.

b. In the conclusion of a contrary-to-fact condition.

> **Se eu pudesse, eu fazia o que êle quer.**
> If I could, I would do what he wishes.

Note 1. **Gostaria**, when used with modal force, is seldom replaced by the imperfect.

Eu gostaria de ir à Europa.
I would like to go to Europe.

Note 2. But **querer,** when used in the same situation and with a very similar meaning, is nearly always in the imperfect.

Eu queria ir à Europa.
I would like to go to Europe.

The compound present perfect

§210. Form of the compound present perfect. This tense is formed of the past participle of the verb and the auxiliary **ter** in the present tense. The auxiliary **haver** is not used at all in BF and is archaic even in literary Portuguese. The past participle in the perfect tenses is invariable.

§211. Uses of the compound present perfect. This form is used in only limited cases, in either speech or writing. However, in those situations, it cannot be replaced by any other form. The line between it and the preterite, for example, is clearly drawn, and there is little or no overlap. The relation between the compound present perfect and the preterite, when the latter is used as a perfect tense, is somewhat similar to the relationship between the imperfect and the preterite when the latter is used as a past definite or aorist tense. The compound form is used:

a. Of a state begun in the past and continued up to the present. It is important to note that the time involved does not consciously include the present.

Como é que você tem estado?
How have you been?
Tem feito calor ùltimamente.
It has been hot lately.
Você tem parecido triste nestes últimos meses.
You have been looking sad these last few months.

b. Of an action begun in the past and continued up to the present. Again, this form makes no assumption as to whether the action still continues into the present. We are not speaking of the present at all.

Você tem estudado demais.
You have been studying too much.
Tenho andado com êle a tôda a parte.
I have been going everywhere with him.

Êles têm trabalhado como loucos, mas já estão aposentados.
They have been working like madmen, but now they are retired.

c. Of an action repeated indefinitely, up to the present moment. This differs from the use of the imperfect in that the action is considered from the point of view of the present, not of the past, and also in that the action continues up to the present.

Êle tem vindo à cidade com freqüência.
He has come downtown frequently.
Tenho visto o João sempre na rua.
I have been seeing John constantly on the street.
Que é que êle tem feito ùltimamente?
What has he been doing lately?
Onde tem andado, que não nos temos encontrado durante tanto tempo?
Where have you been, that we haven't met for so long?

d. In the expression **tenho dito**. This is a formula sometimes used at the end of a speech. The meaning here is not the usual one in this form of the verb, but that of the simple preterite. It is equivalent to **acabei de falar**.

§212. The compound perfect distinguished from other tenses. This tense must be distinguished from certain uses of the preterite and from one use of the present tense. The preterite speaks of a state which is now finished, or of an action performed at any time in the past up to the present. The time we are concerned with may include all past time, but the act, acts, or state of which we speak occupied a limited part of that time.

O Jorge já esteve na Europa.
George has been to Europe.

The time spent in Europe might be an hour or fifty years. We are not concerned (as far as the verb is concerned) with the exact amount of time occupied by the action or state, except that it is now over. However, we are careful to show that it took place any time up to the present. The person, it is assumed, is not now in Europe, at least not in connection with the trip we are speaking of.

The compound present perfect presents an entirely different situation. When we say, **O Jorge tem estado na Europa**, he has either been there continuously for an indefinite time, or he has been continually in and out of Europe during an indefinite time. While the period we are speaking of comes up to the present, it is not assumed that he is or is not there now. As contrasted with the preceding, the state or acts extend up to the present.

If, on the other hand, we speak of the state or action as still true in present time, the present tense is used. We also give some indication either of the length of time the state or action has continued, or some indication of the time at which it began. Thus when we say, **O Jorge está na Europa há muito tempo,** we assure the hearer that he is still there, and give some information as to the amount of past time during which this has been true.

The pluperfect indicative

§213. The forms of the pluperfect. There are three forms of the pluperfect indicative in Portuguese. There is no difference whatever in meaning among the three forms, nor in the grammatical situations in which they may be used.

a. The synthetic pluperfect. This form is the direct successor of the Latin pluperfect indicative. It is totally unused in BF as a pluperfect, but is still used a great deal in writing, even in some less formal genres.

Ontem eu vi o homem com quem falara no dia anterior.   **Lit**
Yesterday I saw the man with whom I had spoken the day before.

For the use of this form as an imperfect subjunctive, see §222a.

b. Compound form with **haver.** This form of the pluperfect is only slightly less literary than the synthetic form. It is used to a considerable extent in less formal types of writing, such as newspapers, some books, etc., in which the writers avoid the synthetic form as too far removed from speech. Some speakers also make use of it, especially in formal speeches or similar occasions, in order to give a more literary tone to the occasion. Its use in conversation is affected and noticeably unnatural.

O presidente já havia dito que apoiava o projeto de lei.   **Lit**
The president had already said that he supported the bill.

c. Compound form with **ter.** The form of the pluperfect used in BF is formed with the auxiliary **ter** in the imperfect tense and the past participle. It is also becoming somewhat more frequent in the literary language but is still not common there.

Quando eu cheguei, os outros já tinham saído.   **BF**
When I arrived, the others had already gone.

d. The preterite of the auxiliaries. The preterites of **haver** and **ter** are not used as auxiliaries to form a compound perfect tense. Such a construction is unknown in BF and very rare in the literary language.

§214. Use of the pluperfect. The pluperfect indicates in Portuguese, as in other European languages, an action which was regarded as complete at a point in past time. For its use in place of the conditional perfect, see §220.

The future perfect indicative

§215. Forms of the future perfect. The auxiliary of the future perfect is the future form of the verb **ter**. In literary style, **haver** is sometimes used, but it is infrequent in modern literature.

a. The periphrastic auxiliary. The periphrastic future of **ter**, **há de ter**, exists as an auxiliary, but it is infrequent and usually expresses some obligation, promise, or previous arrangement, as well as future time.

Vocês hão de ter lido êste livro até quinta-feira.
You are to have read this book through by Thursday.

§216. Use of the future perfect.

a. The future perfect generally speaks of an action that is to be completed before another future action, or before a point in future time.

Êle terá chegado antes de eu ter meu trabalho terminado.
He will have arrived before I have my work finished.

b. It may indicate conjecture or probability concerning action or condition which would otherwise be expressed in the preterite, rarely the imperfect.

Êles terão entrado no cinema já, porque não estão na calçada.
They have probably gone into the movie already, because they are not on the sidewalk.

§217. Use of the future for the future perfect. The simple future or an equivalent is often used instead of the future perfect.

Ela receberá minha carta antes que você fale com ela.
She will get my letter before you talk to her.

But if the second future action is expressed by a verb following **quando**, no substitution is possible.

O trem já terá chegado quando você chegar na estação.
The train will have arrived before you get to the station.

The conditional perfect

§218. Form of the conditional perfect This tense is formed from the conditional tense of the auxiliary **ter** combined with the past participle.

§219. Use of the conditional perfect. The conditional perfect is more frequent in BF than the simple conditional. This is explained by the fact that the auxiliary **ter**, being very short, easily assumes the conditional form. The conditional perfect is used:

a. In conditional sentences. The condition itself is expressed in the pluperfect subjunctive, and the conclusion in the conditional perfect.

Se eu tivesse visto a onça, teria caído morto só de susto.
If I had seen the jaguar, I would have fallen dead from sheer fright.

The supposition may be in the past, but the conclusion in the present. In this case, the simple conditional (or the imperfect) is used.

Se você tivesse trazido o casaco, não estaria (estava) com frio.
If you had brought the coat, you wouldn't be cold.

The supposition may be implicit in a phrase or in a situation, without being formally expressed.

No caso de você, eu teria feito o mesmo.
In your case, I would have done the same.
Eu não teria feito o que êle fêz.
I would not have done what he did.

b. To express conjecture or probability. The time of the conjectured action corresponds to the pluperfect tense.

Êle teria surrado a mulher? (=Você acha que êle tinha surrado?)
Do you suppose he had beaten his wife?

c. Other than this case, the conditional perfect expresses only the conclusion resulting from a contrary-to-fact supposition, expressed or implied. While it is possible to use it following a main clause in the pluperfect, in practice the simple conditional is used.

Paulo tinha dito que faria o trabalho antes das cinco horas.
  (*Not* **teria feito.**)
Paul had said that he would do the work before five.

§220. Replacement of the conditional perfect.

a. Replacement by the pluperfect. The pluperfect may replace the conditional perfect at the will of the speaker, except in its use to express conjecture or probability.

Se êle tivesse chegado a tempo, tinha (*or* teria) podido comer.
If he had come on time, he would have been able to eat.

b. Replacement by the simple conditional. The conditional perfect may be replaced very frequently by the simple conditional, or by the imperfect indicative.

Se eu tivesse ouvido quando você chamou, correria (corria) para lá.
If I had heard when you called, I'd have run to you.

However, in many cases the clarity of the sentence is lost if such a substitution is made.

Se eu tivesse gostado da moça, teria casado com ela.
If I had liked the girl, I would have married her.

In this case, **casaria** or **casava** would seem to apply to the future rather than to the past.

THE VERB: THE SUBJUNCTIVE

§221. Survival of the subjunctive in BF. The subjunctive is a very important part of the living spoken language in Brazil. As in many other Western languages, there is a considerable tendency to reduce the application of the subjunctive, and it is less used in BF than in the literary language. Still, all forms, i.e., all six historical tenses, are constantly used in the speech of all levels of culture. They are learned by young children from the speech of their elders, without the necessity of formal study. While certain constructions are learned only through reading and study, most subjunctives are used regularly by pre-school children as a natural part of their everyday speech. In many cases alternatives to the subjunctive exist, and may be more frequently heard than the subjunctive, but only seldom has a subjunctive construction been completely lost from even the spoken language.

Forms of the subjunctive

§222. Tenses of the subjunctive in use. There are six tenses of the subjunctive in active use in the spoken language—the present, the imperfect, the future, and the three corresponding perfect tenses.

a. The synthetic pluperfect indicative used as a subjunctive. This form, e.g., **falara**, was formerly used to a considerable extent as an imperfect subjunctive in literature. Whether it was ever much used in the spoken language would be difficult to determine. At present only two words are in common use in this form. **Tomara** is treated in § 246b below. The other word is **pudera**, used only as an exclamation. In addition, a few fixed expressions are sometimes heard, although they are somewhat archaic.

> **Quem me dera ser rico!**
> I wish I were rich.
> **Quisera que fôsse eu!**
> I wish it were I.

b. Choice of tense. Since the choice of tense is more dependent upon tense sequence than upon the situations which determine the choice of tense in the indicative, it seems more useful to classify the various situations which determine the use of the subjunctive, after which the criteria of choice of tense will be explained. See §256.

The general types of subjunctives

§223. The three basic uses. The following three situations underlie most of the particular cases in which the subjunctive is used.

a. The influence of one will on another. When the will, wish, or influence of one person, mind, or set of circumstances is imposed upon another—that is, in grammatical terms, one subject imposes its will on another—this situation is indicated by expressing the verb which accompanies the second subject in the subjunctive. The situation which requires the subjunctive may be expressed (1) by a verb whose primary meaning is such that it expresses wish, command, persuasion, etc., (2) by a verb which does not have this primary meaning but is made to express it by the use of a dependent subjunctive clause, (3) by a noun, adjective, etc., in combination with a verb, so that together they express such a meaning, or (4) by a situation in which such a meaning is implicit, even though it may not be expressed at all, as in the use of the subjunctive for the imperative. With this category, only the present and imperfect subjunctives and their respective perfect tenses may be used.

b. Uncertainty or the negation of certainty. Particular cases which determine subjunctives of this category include (1) uncertainty as to the truth of a statement, denial or doubt of the truth of a statement, (3) uncertainty as to who or what is the antecedent of a relative pronoun, (4) denial that the antecedent of the relative pronoun exists, (5) the indefiniteness of the future time of the action of the verb. We should also include under this category (6) assumptions contrary to fact, and (7) assumptions concerning future action which may or may not take place. All tenses of the subjunctive are used to express uncertainty, but the future and future perfect are limited to certain cases of the expression of futurity.

c. The expression of emotion. Expressions of emotion, whether they be verbal, nominal, or adjectival, cause a dependent verb to be in the subjunctive. While this type might be considered to be related with either of the preceding types, it seems distinct enough to be considered a separate category.

The subjunctive of will

§224. General considerations. The subjunctive which expresses the exercise of the will, wish, or influence of one subject on another can be divided, for convenience and clarity, into a number of subcategories. These often overlap, and in some instances they extend somewhat beyond the strict limits of this definition. It must be remembered also that possible expressions of will, wish, influence, etc., are almost innumerable, and that the subjunctive will be used following other expressions similar to those given below. Herein, the most commonly used expressions in each subcategory are given, with one or more illustrative sentences. It follows from the nature of this type of subjunctive that it will be used only if the subject of the main verb and that of the subordinate verb are different. If no verb is used before the subjunctive clause, the form of the subjunctive indicates that a different person is assumed to will or wish that the action be performed.

In many cases another construction exists which is an alternate way of expressing the same meaning as that of the subjunctive. Usually the infinitive, personal or impersonal, is the preferred substitute for the subjunctive, but sometimes it is the indicative. Such cases are also given following each of the verbs or other expressions discussed, with some indication of the relative frequency of each construction in BF. The subjunctive is used following:

§225. An expression of wish: **querer, desejar, ter (sentir) vontade, ter (sentir) desejo,** etc.

a. The subjunctive is obligatory after such verbs; no alternative exists.

> **O que você quer que eu faça?**
>   What do you want me to do?
> **Só desejo que me deixem ir embora.**
>   I merely want them to let me go.

b. But following nominal expressions, while the subjunctive may be used in literary Portuguese or BF, the latter generally prefers **de** and the infinitive.

Eu sentia vontade (de) que ela sorrisse para mim.
I felt a wish that she would smile at me.
Eu tinha vontade de ela sorrir para mim.
I felt a wish that she would smile at me.

§226. Preference: **preferir, ser bom, ser melhor, achar bom, ser preferível, ser vantagem, ser coisa boa, ser boa idéia, escolher,** etc.

Prefiro que você me acompanhe.
I prefer that you accompany me.
Era bom que ela se casasse logo.
It would be a good idea for her to get married right away.

a. **Preferir** must be followed by the subjunctive.

b. **Escolher** rarely takes the subjunctive except in literary style. In BF, the sentence is usually constructed in such a way that the subjunctive is avoided.

Antônio escolheu que lhe dessem a casa em vez do dinheiro.   SLit
Anthony chose that they should give him the house instead of money.
Escolhi que esta companhia construisse minha casa.   SLit
I chose to have this company build my house.
Escolhi esta companhia para construir minha casa.   BF
I chose this company to build my house.

c. A verb with a noun or adjective may also be followed by the infinitive, the more usual construction in BF.

Era bom êles se casarem.
It would be a good idea for them to get married.
Achamos preferível êles irem embora sem demora.
We consider it preferable for them to go without delay.

d. Conditional sentences with similar meanings. Expressions with **ser bom, melhor, preferível,** etc., are often constructed as conditional sentences.

Era bom se êles chegassem amanhã.
It would be nice if they arrived tomorrow.

§227. Persuasion or suggestion: **persuadir, instigar, convencer, aconselhar, induzir, avisar, sugerir, propor, recomendar, incitar, estimular, excitar, impelir, mover (=influir nas emoções).**

a. **Persuadir** may be followed by **a que** and the subjunctive in literary Portuguese but nearly always takes **a** and the infinite in BF.

O homem me persuadiu a que comprasse o quadro.   **Lit**
The man persuaded me to buy the picture.
Êle persuadiu meu irmão a comprar o quadro.   **Lit & BF**
He persuaded my brother to buy the picture.

Note also the different meaning expressed in the following:

Persuadiu o colega (de) que era bom comprá-lo.
He persuaded his colleague that it would be fine to buy it.

b. **Dissuadir** is regularly followed by **de** and the infinitive, usually impersonal.

O Henrique me dissuadiu de aceitar o emprego.
Henry dissuaded me from accepting the job.

c. **Instigar** is similar to **persuadir**.

Instigaram-nos para que (*or* a que**) fizéssemos o que não devíamos.
Lit**
They urged us to do what we shouldn't.
Instigaram-me a prender fogo ao paiol.   **BF**
They urged me to set fire to the shed.

d. **Animar, encorajar, alentar, incitar, estimular, excitar, impelir, mover** are constructed with **a** and the infinitive.

Minha mãe sempre nos encorajava a estudar.
My mother always encouraged us to study.
Os fãs animavam os jogadores a ganhar.
The fans encouraged the players to win.

e. **Convencer** is regularly followed by **a** and the infinitive.

Convenci os três a ficar comigo.
I convinced all three to stay with me.

Note, however, the following construction, used when one is convinced of something which turns out to be untrue, or when one is not convinced.

Não me convenço de que seja êle.
I am not convinced that it is he.
Eu estava convencido de que fôsse você, mas não era.
I was convinced that it was you, but it wasn't.

f. **Aconselhar** may be construed with the subjunctive or the infinitive.

Aconselho o João (*or* ao João) que não apareça no quartel.   SLit
I advise John not to show up at the barracks.
Aconselhei o João a não aparecer.   BF
I advised John not to show up.

g. **Induzir** may be followed by **a que** and the subjunctive, but this is rare and literary. In BF it is almost always followed by **a** and the infinitive.

Induzi o gato a sair da árvore.
I persuaded the cat to get down out of the tree.

h. **Avisar, advertir.** The subjunctive may be used, even in BF, but it is more usual to hear a preposition and the infinitive or an extra verb which enables one to avoid the subjunctive.

Avisei o empregado que mandasse o embrulho a Copacabana. SLit
I told the clerk to send the bundle to Copacabana.
Avisei o empregado a (*or* para) mandar o embrulho.   BF
I told the clerk to send the bundle.
Avisei o empregado que devia mandar o embrulho.   Lit & BF
I told the clerk that he should send the bundle.

i. **Sugerir** is followed by the subjunctive.

Ela sugeriu que eu ficasse escondido atrás da porta.
She suggested that I stay hidden behind the door.

j. **Propor** also takes the subjunctive.

Proponho que organizemos uma festa.
I propose that we get up a party.

k. **Recomendar** usually takes the subjunctive. But when the logical subject of the dependent verb is a pronoun, it may be expressed as the indirect object of **recomendar**, and the infinitive used.

Recomendo que tenha cuidado.
I recommend that you be careful.
Recomendo-lhe ter cuidado.
I recommend to you to be careful.

§228. Expressions of resolve or decision: **decidir, resolver, determinar.** These verbs may have a meaning which amounts to **ordenar**. In this case the subjunctive follows.

O gerente decidiu (determinou, resolveu) que não trabalhássemos
no dia seguinte.
The manager decided that we would not work the next day.

When the meaning is **persuadir**, they are followed by **a** and the
infinitive.

Isto nos decidiu a fugir.
This made us decide to run away.

When the meaning is **chegar a uma conclusão**, the indicative follows.

Fátima decidiu que as amigas não queriam esperar.
Fatima decided that her friends did not want to wait.

§229. Expressions of command, ordering, insisting: **mandar, ordenar, decretar, prescrever, insistir, instar, urgir (=instar), intimar,
dar ordem, teimar, fazer questão**, etc. The constructions and the
relative frequency of each vary from one expression to another.
Most of them can be followed by the infinitive, and some of them
are generally followed by it.

a. **Mandar.** If the subject of the second verb is a pronoun, it is
generally expressed as an impersonal infinitive. However, the subjunctive is also heard in BF, as well as encountered in the literary
language.

Êle mandou que eu saísse.
He ordered me to leave.
João nos mandou calar a boca.
John told us to shut up.

If the subject of the dependent verb is a noun, however, the infinitive is less frequent than the subjective. If the infinitive is used,
it is personal.

O passageiro mandou que o carregador levasse as malas.
The passenger ordered the porter to carry the bags.
O passageiro mandou os carregadores levarem as malas.
The passenger ordered the porters to carry the bags.

b. **Ordenar** may take either of the constructions which follow
mandar but tends to prefer the subjunctive.

O capataz ordenou que acabássemos o trabalho antes da merenda.
The foreman ordered us to finish the work before lunch.

O tenente ordenou fazer uma trincheira.
The lieutenant ordered a trench dug.

c. **Dar ordem, fazer questão** may be followed either by **(de) que** and the subjunctive or by **de** and either infinitive.

O delegado deu ordem (de) que ninguém saísse de casa.
The police chief gave an order that no one should leave home.
Êle faz questão de ficarmos para almoçar.
He insists that we remain for lunch.

d. **Decretar, prescrever** are followed by the subjunctive if the verb denoting the action decreed or prescribed follows directly.

O presidente decretou que o salário mínimo fôsse aumentado.
The president decreed that the minimum wage should be increased.

However, more often the expression is stated more indirectly, in the indicative.

Decretou-se que ninguém devia sair depois das dez horas.
It was decreed that no one should go out after ten.

e. **Insistir** is followed by the subjunctive, with or without the use of the preposition **em.**

A mulher insistiu (em) que o marido voltasse para o jantar.
The woman insisted that her husband should come back for dinner.
Also: **Insistiu com o marido para que voltasse. (***Or* **para voltar.)**

When the verb has the sense of sticking to a statement, the indicative is used.

Ela insistiu e teimou que o marido voltaria para o jantar.
She insisted and stuck to it that her husband would come back for dinner.

f. **Urgir** is little used in BF, and only very rarely in the sense of **instar, insistir.**

Ela sempre urgia que eu acabasse o curso.   **Lit & rare**
She always urged me to finish the course.
Ela me urgia a acabar.   **BF, rare**
She urged me to finish.

g. **Dizer,** in the meaning **mandar, ordenar,** is nearly always followed by the subjunctive in literary style but more frequently by

para and the personal infinitive in BF. The subjunctive is also heard.

> **Disse-nos que ficássemos quietos.**   Lit & BF
> He told us to keep still.
> **Êle nos disse para ficarmos quietos.**   BF
> He told us to keep still.

§230. Verbs and expressions which may accidentally mean "to order."

Many other verbs and other expressions may have accidentally the sense of transmitting a command, and thus be followed by the subjunctive.

a. **Escrever.**

> **O dono me escreveu que eu vendesse a casa logo.**
> The owner wrote me that I should sell the house at once.

b. **Telegrafar.**

> **O pai do aluno tinha lhe telegrafado que voltasse logo para casa.**
> The student's father had telegraphed to him that he should go back home at once.

c. **Responder.**

> **O médico respondeu que eu ficasse de cama.**
> The doctor answered that I should stay in bed.

d. **Indicar.**

> **O guarda indicou com a mão que parássemos.**
> The policeman gave a signal with his hand for us to stop.

e. **Fazer sinal.**

> **Êle fêz sinal (de) que ela esperasse.**
> He made a signal for her to wait.

f. **Gritar.**

> **Manuel gritou que lhe acudissem.**
> Manuel shouted that they should come to his aid.

g. **Piscar ôlho.**

> **Ela piscou ôlho (para) que eu calasse.**
> She winked at me to be quiet.

§231. Expressions meaning compel, demand, bring about: **exigir, fazer, obrigar, forçar**, etc.

a. **Exigir** is followed regularly by the subjunctive.

>**Exijo que todo mundo contribua.**
>I demand that everybody contribute.
>**Êle exige que entreguemos o cachorro.**
>He demands that we hand over the dog.

b. **Fazer** is followed by the subjunctive only when used in the expression **fazer com que**. Otherwise it takes the impersonal infinitive, without a preposition.

>**O empregado fêz com que esperássemos o chefe de repartição.**
>The employee had us wait for the head of the office.
>**Também fêz o Sr. Gomes esperar.**
>He also had Mr. Gomes wait.

c. **Obrigar, forçar, constranger, compelir, coagir** (the last two rare in BF), are regularly followed by **a** and the infinitive, personal or impersonal.

>**Obrigou-nos a calar.**
>He obliged us to be silent.
>**A enchente forçou os transeuntes a passarem pela outra rua.**
>The flood forced the pedestrians to go by the other street.

However, they may be followed by **a que** and the subjunctive.

>**O cangaceiro obrigou o padre a que rezasse pela alma do camarada.**
> **SLit**
>The bandit obliged the priest to pray for the soul of his companion.

§232. Expressions of permission or prohibition: **deixar, permitir, consentir, proibir, vedar, evitar, ser inevitável**, etc.

a. **Deixar, permitir** may be followed by either the subjunctive or the infinitive, but the latter is far more frequent in BF. The infinitive is generally impersonal.

>**Deixa que eu arrume o quarto antes de sair.**
>Let me straighten up the room before I go out.
>**Deixa-me fazer isso.**
>Let me do that.
>**Podemos deixar o chofer esperar um pouco.**
>We can let the driver wait a while.

Ela nos permitiu ir ao cinema.
She let us go to the movies.
Note: **Deixa, que eu faço. (que=e.)**
Let it alone, I'll do it.

b. **Consentir** is followed by the subjunctive and by the personal infinitive with about equal frequency. The preposition **em** may be used or omitted before the clause.

Consenti (em) que o menino brincasse lá fora.
I consented to the child's playing outside.
O pai consentiu nos rapazes irem à praia.
The father consented to the boys' going to the beach.

c. **Proibir** usually takes the subjunctive. The construction with **de** and the infinitive (usually impersonal) is somewhat less used.

Proíbo que você faça isso.
I forbid you to do that.
Ela me proíbe de fazer isso. (*Also* **me proibe fazer.**)
She forbids my doing that.

d. **Impedir** is followed by either the infinitive or the subjunctive, more frequently by the former in BF. The infinitive is usually personal.

Vou impedir que os vendedores entrem em casa.
I am going to prevent salesmen from getting into the house.
A polícia impediu os mendigos de pedirem na cidade.
The police prevented the beggars from begging in town.

e. **Vedar** takes the infinitive more often than the subjunctive.

O pai vedou que a filha se casasse.
The father forbade that his daughter should marry.
Vedou a filha de casar.
He forbade his daughter to marry.

f. **Evitar** may be followed by the subjunctive in the following construction:

Fugindo do país, o capitão evitou que prendessem.
Fleeing from the country, the captain avoided arrest.
O senhor não pode evitar que chova.
You can't prevent its raining.

This usage is not frequent in BF. It would be avoided in most cases by a different construction of the sentence.

g. For **ser inevitável** and similar expressions, see §255.

§233. Expressions of requesting: **pedir, rogar, encomendar, encarregar, incumbir,** etc.

a. **Pedir** usually takes the subjunctive in literary Portuguese, but in BF, while the subjuncive is heard, the usual construction consists of **para** and the infinitive, personal when its subject is different from that of **pedir**.

> **Eu peço que você venha amanhã.**   Lit & BF
> I ask you to come tomorrow.
> **Pedi ao João que trouxesse a mala.**   Lit & BF
> I asked John to bring the suitcase.
> **Êle pede para vermos o apartamento dêle.**   BF
> He asks us to see his apartment.
> **Vou pedir ao guarda para nos mostrar o caminho.**   BF
> I am going to ask the policeman to show us the way.
> **As crianças pedem para sair ao alpendre.**   BF
> The children ask to go out on the porch.

b. **Rogar, suplicar, implorar, solicitar** are confined largely to literary, semi-literary, and religious usage. They are most frequently followed by the subjunctive.

> **Roguei que Deus me perodasse.**
> I begged that God would pardon me.
> **O matuto suplicou que não lhe matassem a vaca.**
> The countryman implored them not to kill his cow.
> **O coitado implorou que não batessem mais nêle.**
> The poor fellow implored them not to beat him any more.
> **O candidato solicitou os eleitores a que votassem nêle.**
> The candidate solicited the voters to vote for him.

Implorar and **solicitar** may also be followed by **a** and the infinitive, personal or impersonal.

> **Solicitamos todos os cidadãos a auxiliarem na campanha.**
> We solicit all citizens to help in the campaign.
> **Imploramos os amigos a ajudar-nos.**
> We implore our friends to help us.

Rogar and **solicitar** often take **a que** before the subjunctive if an object, noun or pronoun, intervenes between the two verbs.

> **Rogou-nos a que contássemos tudo.**   Lit
> He begged us to tell everything.

c. **Encomendar** is followed by the subjective if the subject of the dependent verb is a noun. The person to whom the charge is given is the indirect object of **encomendar**.

Encomendei a Paulo que levasse os refrescos.
I put Paul in charge of taking the refreshments.

But when the verb does not have a noun object, the following construction is more usual:

Encomendei-lhe para fazer o trabalho.
I put him in charge of doing the work.

With either noun or pronoun object, the use of the preposition **de** and the infinitive (usually impersonal) is the most frequent of all.

Encomendei-lhe (a Paulo) de fazer o trabalho.
I put him (Paul) in charge of doing the work.

d. **Incumbir** and **encarregar** usually take **de** and the infinitive.

Incumbi Das Dores de preparar o almôço.
I made Das Dores responsible for preparing the lunch.
Êle encarregou a mulher de tomar conta do orçamento da casa.
He put his wife in charge of handling the household budget.

§234. Expressions of necessity: **precisar, necessitar, urgir, convir,** and **ser** with numerous adjectives of various shades of meaning.

a. **Precisar** and **necessitar** are followed by the subjunctive in circumstances in which one subject has need that another perform an act.

Preciso que voce me ajude.
I need you to help me.
Necessitava que alguém lhe acudisse.
He needed someone to come to his aid.

However, the same sense is more often expressed thus:

Preciso de voce para me ajudar.
I need you to help me.
Necessitava de alguém para lhe acudir. (*Also* que lhe acudisse.)
He needed someone to come to his aid.

b. **Urgir** (impersonal) is rare in BF. It takes the subjunctive if the verb which follows has a definite subject. It may also take the infinitive, especially if the dependent verb has a pronoun subject.

Urge que João chegue já.
It is urgent that John arrive at once.
Urge arranjarmos casa.
It is urgent for us to get a house.

c. **Convir** (impersonal) may take the subjunctive or the infinitive, usually the former if the subject of the second verb is a noun.

Convém que todos se reúnam.
It would be a good idea for all to hold a meeting.
Convém reunir-nos já.
We should hold a meeting at once.
Convém estarmos quietos.
We had better be quiet.

d. **Preciso, necessário, mister, forçoso, indispensável, inevitável, essencial, fatal, imprescindível, urgente** when used with an impersonal form of the verb **ser**, express necessity and similar ideas. They are followed either by the subjunctive or by the infinitive without a preposition. The infinitive becomes the subject of the verb **ser**.

É preciso que trabalhemos amanhã.
It is necessary that we work tomorrow.
É (*or* será) preciso trabalharmos amanhã.
It will be necessary for us to work tomorrow.
Foi necessário que corressem.
It was necessary for them to run.
Foi necessário correrem.
It was necessary for them to run.

§235. Expressions of importance: **importar, ser importante** (both expressions impersonal). Both take either the subjunctive or the infinitive.

É importante que tenhamos água potável.
It is important that we have drinking water.
Importa termos água potável.
It is important for us to have drinking water.
Importa que seja homem de confiança.
It is important that he be a trustworthy man.

The subjunctive of uncertainty

§236. Verbs and expressions of uncertainty, negation of certainty, disbelief, and doubt are followed by the subjunctive.

a. Expressions of certainty and belief, such as **crer, acreditar, pensar, achar, julgar, suspeitar, imaginar,** and expressions consisting of a verb and an adjective or noun with similar meanings are followed by the indicative as long as they express belief rather than disbelief or doubt.

> **Creio que Deus ajuda os pobres.**
> I believe that God helps the poor.
> **Acho que foi o Hélio que passou.**
> I think it was Helio who went by.
> **Já suspeitava que era êle.**
> I already suspected it was he.
> **Eu imaginava que você ia dizer isso.**
> I imagined you were going to say that.

b. Negative expressions of belief. When the verb of belief is negative, the subjunctive follows.

> **Não creio que seja êle.**
> I don't believe it is he.
> **Nunca pensei que você fôsse capaz disso.**
> I never thought you were capable of that.
> **Nunca suspeitei que êsse fôsse o ladrão.**
> I never suspected that he was the thief.

c. Transfer of the negation. These expressions very often avoid the subjunctive in BF by transferring the negation from the main to the subordinate clause.

> **Creio que não é êle.**
> I believe it is not he.
> **Eu achava que você nunca seria capaz disso.**
> I thought that you would never be capable of that.

d. Infinitive with verbs of belief. These verbs may often use the infinitive instead of the indicative, less often instead of the subjunctive. However, no clear-cut rule can be stated which will explain exactly when this is likely to be done.

> **Creio ter sido você que abriu a janela.**
> I think it was you who opened the window.
> **Alguém vem, mas não creio ser o Gilberto.**
> Someone is coming, but I don't think it is Gilbert.
> **Nunca suspeitel ser êsse o ladrão.**
> I never suspected his being the thief.

e. Expressions of less than full belief. Other expressions containing the verbs of belief are followed by the subjunctive if they express something less than full belief.

Custa-me crer que você esteja de volta.
It is hard for me to believe that you are back.
Mal posso acreditar que seja êle.
I can hardly believe that it is he.
É difícil compreender que um homem só possa fazer tanto.
It is difficult to understand that one man can do so much.

f. Erroneous belief. An affirmative statement of belief is followed by the subjunctive if the belief is known to be, or has turned out to be, erroneous.

Ouvi alguém chamar, mas pensei que fôsse o carteiro.
I heard somebody call, but I thought it was the mailman.
Êle imagina que eu seja (*or* sou) o herdeiro de milhões.
He imagines that I am the heir to millions.
Quincas sabe que o filho tem namorada, e suspeita que seja você.
Quincas knows his son has a girl-friend, and suspects that it is you.

g. Verbs of belief in questions. The indicative is generally used in questions, unless the verb is negative, or the speaker wishes to suggest his own disbelief.

Você não pensa que seja êle?
Don't you believe that it is he?
Você crê mesmo que isso seja verdade?
Do you really believe that that is true?

h. **Compreender** expresses a meaning similar to belief, and takes the subjunctive in the same situations.

Não compreendo que o senhor demore na rua.
I don't understand your staying so long on the street.
O senhor compreende que um homem possa ser tão indolente?
Do you understand how a man can be so lazy?

i. Expressions of doubt: **duvidar, desconfiar,** and similar expressions resulting from combinations of verb and adjective or noun take the subjunctive regularly, whether they are affirmative or negative.

Duvido que você possa abrir a porta.
I doubt that you can open the door.

Ninguém duvidava que chegássemos atrasados.
Nobody doubted that we would arrive late.
Desconfio que o sujeito esteja falando de mim.
I rather suspect that the fellow is talking about me.

j. Expressions of denial: **negar, não que**, etc., always require the subjunctive.

Não nego que o culpado fôsse eu.
I don't deny that I was at fault.
O Brúni é sabido; não que seja um gênio, mas experto êle é.
Bruni is smart; not that he is a genius, but he is clever.

k. Subjunctive without change of subject. Expressions of uncertainty, disbelief, and doubt may be followed by the subjunctive even if the subject of both verbs is the same. However, the infinitive may also be used in this case.

Não creio que tenha visto o Sr. Carvalho na praia.
I don't believe that I have seen Mr. Carvalho at the beach.
Não creio ter visto o Sr. Carvalho na praia.
I don't believe I have seen Mr. Carvalho at the beach.

§237. Assumptions contrary to fact, with **se**. From the negation of belief or certainty, it is an easy step to conditions contrary to fact. The imperfect subjunctive is used, as in English and Spanish, to make a contrary-to-fact assumption in present time. The pluperfect is used if the asssumption refers to past time. The conclusion is in the conditional or conditional perfect respectively or, more frequently in BF, in the imperfect or pluperfect indicative.

Se eu pudesse ficar, ficava.
If I could stay, I would.
Se êle tivesse visto o buraco, teria (tinha) parado o carro.
If he had seen the hole, he would have stopped the car.

a. Imperfect subjunctive for the pluperfect. The imperfect subjunctive is often heard in conditional sentences which would logically require the pluperfect. The substitution is not made in cases where confusion would result, nor where an expression of time would make the imperfect illogical.

Se eu visse (*for* tivesse visto) o rapaz, teria falado com êle.
If I had seen the boy, I would have spoken to him.

b. Omission of **se**. In literary Portuguese the conjunction may be omitted with reversal of the normal positions of subject and verb. This construction is rare, even in literature.

Tivesse Célia chamado, Antônio teria corrido para socorrê-la. Lit
Had Celia called, Anthony would have run to help her.
Fôsse eu, não teria feito o que você fêz.   Lit
If it were I, I would not have done what you did.

c. **Conditional clause of admitted fact.** If the clause following **se** expresses an admitted fact, or what is considered as possibly fact, the indicative is used.

Se mais disse, eu não lhe ouvi mais nada.
If he said more, I didn't hear another word from him.
Se ela já estava com compromisso, está tudo acabado.
If she was already engaged, it's all over (between us).
Se a mala está aqui, é porque alguém deixou.
If the bag is here, it is because someone left it.

d. **Alternative conditions.** When **se** is followed by alternative conditions, one of which is true, the indicative is used.

Não sei se êle já foi ou não.
I don't know whether he has gone or not.
Estamos na dúvida, se pagamos ou não pagamos.
We are hesitating as to whether we will pay or not.

But when the alternative conditions both lead to the same conclusion, and both are assumptions, the verbs of both alternatives are expressed in the subjunctive, present or imperfect, with the omission of **se**.

O amor de Deus é coisa que já tenho, dê ou não dê o gato.
—Suassuna, *Auto da Compadecida*.
The love of God is something I already have, whether I give the cat or not.
Assistissem ao jôgo ou fôssem embora, tudo era igual para nós.
Whether they attended the game or went away, it was all the same to us.

e. **Se** and a verb referring to present time. When the time is present, without any assumption contrary to fact, the present indicative is used.

Se a gente trabalha todos os dias sem férias, fica aborrecida.
If one works every day without a vacation, he gets bored.

Se estou estudando, é porque tenho exames amanhã.
If I am studying, it is because I have examinations tomorrow.
Se não conhecemos bem o país, é porque o Brasil é grande.
If we don't know the country well, it is because Brazil is big.

f. **Se** and future conditions. If the assumption following **se** refers to the future in any way, giving even the slightest suggestion of futurity, BF tends to express it in the future subjunctive. The conclusion may be in the future indicative, the present indicative, or the imperative. Occasionally, in the conclusion, we may use the conditional (or its substitute, the imperfect) to express a wish which is logically in present time.

Então, vamos ver a nossa doentinha, se você quiser.
Well, then, let's go see our little sick girl, if you wish.
Se chover, temos que ficar em casa.
If it rains, we have to stay at home.
Vem me ajudar, se puder.
Come help me, if you can.
Eu queria comprar um dicionário, se tiver.
I'd like to buy a dictionary, if there is one.

g. Future less vivid. In this type of sentence, the speaker makes an assumption concerning the future, rather than stating a possibility. The **se**-clause is put in the imperfect subjunctive and the conclusion in the conditional or the imperfect indicative.

Se eu fôsse contar-lhe histórias, seria um nunca acabar.
If I were to tell you stories, it would be an endless process.
—E se fôssemos a São Paulo amanhã?
And if we were to go to São Paulo tomorrow?

h. Use of **como se.** This expression is always followed by either the imperfect or the pluperfect subjunctive.
Rinaldo recuou, como se estivesse com medo.
Rinaldo backed off, as if he were afraid.

§238. Other conditional sentences.
a. Use of **quer . . . quer.** These correlatives introduce alternative conditions, one of which will be fulfilled. However, the conditions are posited as assumptions, and the verb or verbs are in the subjunctive. The construction is seldom used in BF.

Você vai comigo, quer queira, quer não.
You are going with me, whether or no.

b. The negative conjunctions of assumption. These take the present or the imperfect subjunctive, according to the rules for the sequence of tenses. Their usage in BF is limited, being replaced by the usual conditional sentences with **se** most of the time, with a negative verb. The conjunctions are: **a não ser que** and **a menos que**.

> **Esta casa vai ruir, a não ser que façam reformas. (BF=se não fizerem reformas.)**
> This house is going to fall down, unless they make repairs.
> **Eu avisei que não lhe pagava, a menos que trabalhasse. (BF=se não trabalhasse.)**
> I notified him that I wouldn't pay him, unless he worked.

c. **Dado que.** This conjunction may be used to introduce a contrary-to-fact assumption. In such cases it is followed by the same forms as **se**, i.e., the imperfect or the pluperfect subjunctive.

> **Dado que êle tivesse um carro, não poderia viajar até Cuiabá.**
> Provided he had a car, he couldn't travel to Cuiabá.

d. **Contanto que** introduces assumptions only in the future with respect to the main verb, and consequently is followed by either the present or the imperfect subjunctive, according to the rules for sequence.

> **Êle pode se livrar da cadeia, contanto que pague a multa.**
> He can get out of jail, provided he pays the fine.

BF is much more likely to use **se** with the meaning clarified by the intonation.

e. **No caso que** and **caso** are used as conjunctions with a meaning similar to **se**, which often replaces them. They introduce a condition in the future with reference to the main verb, and consequently take the present or the imperfect. However, **caso** is used to a considerable extent in BF, and following a main verb in the present it usually takes the future subjunctive.

> **No caso que seu primo venha, vamos juntos à praia.**
> In case your cousin comes, we will go to the beach together.
> **Caso seu primo vier, vamos todos à praia.**
> In case your cousin comes, we'll all go to the beach.

f. Several other expressions are similar in meaning, although the sentence structure is different. In these, the conjunction **que** is used, followed by the subjunctive to indicate that the sentence is condi-

tional. The imperfect indicative in the main clause has the meaning
of a conditional tense, but the latter is very seldom used in such
sentences in BF.

Era melhor que tivesse ficado.
It would be better if he had remained.
Era bom que se casasse logo.
It would be a good idea for her to get married at once.
Era milagre que tivesse saído com vida.
It was a miracle that he had come out of it alive.
Que tinha que ela saísse com êle?
What was wrong with her going out with him?
Quanto mais trabalhasse, mais depressa realizaria o que sonhava.
The more he worked, the sooner he would get what he dreamed of.
Você não podia escapar dessa, nem que fôsse campeão de luta livre.
You couldn't get out of that one, even if you were a champion
wrestler.
Mesmo que eu pudesse, não te ajudava.
Even if I could, I wouldn't help you.

It should be noted that the preceding conjunctions may not be
followed by the future subjunctive. The present is used when referring to future time.

§239. Subjunctive with conjunctions of concession. These adverbial conjunctions are often followed by a clause expressing a
contrary-to-fact assumption. However, whether this is true or not,
they are always followed by the subjunctive. The difference is clarified by the verb of the conclusion, which is in the conditional or
an equivalent as the conclusion of a contrary-to-fact assumption.
The future subjunctive is never used with these conjunctions.

   a. **Embora**

   Embora você fôsse com êle, não iria gostar da viagem.
   Even if you went with him, you probably wouldn't like the trip.
   Embora eu estivesse na festa, não dancei com ela.
   Although I was at the party, I did not dance with her.

   b. **Posto que**

   Posto que chova amanhã, vou sempre.
   Even if it rains tomorrow, I'm still going.

   c. **Bem que.** This conjunction may be equivalent to **embora**, but
this meaning is literary. When it means **seguramente**, the indicative
is used.

Êsse mugido me impressionava, bem que soubesse de onde vinha.
Lit
That moo impressed me, although I knew where it came from.

d. Ainda que

Saimos à noite, ainda que fizesse frio.
We went out at night, although it was cold.

§240.   Conjunctions of purpose. The conjunctions of purpose and those of result and negative result, when they also have some suggestion of purpose, are followed by the subjunctive. Only the present and imperfect subjunctive may follow them, never the future. By replacing the conjunction with the corresponding preposition and using the personal infinitive, BF usually manages to avoid the subjunctive.

a.   **Para que** is always followed by the subjunctive.

Godofredo nos fêz esperar, para que apreciássemos a paisagem.
Godfrey made us wait, so that we could enjoy the landscape.

This conjunction may always be, and in BF usually is, replaced by the preposition **para**, which is followed by the infinitive.

Só disseram isso para ficarmos com medo.
They only did this so that we would be scared.

b.   **A fim de que** is little used in BF. It always requires the subjunctive.

O Zé nos explicou os pontos, a fim de que saíssemos bem no exame.
Joe explained the questions to us, so that we would pass the examination.

The corresponding preposition, **a fim de**, rarely takes a personal infinitive. To express the meaning, one may use **para** and the personal infinitive or add another verb which makes it possible to use the impersonal infinitive.

O Zé nos explicou os pontos, para sairmos bem.
Joe explained the questions to us, so that we could pass.
O Zé nos explicou os pontos, a fim de ajudar-nos a sair bem.
Joe explained the questions to us, in order to help us pass.

c.   **De modo que, de maneira que, de jeito que** are three synonymous conjunctions which are followed by clauses of result, usually in the indicative.

De modo que você já vai à escola?
So you are already going to school?
Êle caiu numa vala, de jeito que quebrou uma perna.
He fell into a ditch, so that he broke a leg.

However, when any purpose is implied by these conjunctions, the verb is put in the subjunctive.

O caçador preparou a trampa de modo que a onça caísse sôbre as estacas.
The hunter prepared a trap in such a way that the jaguar would fall on the stakes.

These conjunctions may be transformed into prepositions by substituting a for que. However, they usually take the impersonal infinitive, which may require that an additional verb be used to express the meaning.

Preparou a trampa de modo a fazer a onça cair sôbre as estacas.
He prepared the trap in such a way as to make the jaguar fall on the stakes.

d. Sem que is always followed by either the present or the imperfect subjunctive. However, it may always be, and in BF usually is, replaced by the preposition sem and the personal infinitive.

Passamos pela frenta da janela, sem que os moradores nos vissem.
We passed in front of the window without the residents' seeing us.
Passamos pela frente da janela, sem os moradores nos verem.
We passed in front of the window without the residents' seeing us.

§241. Verbal and adverbial expressions of conjecture. These require the subjunctive of a verb which follows, if the conjecture applies to the verb. If the verb precedes, or the conjecture applies to something else, while the verb expresses a factual action, the indicative is used.

a. Talvez

Talvez tenhamos sol amanhã.
Perhaps we will have sunshine tomorrow.
Teremos sol amanhã, talvez.
We will have sunshine tomorrow, perhaps.
Talvez por isso mesmo, ela ficou zangada.
Perhaps for that reason, she became angry.

b. **Pode ser que**

> **Pode ser que êste médico me cure.**
> It may be that this doctor will cure me.

c. **Quiçá, porventura.** These words are mostly limited to literary usage.

> **O Erlindo quiçá esteja lá em casa já.**　　**Lit**
> Perhaps Erlindo is already at home.

§242. In relative clauses. The source of the subjunctive in a relative clause is the uncertainty as to the identification of the exact person or thing which is the antecedent of the relative pronoun.

a. The antecedent may be indeterminate. The individual to which the relative pronoun refers may be any one of a group or class, the specific one not having been determined as yet.

> **Eu sonhava com uma namorada que gostasse de mim.**
> I dreamed of a girl-friend who would love me.
> **Corri com o pavor de quem fugisse de uma multidão.**
> I ran with the terror of one who was running from a multitude.
> **Procura então quem queira você para esposo.**
> Then look for someone who will want you for a husband.

Compare the following, in which the speaker knows the exact person to whom he refers.

> **Êle tem uma namorada que gosta dêle.**
> He has a girl-friend who loves him.
> **Estou procurando um amigo que devia estar aqui.**
> I am looking for a friend who should be here.

In the following, all possible antecedents are included.

> **Todo o brasileiro que sabe ler tem que votar.**
> Every Brazilian who knows how to read has to vote.

b. The person named as antecedent is nonexistent. If the antecedent is negative, or it is otherwise stated that he does not exist, the verb is in the subjunctive.

> **Não há ninguém que se lembre de mim.**
> There is no one who remembers me.
> **Não conheço nenhum brasileiro que saiba falar tupi.**
> I don't know any Brazilian who can speak Tupi.
> **Estou sem ninguém que me auxilie.**
> I have no one to help me.

A relative adverb which is negated is also followed by the subjunctive.

Não havia onde o rapaz se metesse.
There was nowhere for the boy to hide.

The expression **que eu saiba** is in the subjunctive because of a negative antecedent, expressed or implied, often placed after it.

—O que tem nesta caixa? —Que eu saiba, nada.
What is in this box? As far as I know, nothing.

c. Tense of the subjunctive, referring to the future. When the relative clause refers to future time, and the relative pronoun refers to any one individual or to a limited number of individuals of the class, the present subjunctive is used.

Êle está procurando duas môças que possam servir de modelos.
He is looking for two girls who can serve as models.

But when the relative pronoun may refer to any or all of the individuals of the class, the future subjunctive is used.

Ai de quem cair nas mãos dos cangaceiros.
Woe to whoever falls into the hands of the bandits.
Toma nota dos nomes de todos os que estiverem lá.
Take note of everybody who is there.
Farei o que eu puder.
I will do whatever I can.
Quem chegar atrasado fica do lado de fora.
Anyone who arrives late stays outside.

This construction regularly follows the optative subjunctive in expressions such as the following:

Suceda o que suceder.
Happen what may.
Façam o que fizerem.
Let them do what they may.
Seja como fôr.
Let that be as it may.

§243. Subjunctive of indefinite future time. The subjunctive is used in any dependent clause if the future action expressed in it is uncertain or the future time vague. It should be noted that it does not matter whether the clause expresses futurity from the point of view of present time or from the time of the main verb. The conjunction, most frequently an adverb of time, influences to some extent the construction which follows it. For this reason, it is necessary to treat each conjunction separately.

a. **Quando** takes the future subjunctive when the subordinate clause refers to the future, following a main verb in the present or future. It is seldom, if ever, followed by the present subjunctive.

> **Eu peço a enxada quando precisar.**
> I'll ask for the hoe when I need it.
> **O que diria êle quando soubesse?**
> What would he say when he found out?

Note that definite future time is expressed in the indicative.

> **Vamos nos encontrar às quatro, quando iremos à praia.**
> We will meet at four, when we will go to the beach.

b. **Antes que**, whose meaning insures that the dependent clause will always refer to future time, always takes the subjunctive but may not take the future tense. The conjunction may always be replaced by **antes de** and the infinitive, personal or impersonal. Both conjunction and preposition are frequently used in BF.

> **Vamos entrar antes que chova.**
> Let's go in before it rains.
> **Chegamos antes de darem quatro horas.**
> We arrived before it struck four o'clock.
> **Comeram antes de sair.**
> They ate before going out.

c. **Depois que** may take either the present or the future subjunctive in a clause which refers to future time, at the choice of the speaker. But BF tends to prefer the future, as it does in all cases in which there is a choice. The conjunction may also be replaced in all cases by the preposition **depois de**, with either the personal or the impersonal infinitive.

> **Eu lhes pago depois que acabarem (*or* acabem) o trabalho.**
> I'll pay them after they finish the work.
> **Êle disse que vinha depois que acabasse de se vestir.**
> He said he was coming after he finished dressing.
> **Vamos sair só depois dos meninos dormirem.**
> Let's go out only after the children go to sleep.

d. **Até que** may be followed by the present or the imperfect subjunctive, but never by the future. It may always be replaced by the preposition **até** and the personal or impersonal infinitive.

Eu espero aqui até que você volte.
I'll wait here until you return.
Tive que escorar os galhos até colhermos a fruta.
I had to prop up the branches until we picked the fruit.

e. **Logo que, assim que, tão logo, tão depressa** are synonymous, but the last two are almost purely literary. All of them may take either the present or the future when the clause refers to future action. The literary language generally prefers the present subjunctive, BF the future.

Diga-lhe que me chame logo que chegar (*or* chegue.)
Tell him to call me as soon as he arrives.
Vem logo que puder.
Come as soon as you can.
Vamos à serra assim que tirarmos férias.
Let's go to the mountain as soon as we get a vacation.
Ela irá morar na cidade, tão logo os filhos a deixem sòzinha.
Lit
She will go live in the city as soon as the children leave her.
Serei promovido, tão depressa se reforme a minha repartição.
Lit
I will be promoted, as soon as my department is reorganized.

f. **Enquanto** is heard followed by the present indicative and by the future subjunctive, when the clause refers to future action. The present subjunctive is rare. When the action to take place will parallel another, simultaneous action, the present indicative may be heard, although the future subjunctive is more frequent in this situation. The indicative emphasizes the fact that the action will really be carried out and is not merely conjecture.

Espera aqui, enquanto vou à loja.
Wait here while I go to the store.
Espera aqui enquanto eu fôr à loja.
Wait here while I go to the store.

If the duration of future time is indicated, the future subjunctive is required.

Não vai embora enquanto eu estiver aqui.
Don't go away while I am here.

Enquanto with a negative verb is often used as an equivalent of **até que** or **até**. It requires the future subjunctive always when referring to the future.

> **Vamos ficar cá fora enquanto não chover.** (=até que chova *or* até chover.)
> We are going to stay out here until it rains.
> **Não podem jantar enquanto Papai não chegar.**
> You can't have dinner until Father gets here.

g. **Ao passo que, à medida que, ao mesmo tempo que.** In these expressions the word **que** is doubtless a relative pronoun in origin. This would seem to require the present subjunctive after it before a future clause. However, doubtless because of the similarity of their meaning to that of **enquanto**, the future subjunctive is also heard after them.

> **Vão compreender melhor à medida que vão (forem) adiantando nos estudos.**
> You will understand better as you make progress in your studies.

h. **Sempre que** has two distinct meanings—**em qualquer época em que** and **provisto que**. The former takes the future subjunctive in clauses referring to the future, the latter takes the present. There is naturally a certain amount of confusion between the two constructions.

> **Eu devolverei o livro sempre que (=quando) o homem exigir.**
> I will return the book whenever the man demands it.
> **Eu devolverei o livro, sempre que (=provisto que) o homem exija.**
> I will return the book, provided that the man demands it.

i. **A que** after some verbs has the meaning **até que**, while after others it is equivalent to **para que**. In either case it is followed by the subjunctive, but never by the future. It is largely literary.

> **Esperarei aqui a que venham.**
> I will wait here until they come.
> **Obrigou os moleques a que deixassem de amolar.**
> He obliged the kids to stop annoying us.
> **Rogou-nos a que contássemos tudo.**
> He begged us to tell everything.

§244. The relative adverbs with indefinite reference. The relative adverbs **como, quando, onde, quanto** are given an indefinite meaning referring to any manner, time, place, etc., when the subjunctive follows. If any suggestion of future time is implied in the sentence, the future subjunctive is used. The present subjunctive is quite rare.

> **Faz isso como quiser.**
> Do this however you wish.
> **Fôsse quando fôsse, sei que já houve uma casa aqui.**
> No matter when it was, I know there was once a house here.
> **Cada um deve ficar onde estiver.**
> Each one should remain wherever he is.
> **Pode caçoar quanto quiser.**
> You may tease as much as you wish.

a. Use of **quer que** with relatives. The indefinite reference of a relative adverb or pronoun may be reinforced by the words **quer que** placed immediately after them. This construction is little used in BF. With these phrases, the verb may be in any tense of the subjunctive.

> **Você será feliz onde quer que fôr.**
> You will be happy wherever you may go.
> **Êle pode falar com quem quer que seja.**
> He may speak to anyone at all.

b. **Qualquer**, written as one word, is usually an adjective but occasionally is used as a pronoun in BF. Ordinarily, to preserve its quality of adjective, the pronoun **um** is used to replace a missing noun. When it is an adjective, the noun or pronoun intervenes between it and **que.**

> **Qualquer um que se atrevesse a entrar aí morria na certa.**
> Anyone who should dare to enter there would certainly die.

The subjunctive of emotion

§245. General considerations. Expressions of emotion are, in general, followed by the subjunctive, especially if the subject of the dependent verb is different from that of the main verb. If the subjects are the same, the subjunctive may be used, but the infinitive is much more frequent. It is interesting to note that in most of these expressions the emotion is the result, rather than the cause, of the action of the dependent verb. The future subjunctive is never used with this type of sentence. The present tense replaces it.

§246. Expressions of hope: **esperar, ter esperança**, etc., require the subjunctive.

a. **Esperar** has three distinct meanings, and the construction differs in each case.

With the meaning "hope," the subjunctive follows universally in BF.

> **Espero que vocês possam vir.**
> I hope you can come.
> **Êle esperava que o Papai Noel trouxesse um trenzinho.**
> He hoped that Santa Claus would bring a little train.

In the sense of "wait," the subjunctive may follow with a conjunction of time, such as **a que** or **até que**, or one may use **até** and the infinitive.

> **Esperarei a que (até que) venha o gerente.**
> I will wait until the manager comes.
> **Vou esperar aqui até êles virem.**
> I am going to wait here until they come.

When the meaning is "expect," which denotes a reasonable amount of belief, the indicative is used.

> **Espero que amanhã será um dia de sol.**
> I expect tomorrow to be a sunny day.

b. **Oxalá, tomara.** These words may express a hope or a wish. The former has become quite rare in the speech of Rio de Janeiro and vicinity. It is replaced by **tomara**, which has exactly the same meaning. With the present subjunctive they express a hope that something may happen; with the imperfect, they express a wish that something which is not true were true.

> **Tomara que faça bom tempo amanhã.**
> I hope the weather is good tomorrow.
> **Tomara que eu pudesse ir à Europa.**
> I wish I could go to Europe.
> **Tomara que João tenha chegado já.**
> I hope John has already arrived.
> **Tomara que tivesse conhecido você antes.**
> I wish I had known you before.

The imperfect may also express a wish for the future which is unlikely to be fulfilled.

Tomara que esta pobreza acabasse.
I wish this poverty would end.

c. **Antes.** This adverb may be used with the imperfect subjunctive to express a wish that something were true, rather than the existing situation.

Não, aquêle não é meu namorado. Antes fôsse.
No, that is not my boy-friend. I wish he were.

§247. Expressions of fear: **temer** and similar verbs, and expressions in which the sense of "fear" is given by a noun.

a. **Temer, recear, espantar** are regularly followed by the subjunctive.

Temo que me prendam.
I am afraid they will arrest me.
Espantou-me que êle não tivesse mais vergonha.
It astounded me that he didn't have any more decency.

b. Expressions formed with nouns. If the sense of "fear" is given a noun such as **medo, receio, temor, horror, pavor**, either the subjunctive or the infinitive may be used. The infinitive is preceded by **de**, which may be kept or dropped before **que** and the subjunctive.

Tenho medo (de) que me descubram.
I am afraid they will discover me.
Carlos ficou tremendo de pavor dos meninos darem uma surra nêle.
Charles was trembling with terror that the boys would beat him up.

§248. Expressions of regret and sorrow: **sentir, doer** (impersonal), **lamentar**, and expressions formed with nouns such as **pena, lástima**, and **tristeza**, may take the subjunctive or the infinitive. The two subjects may be different or identical.

Sinto que o Durval não possa ir.
I am sorry that Durval can't go.
Êles sentiam que estivessem longe de você nessa crise.
They regretted that they were a long way from you in this crisis.
Sentiam estar longe.
They were sorry to be so far.
Lamento vocês terem perdido o jôgo.
I regret that you lost the game.
Dói-me na alma que êle ande em más companhias.
It breaks my heart that he keeps bad company.

É pena êles não poderem estar conosco.
It is a pity that they are not able to be with us.
A coitada da mulher sente muito os filhos estarem de mal.
The poor woman feels very bad that her sons are at odds.

§249. Expressions of pleasure. These take the subjunctive, but it can nearly always be avoided by one means or another.

a. **Alegrar** (impersonal), **alegrar-se** may take either the subjunctive or the infinitive. The verb is not very frequent in conversation.

Alegra-me que você tenha ganho.
I am glad that you won.
Amado se alegrou (de) que os filhos estivessem de volta.
Amado was glad that his sons were back.
Alegra-me terem chegado sãos e salvos.
I am glad you have arrived safe and sound.

b. **Estar (ficar) contente** may take either the subjunctive or the infinitive.

Fiquei contente de que você gostasse de mim.
I was glad that you liked me.
Êle está contente dela estar aqui.
He is glad she is here.

Both constructions are often bypassed by a very common device in BF—using an extra verb which can be put in the impersonal infinitive.

Êle está contente de saber que ela está aqui.
He is glad to know that she is here.

c. **Gostar** takes either the subjunctive or the infinitive, much more often the latter.

Não gosto que você se comporte mal.
I don't like for you to misbehave.
Não gosto de você se comportar mal.
I don't like for you to misbehave.

d. **Agradar** rarely takes the subjunctive. It usually is followed by an infinitive or noun which permits a change of sentence structure.

Agradou-lhes saber que você estava aqui.
It pleased them to know that you were here.
Agradou-lhes o fato de você estar aqui.
The fact that you were here pleased them.

§250. Expressions of surprise and wonder: **surpreender, estranhar, admirar, espantar, assombrar, maravilhar.**

a. **Surpreender** (impersonal), **surpreender-se.** This verb is used either impersonally or reflexively, followed wtih approximately equal frequency by the subjunctive or the infinitive.

> **Surpreende-me que êle queira me ver.**
> It surprises me that he wants to see me.
> **Surpreendo-me (de) que você não se esconda de pura vergonha.**
> I am surprised that you don't hide from pure shame.
> **Surpreende-me êles ainda estarem aqui.**
> It surprises me that they are still here.
> **Surpreendo-me de você ter feito isso.**
> I am surprised that you did that.

b. **Admirar** (impersonal), **admirar-se.** The second is less frequent.

> **Admira-me que possam dormir sôbre folhas de milho.**
> It astonishes me that they can sleep on corn-husks.
> **Admirou-se de que tivessem pescado o dia inteiro sem pegar nada.**
> He was astonished that they had fished all day without catching anything.

c. **Espantar** (impersonal), **espantar-se.** The subjunctive may be used but is more often avoided after them by the insertion of another word.

> **Espantou a todos que um homem tão manso tivesse reagido.**
> It astounded everyone that such a gentle man had fought back.
> **Espanta-se de que todos fujam.**
> He is astounded that everyone runs away.
> **Espanta-se de ver que todos fogem.**
> He is astounded to see that everyone runs away.

The subjunctive as optative and imperative

§251. Classification of this subjunctive. These usages belong logically with the first of the three preceding types discussed—the imposing of the will of one subject on another. They contain within them implicitly the idea that the speaker is urging, suggesting, or ordering that something be done. He may suggest that he himself do something (first person singular), or that he and others do it (first plural); he may suggest that the person or persons spoken to do it (second person); or that a third person or persons do it. These expressions differ from those previously discussed in that the main clause is absent. The person whose will is imposed is normally the speaker. The exact form which the exercise of will takes (command, wish, request, etc.) is not specified. It seems best to treat these subjunctives separately, since a different type of analysis of usage is required.

§252. Use of optative subjunctive and subjunctive for imperative.

a. The first person singular. The subjunctive is used here only to a very limited extent. There are no specific cases in which it must be used. It appears to be a survival of past usage which has not yet been entirely lost, or possibly an occasional analogy from the third person.

> **Discutam a política se quiserem; só que eu esteja quietinho aqui com o meu café.   SLit**
> Let them discuss politics if they wish; just let me be quiet here with my coffee.

The usual construction is formed from **deixar** and the infinitive. See §260b.

b. The first person plural. The subjunctive may be used, but in BF it is heard only in the verb **ir**, where **vamos** is the only form. The subjunctive of other verbs is frequent in literature, however.

> **Não nos percamos neste bairro, que eu não conheço.   Lit** *or* **SLit**
> Let's not get lost in this district, which I am not acquainted with.
> **O jantar está pronto; sentemo-nos.   Lit**
> Dinner is ready; let's sit down.

In BF, the word **vamos**, the subjunctive of **ir**, is used before the infinitive of any verb except **ir**, both in the affirmative and the negative. This construction is also found in the literary language.

> **Vamos à praia.**
> Let's go to the beach.
> **Não vamos cair naquele buraco.**
> Let's not fall into that hole.

c. The second person. The literary language requires the subjunctive for the imperative with the subjects **você**, **o senhor**, etc.

> **Venham comigo.   Lit**
> Come with me.
> **Traga-me um copo de água.   Lit**
> Bring me a glass of water.

The subjunctive is used universally in writing, with the exception of letters to friends. But in speech it is seldom used except in the verbs noted below. The **carioca** feels that the subjunctive is harsher and more abrupt than the imperative. Even in the plural, where the imperative has been lost, he seldom uses the subjunctive. However, the verbs **ser, estar,** and **querer** have lost the imperative singular forms, and these verbs employ the subjunctive both in the singular and the plural.

> **Seja bonzinho, meu filho.**
> Be good, my son.
> **Estejam quietinhos.**
> (You all) be quiet.
> **Oh! Senhora viuva, comigo não queira casar. —Canção.**
> Oh widow lady, don't want to marry me.

In the verb **dizer** the subjunctive and the imperative are heard with about equal frequency.

> **Diga-me o que viu na feira.**
> Tell me what you saw at the market.
> **Me diz o que é.**
> Tell me what it is.

A few other expressions are more or less traditional in the subjunctive, even though the imperative of the same verbs might be used in other expressions.

> **Veja só.**
> Just look.
> **Desculpe.**
> Excuse me.

The use of the subjunctive with an expressed subject, formerly heard to a considerable extent in situations in which the speaker was unwilling to be "incorrect," has largely disappeared.

> **O senhor siga direito em frente e verá a marquise no próximo quarteirão.   Now rare**
> Go straight ahead and you will see the marquee on the next block.

d. The third person. The subjunctive is used regularly in the third person, in several different situations.

(1) To express a wish, a prayer, or a curse.

Bons olhos o vejam.
  You are a sight for sore eyes.
Deus lhe pague.
  May God repay you.
Louvado seja Deus.
  Praise God.
Viva!
  Hurrah!
O diabo te carregue.
  The devil take you.

These are mostly fixed formulas, with only limited application to new expressions.

(2) To express a wish or suggestion that a person perform an act. It is heard most often in reply to a statement that someone has the intention of performing the act, but has much broader use in literature.

Vá [êle] lavar as mãos.
  Let him go wash his hands.
A Neusa vai tomar um táxi. —Pois, tome.
  Neusa is going to take a taxi. Well, let her.

Occasionally the verb is preceded by **que**, but usually not.

Pois, que tome.
  Well, let her (take it).

If an expression such as **em quanto a** precedes the subject, or is implied by the speaker, **que** is placed between the subject and the verb.

O Manuel que se agüente.
  As for Manuel, let him bear it.

(3) To posit a condition. This type of expression includes the present subjunctive followed by the future, and is followed by a conclusion which is not affected, no matter how the condition may vary.

Seja como fôr, eu não acredito nêle.
  Let that be as it may, I don't believe in him.
Esteja onde estiver, vamos achá-lo.
  Let it be where it may, we are going to find it.
Chame quem chamar, não atendo o telefone.
  Let anybody at all call, I won't answer the telephone.

e. Optative expressions in past time. Whenever any of these expressions refer to the past, the imperfect subjunctive is used. This situation usually is found in a narration of past events.

Êle não queria ouvir falar no Tonico; que batesse noutra porta.
He didn't want to hear Tony mentioned; let him appeal to someone else.
Eu não ia atender o telefone; atendesse quem quisesse.
I wasn't going to answer the telephone; let anyone who wanted to answer it.
Fôsse como fôsse, a gente logo saberia como acabava.
Let that be as it might, people would soon know how it came out.
Protestamos que não aceitávamos tais condições; antes deixássemos o país.
We protested that we would not accept such conditions; we would sooner leave the country.
Fizessem o que bem quisessem; só que eu ficasse fora.
Let them do whatever they wished; just let me remain out of it.

Miscellaneous subjunctives

§253. Subjunctive with **por.** The preposition **por** is used with certain adjectives and adverbs of quantity in expressions of large, but indefinite, quantity or degree, followed by the subjunctive.

Por mais que seu pai dissesse que você estudasse, nunca quis fazer esfôrço.
No matter how much your father told you to study, you never wanted to make the effort.
Por muito dinheiro que êle tenha, não pode comprar o que não existe.
No matter how much money he has, he cannot buy what does not exist.
Por maior que fôsse o bicho, não chegava ao tamanho da onça.
No matter how big the animal was, it wasn't as big as the jaguar.
Por pobrezinha que ela seja, sempre terá alguma coisa.
No matter how poor she is, she must have something.

254. Subjunctive with superlatives. Normally the subjunctive is not used after superlatives, but it is occasionally found both in the literary language and in BF, to express the very great, though vague, extent of the quality denoted by the superlative.

É a mais bela paisagem que se possa imaginar.
It is the most beautiful landscape that one can imagine.

§255. Subjunctive with impersonal expressions. There are a large number of impersonal expressions, most often consisting of the verb **ser** in the third person singular and an adjective, sometimes a noun, which may take the subjunctive following them. It is also possible in nearly all cases to use the infinitive instead of the subjunctive. Both constructions are normal in BF. Most of these expressions fall into one or another of the categories treated previously, but some do not. Such adjectives and nouns include, among others:

admirável	**incerto**	**necessário**
conveniente	**incrível**	**obrigatório**
desejável	**indispensável**	**possível**
difícil	**inevitável**	**preciso**
duvidoso	**injusto**	**preferível**
essencial	**inútil**	**problemático**
estranho	**inverossímil**	**provável**
fácil	**justo**	**prudente**
forçoso	**lamentável**	**recomendável**
implausível	**mandatório**	**triste**
importante	**maravilhoso**	**urgente**
imprescindível	**milagre**	**útil**
inacreditável	**mister**	

a. When the second verb has no expressed subject. In this case, the verb which follows the impersonal expression is regularly an infinitive.

> **É difícil dominar uma língua estrangeira.**
> It is difficult to master a foreign language.

b. When the second verb has a personal subject. The subjunctive is always permissible, but BF shows considerable preference for the personal infinitive. This infinitive and the phrase of which it is a part are treated as the subject of the main verb, i.e., no preposition is used.

> **É essencial termos cuidado.** (*Or* **que tenhamos.**)
> It is essential for us to take care.
> **É estranho estarem juntos tanto tempo.** (*Or* **que estejam.**)
> It is strange that they have been together so long.
> **Foi pena perderem a festa.** (*Or* **que perdessem.**)
> It was a pity that they missed the party.

c. When **ser** is replaced by other verbs. Numerous other verbs may be used with these words, sometimes in an impersonal form, but more frequently with a personal subject. In such cases, the subjunctive is the more usual construction, although the infinitive is usually possible also.

> **Eu acho possível que saiam pela porta dos fundos. (Eu acho possível sairem.)**
> I think it is possible they will go out the back door.
> **Parece admirável que êle leia tão bem. (Parece admirável êle ler.)**
> It seems admirable that he reads so well.
> **Cremos impossível que nosso empregado seja ladrão.**
> We believe it impossible that our hired man is a thief.
> **Acho conveniente irmos visitar o tio. (que vamos.)**
> I think it is a good idea for us to go visit our uncle.

Choice of tense in the subjunctive

§256. Sequence of tenses. The tense of the verb in the subjunctive is usually determined by the tense of the verb in the main clause. Although one hears an occasional departure from the rules of sequence, it is quite rare and immediately strikes the ear of the hearer as incorrect.

a. Primary sequence. The present indicative or subjunctive, the imperative, and the future are followed by the present or by the future subjunctive, or by the respective perfect tenses. The choice between the present and the future subjunctive does not depend upon the sequence and is dealt with below.

Note: With verbs of emotion, when the emotion is felt in present time, but is a result of events in past time, the imperfect subjunctive follows the present tense.

> **Sinto que êle estivesse doente ontem.**
> I am sorry that he was ill yesterday.

b. Secondary sequence. The preterite, the imperfect, the conditional, the present perfect, and the pluperfect are followed by the imperfect or the pluperfect subjunctive. Either a present or a future subjunctive becomes imperfect if the main verb is changed to a past tense.

> **Irei quando você quiser; eu disse que iria quando você quisesse.**
> I will go when you wish; I said I would go when you wished.

Espero que ela venha; esperava que ela viesse.
I hope she will come; I hoped she would come.

§257. Choice between the present and future subjunctive. The future is never used with the subjunctive of will (see above), nor with the subjunctive of emotion (see above). It can only be used when its clause refers to indefinite future time, and even then it is limited to certain constructions. The following situations require or permit the future subjunctive, provided future time is implied:

a. Adverbial conjunctions which require the future subjunctive. After **quando, se, enquanto,** only the future is used.

Eu lhe dou isto, se você quiser:
I'll give you this, if you wish.
Vem quando quiser.
Come when you wish.
Vai estudando enquanto puder.
Go on studying while you can.

b. Conjunctions which may take either the present or the future. **Assim que, logo que, depois que, tão logo (que), caso, conforme, segundo** may be followed by either the present or the future, at the choice of the speaker. BF nearly always prefers the future.

Sairemos depois que você acabar de jantar. (*Or* acabe.)
We'll go out after you finish eating.
Não iremos, caso chover. (*Or* chova.)
We won't go if it rains.
Pagaremos conforme trabalharem bem ou mal. (*Or* trabalhem.)
We will pay according as they work well or badly.

c. Future subjunctive in relative clauses. See §242c.

§258. Periphrastic future subjunctive. It is always possible to express futurity in the subjunctive, even in situations which require the present tense, by using periphrastic futures. At times this distinction is important.

Sinto que êle não vá poder trabalhar. (*Cf.* não possa.)
I am sorry that he will not be able to work. (is not able.)
É possível que êle haja de ter tudo o que quer. (*Cf.* tenha.)
It is possible that he will have everything he wishes. (does have.)
Espero que êle esteja bem hoje e que vá estar amanhã.
I hope that he is well today and that he will be tomorrow.

The need for such distinction is not frequent, since in most verbs the progressive form serves to clarify the meaning.

É provável que êle trabalhe.
It is probable that he works. (*Or* will work.)
É provável que êle esteja trabalhando.
It is probable that he is working.

THE VERB: THE IMPERATIVE

§259. The forms of the imperative. Portuguese had forms of the imperative in the singular and plural of the old second person. They were used only in the affirmative, being replaced in the negative by subjunctive forms. In regions in which the old second person singular survives, the imperative is still in use with the subject **tu**. However, the simplicity of the form has caused it to survive even where the rest of the old second person has been lost. (See §191f.) The few irregular forms have not survived. The entire second person plural is lost everywhere in Brazil, the imperative along with the other forms.

§260. Present-day usage in the singular.

a. The imperative. The imperative is used in the singular with the subjects of the new second person—**você, o senhor, a senhora**. Although the traditional usage did not permit the imperative in the negative with the second person, it is now also used in the negative.

> **Me ajuda a mover a mesa.**
> Help me move the table.
> **Não fala assim.**
> Don't talk like that.

Formerly the pressure from the schools and the generally accepted public opinion that these forms were incorrect was such that many people were unwilling to use them, and tried in various ways to avoid them. This attitude has largely disappeared. During a recent stay of eight months in Rio, I heard only one Brazilian use subjunctives as imperatives—a teacher of Portuguese. For the subjunctive used with certain verbs, see §252c.

b. Use of **deixar** in the first and third persons. When the speaker wishes to suggest that he himself do something, or that a third person do it, the most usual construction is formed with the imperative of **deixar** as an auxiliary with the infinitive. **Deixar** may, of course, have its full meaning as an independent verb in such constructions.

But in other cases it may be ambiguous, possibly having some of this meaning or not, or it may have no independent meaning at all. We may hear any of the following constructions, ranging from the more to the less literary. In general, the shorter forms also have less force of the verb **deixar** and amount simply to imperatives.

Deixa que eu faça isso. Deixa que a empregada faça isso.
Let me do that.   Let the maid do that.
Deixa-me (me deixa) fazer isso. Deixa a empregada fazer isso.
Deix'eu fazer. Deix'ela fazer.
'X'eu fazer. 'X'ela fazer.

These shortest examples are heard mostly when the dependent infinitive has a pronoun subject.

c. The indicative. It is difficult in many cases to be sure whether the speaker is using the indicative or the imperative, since the forms are identical. There are two clues which point to the indicative: the use of an expressed subject when no emphasis is placed on it, and the tone, which is lower in the indicative than in the imperative. The indicative is fairly frequent in more formal speech, e.g., in commercial situations or in speaking to strangers.

O senhor dá uma telefonada para cá às quatro.
You may call here at four.
O senhor vai até a esquina e dobra à esquerda.
You go to the corner and turn left.

d. Use of circumlocutions. Various verb phrases are used on somewhat more formal occasions when the speaker is unwilling to use the imperative. These vary from one situation to another, since the meaning must fit the occasion.

Poder. In commercial use, one hears **poder** and the infinitive used in a situation in which the imperative would be logical. The meaning, of course, is intended literally. But the situation and the tone of voice give this expression the unmistakable force of the imperative.

Pode pagar na caixa.
You can pay the cashier.
Pode me deixar embrulhar primeiro.
Let me wrap it first.

Dever. This verb is used frequently when the imperative would constitute a command, but the speaker does not wish to seem to give orders.

Você deve estudar o terceiro capítulo.
You should study the third chapter.
O Sr. Prates não está no escritório. O senhor deve voltar amanhã.
Mr. Prates is not in the office. You should come back tomorrow.

Querer. This verb is used to express the meaning in the form of a request. Often the tone of voice counteracts the softening of the expression which the change from command to request might indicate.

Quer se sentar?
Will you sit down?
Você quer ficar calado?
Will you shut up?

§261. **Present-day usage in the plural.** The traditional imperative has completely disappeared from usage. Many educated speakers of Portuguese would not be able to remember the plural imperatives of several common verbs.

a. **New imperative.** In certain verbs which have monosyllabic third person plural forms in the present indicative, these forms are popularly used as imperatives. As in the singular, the criteria of distinguishing imperative from indicative are the tone of voice and the omission or use of subject pronouns.

Meninos, têm juizo.
Boys, behave.
Vêm todos para cá.
All of you come here.
Dão os cadernos ao professor.
Give your notebooks to the teacher.
Vão com Mamãe.
Go with Mother.
Põem os sapatos antes de sair.
Put your shoes on before you go out.

b. **Use of the subjunctive.** The subjunctive is used for the imperative in the plural in the same verbs as in the singular.

c. **Use of the indicative.** Since only a few verbs have forms which may be used as imperatives in the plural, the indicative is used much more than in the singular. There is some trend toward changing these to real imperative use, but it is not very strong thus far.

d. **Use of circumlocutions.** The verbs mentioned in the discussion of the singular as used to form phrases to replace the imperative are also used in the plural, except in the first person.

§262. Use of subjects with the imperative. Normally no subject is expressed with the imperative.

[O senhor] passa lá na pizzaria e pede uma pizza para viagem.
Go down to the pizzaria and order a pizza to go.
Menina, come essa alface.
Girl, eat that lettuce.
Põe os sapatos.
Put on your shoes.

The subject is used for emphasis. It is usually placed before the verb, although it may be put after to emphasize strongly that the person mentioned, rather than another, is to perform the action.

Eu vou ficar aqui; você vai à farmácia e me traz umas aspirinas.
I am going to stay here; you go to the drug store and bring me some aspirins.
Eu não vou de jeito nenhum. Vai você. (*Or* você vai.)
I am not going under any circumstances. *You* go.
Você ajuda êle.
You help him.

§263. The infinitive as an imperative. The infinitive is used as an imperative in certain cases.

a. In commerce. In giving directions in commercial use, as on packages, medicine bottles, etc., the infinitive is used more often than any other form.

Sacudir bem antes de usar.
Shake well before using.
Tomar uma pílula de três em três horas.
Take one pill every three hours.

b. In military commands. The word which activates the command is an infinitive.

Meia volta, voltar!
About, face!

c. In a very few fixed expressions. The following is used when taking leave of an acquaintance:

Passar bem. (=Fica bom de saúde.)
Keep well.

THE VERB: THE INFINITIVE

The forms of the infinitive

§264. Personal and impersonal infinitives. In addition to the form used without a subject, similar to the infinitives of other Romance languages, Portuguese has a personal infinitive, which expresses its subject by means of personal endings. But since the second person is largely lost in BF, and the first and third persons of the infinitive are alike, for all practical purposes we have only one form of the infinitive in the singular, whether it is personal or impersonal. In the plural, however, the personal form has the endings -mos and -em. The forms used in BF are the following:

Impersonal: **falar**   Personal: **eu falar**   **nós falarmos**
                                     você falar   **vocês falarem**
                                     êle, ela falar   **êles, elas falarem**

§265. Active and passive infinitives. Either the personal or the impersonal infinitive can be made passive. The respective infinitives of the auxiliary **ser** are combined with the past participle of the verb indicated.

> **Ser escrito; sermos amados.**
> To be written; for us to be loved.

§266. The perfect infinitive. In addition to the forms of the present infinitive, Portuguese has a full complement of perfect infinitives. They are formed by the use of the infinitives of the auxiliary **ter** (in the literary language, also **haver**) with the past participle.

> **Ter feito; terem compreendido; ter sido feito; terem sido compreendidos.**
> To have done; for them to have understood; to have been done; for them to have been understood.

Nature of the infinitive

§267. The infinitive as a noun. The infinitive is basically a substantive form of the verb, and as such partakes of the qualities of both noun and verb. In the quality of noun it is used:

a. As a pure noun. A good many infinitives have become so thoroughly substantivized in certain usages that they have become pure nouns, without any verbal force at all. The same word may be used elsewhere with part or all of its verbal qualities. These nouns are of the masculine gender and form plurals in the regular way.

Êle tem uma casa de dois andares.
    He has a two-story house.
Não encontraram nenhum ser humano.
    They did not meet a single human being.
O falar carioca tem certas caraterísticas especiais.
    The speech of Rio has certain special characteristics.
Pedimos os pareceres de várias pessoas peritas no assunto.
    We asked the opinions of several people who are experts in the matter.

b. With both nominal and verbal force. Elsewhere, these and other infinitives, both personal and impersonal, may be used as nouns without complete loss of their verbal force. As nouns, they may be used as subjects or objects of a verb or as objects of prepositions. They do not take the plural form of nouns.

Errar é fácil.
    To err is easy.
Proíbo-lhe ir.
    I forbid him to go.
Ouvir é obedecer.
    To hear is to obey.
Êle chegou antes de sairmos.
    He arrived before we went out.

§268. Syntax of the infinitive as a noun. As a noun, the infinitive may be modified by:

a. An adjective. When modified by an adjective, the infinitive also takes an article or other determinant.

Ouvíamos o estourar barulhento dos foguetes.
    We heard the noisy bursting of the firecrackers.
Irritava-me o choramingar aborrecido das crianças.
    The annoying whining of the children irritated me.
Aquêle martelar contínuo da araponga não parava mais.
    That continuous hammering of the araponga never stopped.

b. A prepositional phrase. In this case also it takes an article or other determinant.

O pôr do sol é quase sempre bonito em Minas.
The setting of the sun is almost always pretty in Minas.
Eu gosto de ouvir o bater das ondas na praia.
I like to hear the beating of the waves on the beach.

c.   The definite article. The article is used with the infinitive only in certain circumstances in BF. The infinitive is largely felt as a noun in such cases, but still with a suggestion of action derived from the verb. The result of using an infinitive rather than a pure noun is usually a more graphic and lively description. Thus, **o mugir das vacas** (the mooing of the cows) suggests action, while **o mugido** may refer only to the sound produced. The definite article is used:

When the infinitive is used as a subject or object and is modified by an adjective or a phrase.

O estourar barulhento dos foguetes.
The noisy bursting of the firecrackers.
O mugir das vacas.
The mooing of the cows.

In the expression **ao** plus the infinitive. This construction is largely confined to literature. BF usually employs a clause instead. In spite of the article, the infinitive is here more verb than substantive.

Ao encontrarmos com êle, entramos no restaurante.
   (BF=Quando encontramos com êle.)
When we met him, we entered the restaurant.

If the infinitive is modified only by an adverb, it may take the definite article, but it is usually omitted in BF.

(O) jogar bem exige muito treino.
Playing well demands a lot of training.

d.   The indefinite article.

Isso aconteceu num abrir e fechar de olhos.
That happened in the twinkling of an eye.

§269.   The infinitive as a verb.
As a verb, the infinitive may be modified by an adverb, even when it is used as a subject or object.

(O) jogar bem exige muito treino.
Playing well demands a lot of training.

Note the increased emphasis on action conveyed by changing the modifier in the following from adjective to adverb.

Ouvíamos o bater contínuo do malho na bigorna.
We heard the continual beating of the hammer on the anvil.
Resultou enfadonho o bater continuamente do malho.
The hammer beating continually became annoying.

§270. The subject of the infinitive.
a. The infinitive may have a subject. As a verb, the infinitive may have an expressed subject. The impersonal infinitive does not have a subject expressed in the nominative but often presumes the object of another verb, sometimes its subject, is the subject of the impersonal infinitive.

Quero ver.
I want to see.
Deixa-me ver.
Let me see it.

b. The subject of the personal infinitive. The subject must be in the nominative case if the infinitive is personal. If the logical subject is expressed as the object of the preceding verb, then the infinitive is generally impersonal.

Êle pediu para eu fazer a mudança.
He asked me to do the moving.
Antes dêles entrarem, as portas foram fechadas.
Before they came in, the doors were closed.

There is in popular speech some confusion between the usages in which the pronoun is the object of the main verb and those in which it is the subject of the infinitive. When the pronoun follows the main verb, the subject form is often heard, replacing the more correct object form. Some such expressions are in very general use and attract little notice in colloquial speech. But the use of an object pronoun following a preposition, where the subject of the infinitive should be in the nominative form is definitely substandard.

Deixa eu fazer isso.   BF (*For* **Deixa-me fazer isso.**)
Let me do that.
Êle trouxe um sanduíche para mim comer. Subst (*For* **para eu comer.**)   BF
He brought a sandwich for me to eat.

c. Kinds of words used as subjects. The subject of a personal infinitive may be a pronoun, expressed or implied, or a noun.

> **Em vez de rirem, vocês deviam levar a coisa a sério.**
> Instead of laughing, you ought to take this thing seriously.
> **Ao sairmos nós, as comadres começaram a contar mexericos.**
> When we left, the gossips began to tell tales.
> **Você devia adubar a terra, para as árvores crescerem mais depressa.**
> You ought to fertilize the land, so the trees would grow more.

For the position of the subject of an infinitive, see §2e,f.

§271. The object of an infinitive. Either the personal or the impersonal infinitive may have an object, direct or indirect, noun or pronoun.

> **É urgente passar um telegrama.**
> It is urgent to send a telegram.
> **Entrei à noite, sem ninguém me ver.**
> I came in at night without anyone's seeing me.

For the position of the pronoun object, see §184.

General uses of the infinitive

In addition to the uses given above (268–271), the infinitive is used:

§272. As the complement of a verb. Sometimes the infinitive follows directly without a preposition, but in most cases one is required. The omission or choice of preposition is determined by the main verb which precedes the infinitive.

a. With no preposition. Several common verbs do not require a preposition. They include **querer, dever, ir, vir, ouvir, ver,** and several others.

b. With choice of preposition. Many verbs may take any one of two or more prepositions before an infinitive, usually to express different meanings. Some verbs which are not ordinarily followed by a preposition may take one in special circumstances.

> **Êle acabou de ler o livro.**
> He has just read the book.
> **Êle acabou por entrar em casa.**
> He finished by coming into the house.
> **Êle veio a ser delegado de polícia.**
> He came to be chief of police.

The omission or choice of a preposition is, therefore, a lexical matter, and it is necessary to learn the preposition required by each verb which may be followed by an infinitive. The variety of constructions which have been used by Portuguese and Brazilian writers after certain verbs may be quite large. Frequently BF limits the choice somewhat, or even employs a preposition which is rare in the literary language.

§273. After nouns and adjectives. Nouns and adjectives may also be followed by infinitives, which are always linked to them by a preposition. The most usual preposition is de, but some nouns and many adjectives require another or allow a choice among prepositions.

> **Tenho medo de ficar em casa à noite.**
> I am afraid to remain at home at night.
> **Êle tem horror de mula sem cabeça.**
> He is terrified of the headless mule.
> **Não há razão de irmos prorrogando a data do casamento.**
> There is no reason for us to keep on putting off the date of the wedding.
> **Há entre êles uma tendência a se declararem livres.**
> There is among them a tendency to declare themselves free.
> **Estou pronto para começar.**
> I am ready to start.
> **Você está seguro de saber tirar a mão da cumbuca?**
> Are you sure you know how to get your hand out of the bowl?
> **Êle parece estar decidido a meter o bedelho.**
> He seems to be determined to stick his nose in.

§274. To form periphrastic verb tenses. See the periphrastic future and conditional, §197–199 and §205–208.

§275. As an imperative. See §260.

§276. As vague reference to an action. The infinitive simply identifies the verb concerning which a future statement will be made.

> **Você deve ir lá falar com ela. —Falar, eu falo, mas escutar não quero.**
> You should go there to speak to her. As for speaking, I'll speak, but I don't want to listen.
> **Você pode ajudar a gente amanhã? —Poder, posso, mas querer, não quero.**
> Can you help a fellow tomorrow? As to that, I can, but I don't want to.

Se a gente nadar nessa praia, morre afogada. —Morrer o quê!
    If you swim on that beach, you will drown. What do you mean, drown?

§277. With the preposition **a**, to replace the present participle. This usage is Luso-Portuguese, found only in writing in Brazil, and even there not in very wide use. In the usage of Portugal, this construction may replace the present participle, without change of meaning, in almost any circumstances.

Estou a falar.   **Lus**
    I am speaking.
Viu um cão a latir atrás de um gato.   **Lus**
    He saw a dog barking after a cat.

§278. As an alternative to a clause in the indicative. Both constructions are in use, both in BF and in literature. The clausal construction is more frequent.

a. The dependent verb has the same subject as the main verb. The infinitive is usually impersonal. The infinitive construction is rather frequent, as an alternative to a clause, although the clause is still the more common of the two.

Creio ser o último a chegar.
    I think I am the last to arrive.
Disse ter sido êle quem salvou a moça.
    He said it was he who saved the girl's life.
Desistiram da empresa por não poder (*or* poderem) acabá-la.
    They gave up the project because they could not finish it.
O arquiteto declarou ter preparado os planos do prédio.
    The architect stated that he had prepared the plans for the building.

b. The dependent verb has a different subject. The infinitive is less likely to be used here than in the preceding case. If used, it is personal.

Creio estarem de volta já.
    I think they are already back.
João nos contou isso ao sairmos da festa.
    John told us that as we left the party.

§279. As an alternative to a clause in the subjunctive. The personal infinitive makes it possible to extend the infinitive construction to a very large number of cases which would be impossible in other Romance languages. In a large number of the cases, the clausal and infinitive constructions exist side by side, both in frequent use in both the spoken and written forms of the language. Some of the types of subjunctives most frequently replaced by the infinitive are given below. For more specific cases, after specific verbs and conjunctions, see § 224–252.

a. Following impersonal expressions.

É imprescindível partirmos já.
It is absolutely necessary for us to leave now.
Não é provável terem aprendido muito.
It is not likely that they have learned much.
È pena não podermos ir.
It is a pity we can't go.

b. Following verbs of ordering, permitting, forbidding, etc.

Amanhã mando consertar os sapatos.
Tomorrow I'll have the shoes repaired.
Eu disse para os meninos voltarem até as quatro horas.
I told the boys to come back by four.
Proibiram termos bebidas alcoólicas nos quartos.
They forbade us to have alcoholic drinks in our rooms.
Êle pediu para ajudarmos com o trabalho.
He asked us to help with the work.

c. After verbs of emotion. The infinitive is most likely if only one subject is involved.

Sinto termos magoado nosso anfitrião.
I am sorry that we hurt our host's feelings.
Temo terem vindo cedo demais.
I fear they have come too early.
Espero ser o primeiro.
I hope to be the first.
Êle receia perder o emprego.
He is afraid of losing his job.

d. Whenever an adverbial conjunction may be replaced by a preposition.

Vamos acabar êste jôgo antes de perdermos tudo. (*For* antes que.)
Let's finish this game before we lose everything.
Êle abriu a cancela para os cavalos entrarem no curral. (*For* para que entrassem.)
He opened the gate for the horses to enter the lot.

Vamos esperar aqui até o ônibus chegar. (*For* **até que chegue.**)
We are going to wait here until the bus arrives.
Tudo isso aconteceu sem sabermos nada. (*For* **sem que soubéssemos**)
All that happened without our knowing anything.
O professor partirá para casa só depois de sairem todos os alunos.
(*For* **depois que sairem** *or* **saiam.**)
The teacher will leave for home only when all the students have left.

§280. The infinitive is the verb form used as the object of a preposition.

Eu estou cansado antes de começar o trabalho.
I am tired before beginning the work.
Além de ser feio, êle é antipático.
Besides being ugly, he is disagreeable.
Vamos levar uns presentes, para os meninos não ficarem decepcionados.
Let's take some presents, so the children won't be disappointed.

For the only exception, **em** with the present participle, see §389.

Use of special forms of the infinitive

§281. Use of the passive infinitive. The passive infinitives, formed from the infinitives of **ser** (and frequently **ficar**) and the past participle, are used freely whenever it is important to express the passive voice. The participle agrees in number and gender with the subject, whether the latter is expressed or merely understood.

A obra deverá ser iniciada em breve.
The construction should be begun soon.
Vocês não estão livres de ficarem presos.
You are not free from being arrested.
A criança foi para a cama sem ter sido mandada.
The child went to bed without being sent.

In many expressions the active infinitive may have passive force, or it may be interpreted as either active or passive. Such usage is limited to cases in which there is no ground for confusion.

Êle mandou consertar os sapatos. (=**que alguém consertasse** *or* **que fossem consertados.**)
He had the shoes repaired.
Deixaram-se convencer. (=**ser convencidos.**)
They let themselves be convinced.

Nada há a fazer. (=a ser feito.)
There is nothing to do. (be done.)
Isso é fácil de compreender. (=de ser compreendido.)
This is easy to understand. (be understood.)

§282. Use of the perfect infinitive. The perfect infinitive is used
to stress the fact that the action of the infinitive precedes that of
the main verb.

a. Use without a preposition of time. When the infinitive depends directly upon another verb, or is connected with the main
verb by a preposition which does not indicate time, it is regularly
a perfect infinitive, if its action precedes that of the main verb.

Sinto não ter estado aqui ontem.
I am sorry I was not here yesterday.
Êle cria ter conhecido você nalguma parte.
He thought he had met you somewhere.
Eu devia ter voltado já.
I should have returned already.
Foram para lá sem terem sido mandados.
They went there without having been sent.

b. After prepositions of time. The simple and perfect infinitives
are used interchangeably, if the action of the infinitive precedes
that of the main verb. The simple form is much more frequent.

Depois de dar graças. (*Or* **Depois de ter dado.**)
After giving thanks.
Antes de fazer outra coisa. (*Or* **Antes de ter feito.**)
Before doing anything else.
Trabalho até acabar. (*Or* **até ter acabado.**)
I work until I finish.

§283. The reflexive infinitive. The infinitive may be reflexive,
with the several uses found in other parts of the verb. It may be:

a. Literally reflexive. The subject literally acts upon itself.

O menino é capaz de machucar-se aí.
The boy might hurt himself there.

b. Reciprocal.

**Ao se encontrarem na rua, passaram sem prestar atenção um ao
outro.**
When they met on the street, they passed without paying any attention to each other.

c. An impersonal reflexive.

> **Hora de se chamar padre é a hora da morte.**—Suassuna, *Auto da*
> *Compadecida.*
> The time for one to call the priest is the hour of death.

d. An equivalent of the passive.

> **Costumam falar-se várias línguas no Brás.**
> Several languages are habitually spoken in Brás.

§284. The personal infinitive. This form has existed from the time
of the earliest documents of the Portuguese language. It is found
with considerable frequency in the works of the writers of all
periods. It is in constant use today at all levels, from the most formal literary usage to the lowest levels of speech. However, there are
absolutely no dependable rules governing its use. No rule can be
drawn up which is not violated constantly by the best writers and
by popular speech. There is no meaning which cannot be stated in
correct and current Portuguese without the use of the personal infinitive. However, its existence adds greatly to the variety of expression available to the speaker—one of the most characteristic qualities
of the language. The personal infinitive may be used in any grammatical situation in which the impersonal infinitive is usable, with
the single exception that it does not form pure nouns without any
verbal force.

The following are statements of the most frequent usage of the
personal infinitive. They are not to be taken as fixed rules in either
literary Portuguese or BF.

a. The infinitive has a logical subject, not previously expressed.
If the infinitive is the first verb form of the sentence, or a previous
verb has a different subject, the personal form is used. However,
note the exception mentioned below.

> **Ao sairmos do hotel, demos com o corpo de bombeiros.**
> As we left the hotel we ran into the fire department.
> **Eu admiro é êles correrem tanto, sem se apartarem.**—Suassuna,
> *Auto da Compadecida.*
> What surprises me is their running so far without separating.
> **É preciso combinarmos.**
> It is necessary for us to agree.
> **É capaz de nós irmos.**
> We may possibly go.

b. The subject of the infinitive is expressed as the object of a preceding verb. The infinitive tends to be impersonal if it follows immediately.

Deixa-nos ir embora.
Allow us to go.
Êle nos manda entregar os pacotes em casa.
He orders us to deliver the packages to his house.

But if the infinitive is separated from the conjugated verb by a noun object of the main verb or other words, there is more probability that the infinitive will be personal. The greater the separation, the more likely one is to use the personal form.

Papai nos deu ordem de irmos passear.
Daddy gave us orders to take a walk.
Isso não impediu os transeuntes de passarem para o outro lado.
This did not prevent the pedestrians from crossing to the other side.
Aconselharam os índios a plantarem mandioca.
They advised the Indians to plant manioc.

c. The subject of the infinitive is also the subject of a preceding conjugated verb. The infinitive tends to be impersonal. This is especially true after the common verbs which are so often followed by the infinitive. However, even there the personal form is sometimes heard and found in good authors. Apparently the speaker or writer wishes to emphasize that the identification of the subject of the infinitive is important.

Os oficiais do exército não podem ser presos pela polícia.
The officers of the army cannot be arrested by the police.
Apanhamos uma maçã ao sair do pomar.
We picked up an apple as we left the orchard.
As crianças ouviram sem querer.
The children overheard without wanting to.
Não podem serem iguais.   Rare
They cannot be alike.

d. After **ver** and **ouvir**. The impersonal form is the usual one, but the personal infinitive is by no means unheard.

Ouvi os meninos dizer (*Less often* dizerem) que iam à praia.
I heard the boys say they were going to the beach.

§285. Special expressions with the infinitive. There are several expressions formed with the infinitive which do not fit into any of the previously mentioned patterns, but which are in common use.

a. **Ter que** and **ter de** with the infinitive. These two expressions, which are interchangeable, indicate compulsion, real or figurative, to perform the action named by the infinitive.

> **Tenho que** (*or* de) **pagar a conta, sem falta.**
> I must pay the bill, without fail.

b. **Ter para.** The use of a verb (most often **ter**) with a noun object, followed by **para** and the infinitive, indicates that the action named by the infinitive is to be performed upon the noun.

> **Êle não tem sapatos para usar.**
> He has no shoes to wear.
> **As visitas me deixaram com bastante trabalho para fazer.**
> The visitors left me with a lot of work to do.

c. **Por** and the infinitive. This preposition indicates that the action named by the infinitive is yet to be performed.

> **Êle tem uma casa nova, mas por pintar.**
> He has a new house, but still unpainted.

d. **Sem** and the infinitive. This preposition with the infinitive may indicate that the action has not been performed, possibly never will be.

> **O milho ficou sem cultivar.**
> The corn remained uncultivated.

THE VERB: PASSIVE VOICE

§286. Frequent use of the passive. In contrast to Spanish, French, and Italian, BF makes very extensive use of the passive voice. For a number of reasons, Portuguese does not shift the positions of subject and object with the facility that exists in Spanish. By shifting the use of a noun or pronoun from object to subject, a shift in sentence order is made natural. The performer of the act, which is the logical subject, now becomes the agent and comes last in the sentence—a more emphatic position.

Although the reflexive is used with the verb in certain cases with meaning equivalent to the passive voice, the usage is limited in Portuguese; and even in those situations in which it is often used, it alternates with the passive.

§287. Logical objects as subjects of the passive. In the passive, the subject is the person or thing which would be the object if the verb were active.

O João viu o Jorge.
John saw George.
O Jorge foi visto pelo João.
George was seen by John.

Normally, the indirect object is not shifted to become the subject of a passive verb. The direct object takes this position, leaving the indirect object unchanged.

João deu um livro a Jorge.
John gave a book to George.
Um livro foi dado a Jorge por João.
A book was given to George by John. (George was given a book.)

However, either the participle alone or the full passive voice can sometimes be heard or read, with a subject which is a logical indirect object. This usage is not frequent and is considered illogical by most speakers.

O ministro, quando perguntado sôbre o novo decreto, explicou . . . .
—Jornal
The minister, when questioned about the new decree, ex-
plained . . . .
Êle foi pedido para fazer um discurso.
He was asked to make a speech.

§288. **The passive with the auxiliary ser.** The passive voice is
usually formed by combining the auxiliary verb **ser** with the past
participle. By varying the tense and mood of **ser** we can produce a
passive form of any tense, indicative or subjunctive.

A canoa é apanhada pela corrente.
The canoe is caught by the current.
Você será castigado.
You will be punished.
João foi apanhado em flagrante.
John was caught red-handed.
Êle tinha sido visto na cidade, antes que fôsse preso.
He had been seen in the city, before he was arrested.

Since no imperative of **ser** exists in BF, there is no passive imperative. However, the present subjunctive of **ser** is used to compose
a form with the meaning of the imperative.

Sejam vacinados antes de entrar na escola.
Be vaccinated before entering school.

The past participle used to form the passive agrees in number and
gender with the subject.

Os animais foram atrelados às carroças.
The animals were hitched to the carts.

Note: The combination of **ser** and the past participle does not
necessarily form the passive voice. It may represent a more or less
permanent state resulting from previous action.

A casa é feita de pedra.
The house is built of stone.
Cf. A casa está sendo feita de pedra.
The house is being built of stone.

§289. **The passive with the auxiliary ficar.** A second passive is
made by using **ficar** as the auxiliary of the past participle, which
agrees with the subject. **Ficar** usually retains the essential meaning
of "to become."

Êle ficou ferido quando caiu.
He was hurt when he fell.
Fiquei cansado de tanto esperar.
I got tired from so much waiting.
A casa fica enfeitada para o Natal.
The house is decorated for Christmas.

In this last case, the meaning may be either that of the passive or the state resulting from previous action.

§290. Avoidance of the passive with an impersonal subject. The passive is rarely used in BF if the verb is impersonal or refers to people in general. One may use a reflexive verb.

Vê-se logo que você não quer ir.
It is easy to see that you do not want to go.
Não se sabia se Gilberto jogava ou não.
It was not known whether Gilbert would play or not.

Or one may use an active verb in the third person plural, with no expressed subject.

Dizem que o general vai se candidatar. (*Not* é dito que . . .)
They say that the general is going to be a candidate.

THE VERB: PROGRESSIVE FORMS

Forms and scope of the progressive

§291. The forms. The principal form of the progressive is made with the auxiliary **estar**, combined with the present participle of the verb concerned. **Estar** may be used in any tense or mood. Both voices exist in the progressive.

a. Use of **a** and the infinitive. In literary Portuguese, and in the spoken language of Portugal, one may use the preposition a and the impersonal infinitive instead of the present participle. In BF this form is not used and it is considered quite amusing when used by the Portuguese.

> **Eu estava a falar com êle.** Lus & Lit
> I was talking to him.
> **Eu estava falando com êle.** BF and Lit

b. Use of other auxiliaries. In addition to **estar**, other auxiliaries are used, but with added connotations derived from the meanings of these verbs. They are **ir**, **vir**, and **andar**. Their use is treated in more detail in §310–312.

§292. Required use of the progressive. The progressive forms of the verb are distinguished from the simple form in BF with great regularity, although the literary language has not yet reached the point of requiring the differentiation. It still assumes that the progressive form is optional and may always be replaced by the simple form. But in BF the distinction is obligatory, and necessary to avoid misunderstanding. Only in very special circumstances is it permissible to use **eu falo**, if the meaning intended is **eu estou falando**.

§293. Verbs lacking progressive forms. Certain verbs lack progressive forms, for all practical purposes. Others use them quite rarely, and still others allow them only in certain meanings of the verb, but not in other meanings.

a. **Estar** is very seldom put in the progressive.

b. **Ser** as a main verb is normally in the simple form. On occasion it may have a somewhat more active meaning, such as "to act," or "to behave," in which case it occurs in the progressive.

> **Você está sendo impossível.**
> You are being impossible.
> **Êle está sendo mau hoje.**
> He is being bad today.

As an auxiliary, **ser** regularly takes the progressive form. See the progressive form of the passive, §308 below.

c. **Poder** is quite rare in the progressive but is sometimes heard.

> **O pai chega cansado do trabalho; não está podendo dar atenção aos filhos; não está podendo brincar com êles.**
> The father arrives tired from work; he is not able to give attention to his children; he is not able to play with them.
> **Sente inveja dos três homens que estão podendo subir e descer a escada.**
> He feels envy of the three men who are able to go up and down the stair.

d. **Ir.** When used as an auxiliary with the infinitive, this verb is always in the simple form. But as a main verb, it may assume progressive forms. In this verb, the progressive is rarely, if ever, necessary, but it strengthens the expression of action in progress. The most frequent auxiliary of this verb is **ir**, but **estar** is also sometimes used.

> **Vem cá já! —Estou indo; para que pressa?**
> Come here at once! I'm coming, what's the hurry?
> **Eu já vou indo. (=Estou para ir.)**
> I'll be going.
> **Êle vai indo melhor. (=Está melhorando.)**
> He is getting along better.

e. **Vir** is kept in the simple form as an auxiliary, but may take the progressive forms with the auxiliaries **estar** and **vir** when it is the main verb.

> **O tio vem jantar conosco.**
> Uncle is coming to our house for dinner.
> **O prédio estava vindo abaixo.**
> The building was coming down.
> **Ela vem vindo de mansinho.**
> She comes creeping softly.

f. **Ter** is like ser in that it may be progressive when the meaning is more active. The progressive is not required, but it makes the application to the immediate moment clearer.

> **Estou tendo dificuldades.**
> I am having difficulties.
> **Êle está tendo que trabalhar.**
> He is having to work.

g. **Querer** is put in the progressive only in the senses of "making wishes," or "trying."

> **Você está querendo tomar a chuva.**
> You are trying to get wet.
> **Eu estou querendo entrar em casa. (=Estou procurando entrar.)**
> I am trying to get into the house.

h. **Dever,** in its meaning of "ought," does not assume the progressive form. When it means "owe," the progressive is used, although the meaning is such that the progressive is not often required.

> **Eu já paguei dez mil, e estou devendo mil ainda.**
> I have already paid ten thousand, and I still owe a thousand.

i. Verbs of intellectual or sensory effort. These verbs are used in the progressive form regularly, contrary to usage in English.

> **Eu não estou entendendo nada do que você está dizendo.**
> I don't understand anything of what you are saying.
> **Você está ouvindo? —Estou, mas não estou compreendendo.**
> Do you hear? I do, but I don't understand.
> **Estou te vendo lá embaixo da mesa.**
> I see you down there under the table.
> **Eu estou sentindo o cheiro de pipoca.**
> I smell popcorn.

Use by tenses and moods

§294. Progressive in the present tense, indicative. In the present tense, the progressive indicates an action actually in progress and continuing at the moment of speaking, usually without regard to the length of time involved. The simple present, on the other hand, expresses habitual action or condition which exists from the past, through the present, and into the future. It may also be used as a historical present and very frequently replaces the future tense.

The progressive evidently represents the present time much more accurately than the simple form. The two forms are not interchangeable in BF, and the simple present cannot replace the progressive without changing the meaning.

Você não está ouvindo? (Você não ouve=You are deaf.)
  Don't you hear?
Escuta o que estou lhe dizendo.
  Listen to what I am saying.
Você não adivinhou ainda, mas está esquentando.
  You haven't guessed yet, but you're getting warm.

a. Limitation on use of the progressive. This form is used only if the action or situation is in progress at the moment of speaking. An action which progresses during the period, but not at the moment, of speaking is in the simple tense.

Assisto à escola êste ano, mas hoje estou em casa.
  I am attending school this year, but today I am at home.
As meninas estão assistindo à escola neste momento.
  The girls are attending school at this moment.
Êle trabalha naquela loja, mas hoje não está trabalhando.
  He works in that store, but today he is not working.

b. Frequent or habitual action. The progressive does not express frequent or habitual action, which is a function of the simple present, unless the action is habitually in progress. Usually such cases are accompanied by an adverb, such as **sempre** or **nunca**.

Aquêle menino está sempre brigando com os outros.
  That boy is always fighting with the others.
Êle nunca está dormindo à meia-noite.
  He is never sleeping (asleep) at midnight.

§295. Progressive in the imperfect. The imperfect indicative includes progressive action as one of the types of past action which it expresses. See §193. Therefore, the progressive form is never necessary in this tense, although it must be distinguished in all others. However, it is very frequently used, since it makes the progressive meaning clear and eliminates the other uses of the imperfect as possible meanings.

Eu estava dormindo quando José bateu na porta.
  I was sleeping when Joe knocked on the door.

> **Tôdas as tardes, quando êle chegava em casa, as crianças estavam brincando na rua.**
> Every day, when he arrived at home, the children were playing in the street.

§296. Progressive in the preterite. The progressive is not very frequent in this tense, because of the nature of the preterite. It is needed only when an action was in progress for a limited period of past time, after which it was discontinued. For such a situation, it is the simplest construction.

> **Eu estive falando com o João ontem.**
> I had a talk with John yesterday.
> **Êle esteve lendo em casa o dia inteiro.**
> He spent the whole day at home reading.
> **Êle foi entrando pela floresta adentro.**
> He went on into the forest.
> **Naquela época andei tomando cerveja de noite com os amigos.**
> In that period I went around drinking beer at night with my friends.
> **Vê-se logo que ela esteve chorando.**
> One can see immediately that she has been crying.

§297. Progressive in the future forms. The various forms of the future tense, simple and periphrastic, are discussed in §194–199. Any of these forms may be made progressive, and they are expressed in that form whenever one speaks of action in progress in future time.

> **Estarei descansando quando você chegar.**
> I will be resting when you get there.
> **Às dez horas hei de estar dormindo.**
> At ten o'clock I will be sleeping.
> **Amanhã a estas horas vou estar voando para a Europa.**
> Tomorrow at this time I am going to be flying to Europe.

The present progressive may be used to refer to the future, only if an adverb of time or other expression makes it clear that it refers to the future.

> **Amanhã a estas horas estou tomando banho de mar.**
> Tomorrow at this time I will be bathing in the sea.

§298. Progressive in the compound perfect tense. The compound present perfect indicative is limited in usage and aspectual in nature.

See §211. The present perfect speaks of an action as continuous or continual in the recent past. The progressive would add to that the element of action in progress on each occasion of its happening. This construction is sometimes used, but both the form and the precision of its meaning become quite complex. For this reason, the imperfect indicative is usually the preferred form, in spite of some loss of precision.

> **Tenho estado trabalhando duro quando êle me visitava.**
> I have been working hard whenever he visited me.
> **Você não me tem visto porque tenho estado recuperando de uma doença.**
> You have not seen me because I have been recovering from sickness.

§299. Progressive in the pluperfect indicative. Only the pluperfect which is formed with the auxiliary **ter** is included here, since the other forms are not used in BF. See §213. The progressive is comparatively rare in this tense, since there are few circumstances which require it.

> **Encontramos fàcilmente o mato onde os homens tinham estado derrubando no dia anterior.**
> We easily found the woods where the men had been felling the day before.

It should be noted that the imperfect tense is used if a terminal point is mentioned, and this point is also in past time.

> **Estavam trabalhando entre os pés de café, já havia dois dias.**
> They had been working among the coffee plants for two days already.

§300. Progressive in the future perfect indicative. This tense itself is quite rare in BF, and circumstances in which the progressive would be required are far more so. It is probably never actually required.

§301. Progressive in the present subjunctive. The progressive is used systematically in the subjunctive as well as in the indicative. Since in many situations the present subjunctive must represent both the present and the future, a great deal of clarity is possible through the use of the progressive, which is clearly present.

Eu sinto que êle esteja demorando.
I am sorry that he is delaying.
Pode ser que as crianças estejam brincando na rua.
Maybe the children are playing on the street.

§302. *Progressive in the imperfect subjunctive.* Since the imperfect of the subjunctive does not of itself express the progressive as the indicative does, it is necessary to use this form whenever a progressive meaning is intended. The additional clarity is often useful also.

Pensei que você estivesse falando comigo.
I thought that you were speaking to me.
Era preciso que fôssem abrindo passagem com facões.
It was necessary for them to open a passage with machetes.
Eu esperava que meus pais estivessem chegando quando acendêssemos as luzes.
I hoped that my parents would be arriving when we turned on the lights.

§303. *Progressive in the future subjunctive.* As the future subjunctive is much more used in BF than the future indicative, so the progressive form of the future is more frequent in the subjunctive than in the indicative.

Não quero que chova quando estivermos nadando.
I don't want it to rain when we are swimming.
Se eu estiver falando com alguém, não me interrompe.
If I am talking to someone, don't interrupt me.

§304. *Progressive of the compound tenses of the subjunctive.* These tenses also may be used in the progressive form when the sense requires, but the comparative rarity of their use makes it difficult to hear examples.

Eu duvido que você tenha estado lendo muitas obras brasileiras.
I doubt that you have been reading many Brazilian works.
Você ficará cansado quando tiver estado trabalhando muito.
You will get tired when you have been working a lot.

§305. *Progressive of the imperative.* The imperative of **estar** is not used in BF but is replaced by the subjunctive **esteja**. The progressive form of the imperative is therefore replaced by the subjunctive when **estar** is the auxiliary. The imperatives of **ir**, **vir**, and **andar** are used.

Quando eu voltar, esteja trabalhando.
When I return, be working.
Se você quer que a casa esteja limpa, vai limpando.
If you want the house to be clean, start cleaning.
Vamos andando, que é tarde.
Let's get going, it's late.
Não seja preguiçosa, anda arrumando a casa.
Don't be lazy, get to straightening up the house.

§306. The progressive infinitive. Both the personal and the impersonal infinitives are used in the progressive form. The impersonal one is found depending on either verbs or prepositions. The personal infinitive is heard in this form mostly depending upon prepositions. Both infinitives may also be progressive when used independently.

Êle pode estar jantando.
He may be eating.
Você devia estar estudando as lições de amanhã.
You should be studying tomorrow's lessons.
As crianças hão de estar dormindo antes da meia-noite.
The children are to be sleeping before midnight.
O pior seria estarmos esperando muito tempo.
The worst would be for us to be waiting a long time.
Êle diz para vocês andarem pensando nisso.
He tells you to be thinking about that.

§307. The present participle in progressive form. The present participle itself may assume a progressive form if there is a desire on the part of the speaker to stress the progressive quality, although the participle is usually sufficient by itself.

Andando contando proezas, êle ganhou fama de mentiroso.
By going around recounting his prowess, he got the reputation of a liar.
Estando viajando longe no interior, êle teve uma pane no motor, e teve que passar a noite lá sòzinho.
While traveling far in the interior, he had motor trouble and had to spend the night there alone.

§308. Progressive in the passive voice. Both forms of the passive —that formed with **ser** and that with **ficar**—are put in the progressive as the situation requires.

O pão não é lá muito bom, mas está sendo comido.
The bread is not really very good, but it is being eaten.

O Brasil vai sendo transformado em país industrializado.
Brazil is being transformed into an industrial country.

As terras de Mato Grosso estão sendo cultivadas sempre mais nos
últimos anos.
The lands of Mato Grosso are being ever more cultivated in
recent years.

O jornal está ficando molhado lá fora na chuva.
The paper is getting wet out there in the rain.

Você fica observando o que estiver sendo feito na praça.
You keep watching whatever is being done on the square.

Êles foram ficando contaminados pelas idéias comunistas.
They were being contaminated by communist ideas.

Use of the auxiliaries of the progressive

§309.   Use of **estar**. This is the most usual auxiliary. As a neutral
verb, it usually does not add any connotation to the progressive form.
However, the meaning of being located sometimes affects the sense.
To bring out this sense clearly, the expression of location may be
placed between the auxiliary and the present participle.

Êle está nadando no lago.
He is swimming in the lake.
Êle está no lago, nadando.
He is in the lake, swimming.

§310.   Use of **ir**. This is the most widely used auxiliary after estar.
It expresses progress away from some point in space or time. Within
this general definition, it may express:

a.   Movement in space.

Êle vai andando pela rua acima.
He goes walking up the street.
O carteiro vai entregando cartas de casa em casa.
The mailman goes delivering letters from house to house.

b.   Progress in time.

Êle vai passando os dias o melhor que pode.
He passes the time as best he can.

c.   Progress in the development of an action.

O doente vai melhorando aos poucos.
The patient is improving little by little.
O preço da carne vai aumentando.
The price of meat keeps rising.

d. The beginning of a progressive action.

Êle abriu a porta e foi entrando.
He opened the door and went on in.

§311. Use of **andar**. This auxiliary is similar in meaning to **ir**, but somewhat less used. It is likely to refer to progress in space, rather than time.

a. Movement in space.

Andam procurando alguém que saiba russo.
They are looking for someone who knows Russian.
Êle anda dizendo que eu consegui sua demissão.
He keeps saying that I got you fired.

b. Habitual action, without movement in space.

Eu quase estou acreditando as histórias que êle anda me contando.
I almost believe the stories that he keeps telling me.

§312. Use of **vir**. As an auxiliary, this verb suggests progress in space or time toward the speaker or the point of reference.

a. Progress in space.

Os rapazes vem chegando.
The boys are arriving.

b. Progress in time.

Êle não tem boa letra ainda, mas está praticando e vem melhorando.
He doesn't have a good handwriting yet, but he is practicing and is improving.

§313. Other verbs used with the present participle. Numerous other verbs can be combined with the present participle. This construction always has some similarity to the progressive, but in most cases no weakening of the meaning of the verb can be distinguished. In these circumstances, the conjugated verb should not be considered an auxiliary, nor should the entire expression be classed as a form of the verb represented by the present participle. In such a sentence as, **Êle sai correndo** (He goes out running) the verb **sair** has its full literal meaning. It can easily be demonstrated that this is not a progressive form by placing it alongside the true progressive form of the same expression: **Êle está saindo correndo** (He is going out running). The true auxiliaries of the progressive can only be used in the simple form when they are auxiliaries. In the example given above, **correndo** should be considered an adverbial modifier. It does, however, express an action in progress.

REFLEXIVE VERBS

Definition and forms

§314. Definition of a reflexive verb. A verb is reflexive when its object, always a pronoun, refers to the same person or thing as the subject, whether or not the subject is expressed. However, the reflexive verbs are used in a variety of ways, in some of which the literal meaning of the reflexive is difficult to distinguish, or has been totally lost. Therefore, in such cases, the verb is distinguished as a reflexive only because it is accompanied by a reflexive pronoun.

§315. Forms of the reflexive pronouns. In the first person, and in the old second, the reflexive pronouns are the same as the regular objects: **me, nos, te.** In the new second and in the third, both singular and plural, the reflexive object is **se.**

§316. Direct and indirect reflexive objects. Dative and accusative objects are identical in all reflexive pronouns. There is, in fact, considerable confusion between direct and indirect objects, even in literary Portuguese.

§317. Position of the reflexive objects. In general, the reflexive objects are placed in the same positions relative to the verb as the other objects. There are two exceptions:

a. In the first person plural. The object never follows the verb in BF. A form such as **levantamo-nos** is so far lost in BF that well-educated speakers often fail to drop the final **s** of the verb, if they wish to use this form.

b. At the beginning of the sentence, **se** is not used. This is probably occasioned by confusion with the conjuction **se.**

> **Despede-se e vamos embora.**
> Say good-bye and let's go.

Use of the reflexive

§318. Literal action of the subject on itself. The most obvious and clear-cut usage of the reflexive is found when there is actual action of the verb on its subject.

João se cortou com a navalha.
John cut himself with the razor.
Êle se reservou a melhor parte.
He reserved the better part for himself.
Habituou-se, desde então, à leitura.
He got (himself) used to reading, from then on.

§319. Reflexive kept to retain transitive character of a verb. Many transitive verbs take the reflexive form when there is no other object expressed, thus showing that the action is performed on the subject, rather than on another person or thing.

Cf. **Êle levantou a mão.**	**Êle se levantou.**
He raised his hand.	He got up.
O menino lavou a cara.	**O menino se lavou.**
The boy washed his face.	The boy washed.

a. Loss of transitive character. The difference between the transitive and the intransitive verbs has never been very strictly maintained in Portuguese. Many verbs are used in BF indifferently as reflexives or intransitives. The frequency of the two constructions differs considerably from one word to another. The following sentences illustrate situations in which the reflexive pronoun is frequently omitted.

Êle casou com ela.
He married her.
Carlos e Fátima casaram.
Charles and Fatima got married.
Levantei às oito.
I got up at eight.
Deitamos tarde.
We went to bed late.
Ela veste bem.
She dresses well.
O quadro despencou da parede.
The picture tumbled from the wall.
Você só quer aproveitar.
You just want to take advantage.
Senta aqui, faz favor.
Sit here, please.
Eu estou sentindo bem hoje.
I feel well today.

b. Expressions which avoid the reflexive. Some reflexive verbs are replaced in BF by expressions which do not contain a reflexive verb.

Tomar banho.   *Cf.* **Banhar-se.**
    To take a bath.
Fazer a barba.   *Cf.* **Barbear-se.**
    To shave.

§320. Change of meaning in the reflexive. Some verbs, when reflexive, acquire a meaning which is quite different from that of the same verb when it is not reflexive.

O patrão despediu três operários.
    The boss fired three workers.
Vou me despedir dos amigos à estação.
    I am going to take leave of my friends at the station.
As macacadas dos meninos divertiram a nossa atenção.
    The boys' monkeyshines diverted our attention.
Divertiu-se muito na festa?
    Did you enjoy yourself a lot at the party?
Eu chamei o noivo de felizardo.
    I called the groom a lucky stiff.
Êle se chama Marcolino.
    His name is Marcolino.
Sinto que você esteja doente.
    I am sorry that you are ill.
Parece que ela se sente bem.
    She seems to feel well.

a. Loss of reflexive pronouns, with retention of meaning. With these special meanings, these verbs nearly always retain the reflexive pronoun. However, there are infrequent occurrences of loss of the pronoun in BF, especially in substandard usage.

Vou-me embora, vou-me embora,
Não despeço de ninguém. —Canção folclórica.
    I'm going away, I'm going away,
    I won't take leave of anyone.

Como é que êle chama?   **Subst & Rare**
    What's his name?
Os rapazes não sabem divertir sem brigas.   **Subst & Rare**
    The boys can't have a good time without fights.
Não estou sentindo bem.   **BF**
    I don't feel well.

b. Special meanings of the reflexive. Several other verbs which may be used reflexively with their regular meanings have come to have special meanings in certain situations.

Onde se acha essa casa? (Onde fica?)
Where is that house?
Gregório se viu na necessidade de pedir auxílio. (Estava.)
Gregory saw himself in need of asking for help.
Quando foi que isso se deu? (Aconteceu.)
When did that happen?

§321. Reflexive pronoun of personal interest. At times the reflexive pronoun merely shows that the subject has a more personal interest than is the case when the verb is not reflexive.

Você decide sôbre isto.
You decide about that.
Decide-se de uma vez; não posso esperar.
Make up your mind right away; I can't wait.
Êle vai resolver esta questão.
He is going to decide that problem.
Jaci não pode resolver-se.
Jaci can't make up her mind.
Eu me comprei umas luvas.
I bought me some gloves.

§322. Verbs which are reflexive only. These verbs have no form which is not reflexive.

Êle vai suicidar-se.
He is going to commit suicide.
Você não se atreve.
You don't dare.
Não deve arrepender-se de ter feito uma boa ação.
You shouldn't repent of having performed a good deed.
Não se dignou nos dar uma palavra.
He did not deign to say a word to us.
De que se queixa?
What are you complaining of?

§323. Verbs reflexive with a preposition, often not reflexive without it. Some of these are never reflexive without the following preposition; some may be so but are usually not. Some become transitive without the preposition, some intransitive, some either.

Não se preocupa com isto.   **Isso não me preocupa.**
Don't worry about that.   That doesn't worry me.

Devotar-se a.
   To devote oneself to.
Encarar-se com.
   To face.
Apropriar-se de.
   To take possession of.
Aperceber-se de.
   To perceive.
Esquecer-se de.
   To forget.

Rir-se de.
   To laugh at.
Conformar-se com.
   To become resigned to.
Aproveitar-se de.
   To take advantage of.
Surpreender-se de.
   To be surprised at.
Lembrar-se de.
   To remember.

Note: The preposition in such cases is more often than not omitted before a clause.

Surpreendeu-se (de) que ficassem zangados de coisa tão fútil.
He was surprised that they should be angry at such a trifle.

§324. Reflexive pronoun with adverbial force. The reflexive pronoun is used at times to give a certain connotation to the verb, with what amounts to adverbial force. The exact sense requires definition in each case, and often the difference is quite small. This usage is much more limited than in Spanish.

Você demora muito para voltar?
Will it be long before you return?
Não se demora (mais do que o necessário).
Don't delay (unnecessarily).
A guerra acabou em 1945.
The war ended in 1945.
Acabou-se o açúcar. (Não há mais nenhum.)
The sugar is all gone.
Chega mais para cá.
Come closer.
João chegou-se para perto de mim. (Moveu-se.)
John moved closer to me.

The most frequent example of this usage is found in the verb **ir**, which has several peculiarities of construction and usage. Four expressions exist, with some overlap of usage and meaning.

1. The verb **ir** alone.
2. **Ir-se.**
3. **Ir embora.**
4. **Ir-se embora.**

The verb alone, in its primary meaning of movement, usually indicates movement toward a destination, expressed or implied.

Eu vou para casa.
I am going home.

However, it may indicate movement away from the place where the speaker is located. In the progressive form, it usually means this.

Eu vou agora. (Vou sair.)
I'm going now. (I'm leaving.)
Eu vou indo. (Vou sair.)
I'll be going.

To indicate movement away from the location of the speaker, we may use any of the other three expressions. However, in certain cases the reflexive must be used; in others the adverb is necessary, but the pronoun is not. The pronoun must be used in the following expressions, where the meaning is **sumir, desaparecer.**

Lá se foi o tempo,
Hoje é assim. —Samba
The time has passed,
Today it's this way.

O dinamite explodiu, e lá se foi o edifício.
The dynamite blew up, and there went the building.
Lá se vão meus dentes.
There went my teeth.

Elsewhere the reflexive pronoun is not necessary, but it may be used along with the adverb. It is a peculiarity of this verb that the pronoun object follows it regularly, unless it is drawn before it by a negative or a subordinating conjunction. Even in these cases, many speakers place it after the verb.

Eu vou-me embora.
I am going (away).
Êle vai-se embora.
He is going (away).

As is regular in BF, the reflexive pronoun of the first person plural never follows the verb. As a result, this verb is never reflexive in that form. One says **Vamos embora,** in rapid speech **Vam'bora.**

§325. Reflexive as substitute for passive. The reflexive is used with a third-person subject, generally inanimate, to replace the passive voice. However, since Portuguese has a well-developed passive form and uses it with great frequency, the reflexive is used for it only to a very limited extent.

Só se ouviam os violinos.
Only the violins were heard.
Gastaram-se bilhões de cruzeiros na construção de Brasília.
Billions of cruzeiros were spent in the construction of Brasilia.
Na Europa, fabricam-se objetos antigos.
In Europe, old things are manufactured.
Essa condição é fácil de curar-se.
That condition is easily cured.

Even with animate subjects, the reflexive at times replaces the passive. But this is unusual, and must be used with care.

A humanidade se compõe de miseráveis.
Humanity is composed of unfortunate people.
Vêem-se homens cultivando a terra.
Men are seen cultivating the soil.
O cachorro vai se enterrar.
The dog is going to be buried.
O morto levou-se ao cemitério.
The dead man was carried to the cemetery.

With a subject referring to people in general, the passive voice is seldom used. The reflexive is frequent, or one may use **a gente** with the active voice.

Vê-se logo que você não quer ir.
It is easily seen that you don't want to go.
Não se sabia se Gilberto jogava ou não.
It was not known whether Gilbert would play or not.

§326. The impersonal reflexive. The reflexive is used in the third person singular, with no expressed subject, to refer to an indefinite, unidentified subject. This usage is rather frequent, but is limited by the existence of other constructions (e.g., the subject **a gente**, or the third person plural of the verb, without expressed subject) also widely used, which give an equivalent or similar meaning.

Pode-se ir a Copacabana pelo Túnel Novo.
One can go to Copacabana by the New Tunnel.
Lá em casa, se janta às sete.
Back home, we dine at seven.

a. Overlapping of impersonal reflexive and reflexive for passive. In transitive verbs used in the singular, these two uses are not distinguished. We may take the noun which follows as either subject or object.

Não se aprende isso nos livros.
One doesn't learn this in books. (*Or* This is not learned in books.)
Fala-se português.
People speak Portuguese. (*Or* Portuguese is spoken.)
Aluga-se casa.
House to rent.

But when the subject precedes the verb, and when the verb is plural, one may safely interpret the construction as the reflexive which replaces the passive.

A casa derrubou-se.
The house was torn down.

b. In commercial usage, the impersonal reflexive is used frequently with a plural noun. But most Brazilian speakers feel this to be unacceptable and put the verb in the plural, interpreted as the equivalent of the passive.

Vende-se frutas.   **BF=Vendem-se frutas.**
One (we) sell fruits.   Fruit is sold.

c. Reflexive with a second object. The reflexive used impersonally or otherwise, with a second object referring to the person whom the action affects, is a rare construction in BF. Usage is limited to a few expressions. Elsewhere it is considered to be a rather amusing mannerism of the Portuguese. An example from BF:

Pouco se me dá que o trem parta.
Little does it matter to me if the train leaves.

A supposed definition of "sugar," as stated by a Portuguese:

O açúcar é um pó branco e adocicado que dá muito mau gôsto ao café, quando não se lhe põe.
Sugar is a white and sweetish powder which gives a very bad taste to coffee, when you don't put it in.

d. Impersonal form of reflexive verbs. When the verb is reflexive for another reason, e.g., **atrever-se**, which is always reflexive, or **machucar-se**, which is literally reflexive, the indefinite subject cannot be expressed by a reflexive pronoun. The most usual substitute is the subject **a gente**.

A gente se machuca andando descalça no cascalho.
You hurt yourself by walking barefoot on the gravel.

A gente não se atreve a sair de noite.
You don't dare go out at night.

§327. Reflexive to express ownership. The reflexive is very seldom used to indicate the owner of a part of the body, article of clothing, etc. Even with verbs which may be reflexive to show that the action was performed on the subject, the reflexive is omitted if the direct object is expressed. This includes also those expressions in which ownership is often indicated by an indirect object when the object is not reflexive.

O menino se lavou na lagoa.
The boy washed himself in the pool.
Eu lavei as mãos.
I washed my hands.
Eu lhe quebro a perna.
I'll break your leg.
Quebrei minha perna.
I broke my leg.

§328. Reciprocal use of the reflexive. The plural reflexive pronouns, **nos** and **se**, are also used as reciprocals, indicating that the individuals included in the subject act upon each other.

Nos vemos amanhã na cidade.
We'll see each other downtown tomorrow.
João e Flávio se encontraram na rua.
John and Flavio met on the street.

a. Use of **um ao outro**. Since the reflexive pronoun as a reciprocal is often ambiguous, capable of being interpreted either way, it is often necessary to clarify the reciprocal by adding **um ao outro**.

Vêem-se um ao outro no espelho.
They see each other in the mirror.

The reflexive pronoun is usually omitted when **um ao outro** is used, to avoid redundancy.

Escrevem um ao outro.
They write to each other.

b. Forms and agreement of **um ao outro**. The phrase **um ao outro** retains the preposition both as direct and as indirect object, but in the second case the preposition **para** may be used.

Escrevem um para o outro.
They write to each other.

If three or more individuals are concerned, the expression becomes plural **uns aos outros**. If all things or persons referred to are feminine, the feminine forms are used: **uma à outra, umas às outras**. But if any one of them is masculine, then normally both words are masculine. The assumption is that each person referred to acts upon each of the others, and therefore both **um** and **outro** refer to each noun. Thus, if we speak of João and Maria, **um** refers to each of them in turn, and therefore the masculine form must be used.

§329. Other reciprocal expressions. The reciprocal relationship is, of course, often expressed by other prepositions, without an object pronoun.

Dorotea e Félix gostam um do outro.
Dorothy and Felix love each other.
Os rapazes e as meninas ficam olhando uns para os outros.
The boys and the girls keep looking at each other.
Brigaram um com o outro.
They fought with each other.
Estavam pensando um no outro.
They were thinking of each other.

§330. Reflexive pronouns with participles and infinitives.

a. With the present participle. The reflexive pronoun agrees with the logical subject of the participle. If there is no such subject, the third person form is used.

Ela ficou em casa, queixando-se de dor de dentes.
She stayed at home, complaining of a toothache.
Vendo-nos com freqüência, chegamos a gostar um do outro.
Seeing each other frequently, we came to love each other.
Estou me vendo no espelho.
I see myself in the mirror.

b. With the past participle. The reflexive pronoun is not used, unless the participle is part of a compound tense.

Arrependido das crueldades praticadas, dimitiu-se do comando.
Repenting the cruelties he had practiced, he gave up his command.

c. With the infinitives. The reflexive pronouns are used with infinitives, and agree with the logical subject.

Êle nunca pensou que eu fôsse capaz de atrever-me a tanto.
He never thought I was capable of being so bold.
Antes de nos queixarmos, vamos examinar os fatos.
Before we complain, let's examine the facts.

PARTICIPLES

The present participle

§331. Forms of the present participle. The simple present participle is an active form. It is regular in all verbs, formed by replacing the final **-r** of the infinitive with **-ndo**. Contrary to the practice in other situations, a consonantal **n** is pronounced in this form. In substandard speech in a great part of the interior of Brazil, the ending is **-no**, with loss of **d**, but retaining **n** as a consonant.

> **Cê tá falano (Você está falando.)**　　　Subst
> You are speaking.
> **Êle tava abrino a porta. (Êle estava abrindo a porta.)**　　　Subst
> He was opening the door.

a. Passive present participle. A passive form is made by using the participle of the auxiliary **ser** with the past participle of the verb concerned. The form is not frequently used.

> **Sendo vista no primeiro momento, Dora não pôde escapar-se da visita importuna.**
> Being seen at the first moment, Dora couldn't escape the unwelcome visitor.

b. Reflexive present participle. The present participle may be reflexive, with the usages common to most other forms of the verb.

> **Sentando-se à mesa, começou a comer.**
> Sitting down at the table, he began to eat.
> **Olhando-se um momento, reconheceram-se.**
> Looking at each other for a moment, they recognized one another.
> **Vendendo-se muito caro, os produtos desta companhia não têm muita divulgação.**
> Being sold very dear, the products of this company do not have wide circulation.

c. Progressive form. A progressive form of the present participle is sometimes heard but is rarely needed.

Estando viajando longe no interior, êle teve uma pane no motor, e teve que passar a noite lá sòzinho.
While traveling far in the interior, he had engine trouble, and had to spend the night there alone.

§332. Uses of the present participle. This form (called **gerúndio** in Portuguese) is neither verbal adjective nor verbal noun. Except in one case (i, below), it is always used as a verb form, often possessing adverbial force as well. It is invariable in form. It is used:

a. In the progressive forms of the verb. See §291 ff.

Você está falando.
You are speaking.
Eu vou andando.
I'll be going.
Êle veio correndo.
He came running.
Êle anda dizendo bobagens.
He keeps saying nonsense.

b. Following verbs not used as auxiliaries. These verbs retain their usual meaning and denote the primary action. The present participle is used adverbially, to express an attendant circumstance.

Êle saiu correndo.
He left running.
O menino nos falou soluçando.
The boy spoke to us, sobbing.
Contou-nos a história rindo.
He told us the story, laughing.
Vivia filando a bóia lá de casa.
He spent his life mooching his grub at our house.

c. After **ver** and **ouvir**. One may use either the infinitive or the present participle. The latter expresses more clearly the fact that the action is in progress at the moment of observation.

Vi um homem tocando um cavaquinho.
I saw a man playing a ukulele.
Êle ouviu uma môça gritando pelo irmão.
He heard a girl shouting for her brother.

d. Adverbially. The participle is equivalent to an adverbial conjunction and a conjugated verb. Various adverbial meanings can be expressed, depending on the meaning of the verb of the main clause.

The subject of the main verb is also the logical subject of the participle, but it is seldom expressed.

> **Vendo que o cachorro não mordia, o menino perdeu o medo. (=Quando viu** *or* **porque viu.)**
> Seeing that the dog didn't bite, the boy lost his fear.
> **Apreciando a beleza da paisagem, entretinham as horas da viagem. (=Enquanto apreciavam.)**
> Enjoying the beauty of the landscape, they whiled away the hours of the trip.
> **Não se perdoando esta alma, faz-se é dar mais gôsto ao Cão. (=Se não se perdoa.)** —Suassuna, *Auto da Compadecida.*
> By not pardoning this soul, what you do is please the Devil more.

e. The present participle may take an object.

> **Ficaram parados, olhando-se cara a cara.**
> They stood still, looking each other in the face.
> **Passei uma hora ali, contando-lhe as notícias lá de casa.**
> I spent an hour there, telling him the news from home.

f. The present participle may have an expressed subject. It has an expressed subject, if it is different from that of the main verb. In other situations, the subject is seldom expressed.

> **Ninguém te toca, estando eu aqui.**
> Nobody will touch you, while I am here.

g. The present participle is not used with a preposition, except **em.** This usage has existed since the Middle Ages, but it is rather rare in literature, and even rarer in BF. No situation requires the use of the preposition, but it may add some precision to the adverbial meaning of the participle. It may indicate that the action of the participle ends before the beginning of the action of the main verb, or it may give the participle the meaning of an if-clause.

> **O camarada em lá chegando . . . esqueceu-se da ordem. (=quando chegou lá.)** —Lindolfo Gomes, *Contos populares.*
> When the fellow arrived there, he forgot the order.
> **Em Deus me ajudando, volto amanhã. (Se Deus me ajudar.)**
> If God helps me, I'll return tomorrow.

h. The meaning "by means of." This meaning is expressed by the present participle, without a preposition.

> **Tento subir segurando na corda.**
> I'll try to climb up by holding on to the string.

i. One participle is used as an adjective. It does not agree with its noun.

O lobo mau caiu na água fervendo.
The big, bad wolf fell into the boiling water.

§333. Derivatives of the Latin present participle. These words are quite numerous in Portuguese. They are learned in origin, but many have gained universal currency in BF. They are used mostly as nouns, occasionally as adjectives, but have no verbal force at all. They all end in **-nte**.

Os sete dormintes, o alto-falante, os ouvintes, insignificante
The seven sleepers, the loud speaker, the listeners, insignificant

The past participle

§334. Origin and forms. The form called past participle in Portuguese is the successor of a Latin form which was both passive and past. However, in modern Portuguese, as in other Romance languages, it is often not passive, and sometimes not even past.

a. Verbs with two past participles. A considerable number of verbs have two forms. One of them, usually a regular form, is used with **ter** (or **haver**) to form the compound perfect tenses. The irregular one is then used to form the passive voice and as an adjective. Some of the second forms are purely literary and used only as adjectives, while the regular participle may have any of the uses of any past participle.

Tem morrido muitas vacas por causa da sêca.
Many cows have been dying because of the drought.
O cachorro está morto.
The dog is dead.

b. New irregular participles. Along with the general tendency to reduce the number of irregularities, including irregular participles, there is a certain tendency to form new, short, past participles. There are a few participles of verbs of the first conjugation which are formed merely by the addition of **-o** to the infinitive stem. Popular speech is continually inventing more of this type, and some of them have come into fairly wide use. On the analogy of **gasto**, **ganho**, **pago**, one hears **pasmo**, **pego**, **canso**, etc.

c. Active past participle. An active participle is formed from the present participle of the auxiliary **ter** and the past participle. It is not widely used.

> **Tendo acabado de almoçar, deixaram o restaurante.**
> Having finished eating, they left the restaurant.

§335. Uses of the past participle. It is used:

a. To form the compound tenses. In BF, the auxiliary is always **ter**, although a few speakers affect **haver** in the imperfect indicative and subjunctive. The participle, when used with either, is invariable. It is essentially a formal representative of the infinitive from which it is derived. It is not passive, and no expression of past time in the participle can be isolated from the total verb form.

> **Entramos na casa que ela tinha visto.**
> We entered the house which she had seen.
> **Eu tenho estado muito com êle nestes dias.**
> I have been with him a lot these last few days.
> **Se nos tivesse conhecido, não teria fugido.**
> If he had recognized us, he would not have fled.

b. To form the passive voice. The auxiliary is **ser**, and often **ficar** may also be used. The participle is always passive in this case, but not necessarily past. It always agrees in number and gender with the subject of the verb.

> **As casas foram vistas pelos transeuntes.**
> The houses were seen by the passers-by.
> **A melancia ficou esmagada na rua.**
> The watermelon was smashed on the street.

c. As an adjective. The verbal relation of the word is usually clear, but the element of action varies with the verb and other circumstances. There is always agreement of number and gender with a noun or pronoun.

> **O ovo está quebrado.**
> The egg is broken.
> **Vi uma casa abandonada.**
> I saw an abandoned house.
> **Achei os brinquedos no jardim, atirados no chão.**
> I found the toys in the garden, thrown on the ground.

The participle used as an adjective may, at times, be neither passive nor past.

No sofá havia um homem desmaiado.
  On the sofa there was a man who had fainted.
Vi uma mulher sentada no chão.
  I saw a woman seated on the ground.

At times the meaning does not even suggest a participle.

Sou muito esquecido. (=Eu esqueço com freqüência.)
  I am very forgetful.
Êle é cansado. (=Êle cansa os outros.)
  He is tiresome.

d. In absolute phrases. This construction is found mostly in literature. It is rare in BF.

Feita a paz, os soldados voltaram para os seus lares.   **Lit**
  When peace was made, the soldiers returned to their homes.

USAGE OF CERTAIN VERBS

§336. **Ser** and its agreement. The verb **ser** is used in the plural if either its subject or its predicate is plural. The agreement is with the form of these words, whether the implied meaning is of the same number or not.

Os Estados Unidos são um grande país.
    The United States is a great country.
São duas horas.
    It is two o'clock.
A maior parte dos brasileiros é de ascendência portuguêsa.
    Most of the Brazilians are of Portuguese ancestry.
O pior dêste emprêgo são as velhas rabugentas que querem se meter em tudo.
    The worst thing about this job is the impertinent old women who want to stick their noses in everything.

It is used:

a. To express identity.

É êle.
    It is he.
Somos nós.
    It is we.
João é funcionário público.
    John is a civil servant.
Lagoa é uma porção de água rodeada de terra.
    A lake is a body of water surrounded by land.

b. To express origin.

Êsse brinquedo é de Hong Kong.
    That toy is from Hong Kong.
Neusa é de Juiz de Fora.
    Neusa is from Juiz de Fora.
Estas laranjas são da Quinta Macedo.
    These oranges are from the Macedo Farm.

226

c. To indicate material.

Tôdas as peças são de aço inoxidável.
All the parts are made of stainless steel.
Êstes móveis são de jacarandá de lei.
This furniture is made of genuine rosewood.

d. To express ownership.

Êstes sapatos são meus.
These shoes are mine.
Aquêle carro é do Carlos.
That car is Charles's.

e. Before an expression of permanent or fixed location.

Nova Iorque é longe de aqui.
New York is far from here.
A casa é no Flamengo.
The house is in Flamengo.
Onde é a biblioteca?
Where is the library?

For permanent location, **ficar** is also used, more or less interchangeably with **ser**.

f. To identify a location. The location may be temporary or permanent.

Onde fica o escritório de seu pai? —É aqui.
Where is your father's office? It is here.
Onde é o jôgo de hoje? —É no Maracanã.
Where is today's game? It is the Maracanã Stadium.
Foi aqui que encontramos o Mário.
Here is where we met Mario.

g. With a predicate adjective which indicates a usual quality of a noun. The adjective may classify the noun as to the kind, or it may indicate a quality which, although not necessarily permanent, is not thought of by the speaker as changing. The predicate adjective may be a past participle.

O Sr. Mendes é môço ainda.
Mr. Mendes is still young.
Êstes limões são muito azedos.
These limes are very sour.
O Dr. Feliciano é solteiro.
Dr. Feliciano is a bachelor.

Aquêle camarada é enjoado.
That fellow is boring.
Êste livro é escrito em inglês.
This book is written in English.

Instead of an adjective, **ser** may be followed by a phrase or any word, as long as a permanent quality or a characteristic of the subject is indicated.

Você é de encomenda.
You are ideal.
Essa notícia é de arrasar.
This news is overwhelming.

h. With expressions of time.

É uma hora.
It is one o'clock.
São duras horas.
It is two o'clock.
Agora é primavera.
Now it is spring.
São horas de ir ao trabalho. (*But* **Está na hora de ir.**)
It is time to go to work.

i. To form a passive.

Os camarões são cozidos com chuchu.
Shrimp are cooked with chayotes.
O telegrama foi entregue pelo estafêta.
The telegram was delivered by the messenger.

j. To form impersonal expressions. It is used with either nouns or adjectives, especially the latter.

É possível vencer.
It is possible to win.
É pena ter que ficar.
It is a shame to have to stay.

k. With **que** to introduce questions. **Ser** is used impersonally, except for an occasional use of the infinitive. The present tense is the usual form, but others may be used. **É que** may be used alone to introduce a question, or it may follow an interrogative word. The question is then put in declarative order.

É que você quer me ver fracassar?
Do you want to see me fail?

Quando é que êle chega?
When does he arrive?
Quando foi que êle fêz isso?
When did he do that?
Será que ela quer me enganar?
Do you suppose she wants to deceive me?
Pode ser que êle me ajude?
Can it be that he will help me?

1. To introduce folk tales. The formula is **era uma vez**, with **era** equivalent in this case to **havia**.

Era uma vez uma onça que morava na mata.
Once upon a time there was a jaguar that lived in the forest.

§337. **Estar.** This verb loses not only the initial **e-**, in common with other words which begin with **es-** before a consonant, but the **s** as well, in rapid conversational speech. Forms such as **'tive**, etc., are distinguished in the speech of Rio by the fact that the **t** is never palatalized in such cases, whereas the corresponding forms of **ter** always have a palatal pronunciation of *t* (similar to English *ch*) before the vowel *i*.

Estar is used:

a. Of temporary, accidental, or movable location.

João está em casa.
John is at home.
A cadeira está perto da porta.
The chair is near the door.
Aqui estamos longe da cidade.
Here we are far from the city.

Sometimes **estar** is used of permanent location, of something relatively tall, where the meaning is "to stand."

A igreja está no morro.
The church stands on the hill.

The length of time the location is maintained is not important, as long as it is of a kind that is essentially temporary.

Eu estive muitos anos naquela cidade.
I was in that city for many years.

b. With adjectives of temporary states. The meaning of the adjective may be such that the state or condition is necessarily temporary or changeable, or the use of **estar** may give such a meaning to the adjective.

> **D. Lourdes está adoentada hoje.**
> Lourdes is somewhat ill today.
> **Ela está bonita de vestido de noiva.**
> She is pretty in her bridal gown.
> **Jorge está zangado comigo.**
> George is angry with me.
>
> **Samba Le-lê está doente,**
> **Está de cabeça quebrada.**
> Samba Le-le is ill,
> She has a broken head.
>
> **O tempo está quente hoje.**
> The weather is hot today.

By analogy with the preceding example, **estar** is used with nouns when they describe the temporary state of the weather.

> **Hoje está calor.**
> It is hot today.
> **Está um dia lindo.**
> It is a beautiful day.

c. With past participles denoting a temporary state. When the state resulting from previous action is permanent, **ser** or **ficar** is used.

> **A porta está aberta.**
> The door is open.
> **O nome dêsse cavalo está riscado.**
> The name of that horse is scratched.
> **Aquêle campo não está cultivado atualmente.**
> That field is not in cultivation at present.

d. Before a word expressing a state only recently become true. The word may be a noun or an adjective, or even a phrase may be used. The state or condition may be one which is normally permanent, which would generally require the use of **ser**. One is especially likely to use **estar** in informing a person of the new condition.

> **Ela está noiva.**
> She is engaged.
> **Êles já estão casados.**
> Now they are married.

Você ganhou o prêmio; está rico.
You won the prize; you are rich.
A menina está crescida.
The girl is grown up.
Ela nunca chamava a atenção, mas hoje está bonita.
She was never striking, but today she is pretty.

Sometimes **estar** is used to show that an adjective has a figurative sense which is a temporary state.

Trabalhei tanto hoje que estou morto.
I have worked so hard today that I am dead.

e. As the principal auxiliary of the progressive. See §309.

f. **Estar para**, with an infinitive. This expression is used of an action which is about to begin.

José estava para tomar o trem.
Joe was about to take the train.

g. **Estar com** is a synonym of **ter**. It may be used in almost any situation in which **ter** is an independent verb. The negative form is **estar sem**.

A criança está com dois anos apenas.
The child is only two years old.
Eu estou com frio.
I am cold.
O rapaz estava sem um níquel.
The boy didn't have a nickel.
Eu estou com pena dêle.
I feel sorry for him.

§338. **Fazer.** In addition to its two most usual meanings, **criar** and **executar**, the verb **fazer** has a number of uses of importance in the syntax of BF. It is used:

a. As an equivalent of **arrumar, pôr em ordem**.

Ela já fêz as malas. (*Also* **a mesa, a cama.**)
She has packed the suitcases.
Vou fazer as unhas e a barba.
I am going to trim my nails and shave.

b. With the meaning **chegar a, atingir a soma de**.

Quantos fazem três e três?
How much are three and three?

c. With the meaning **levar até o fim, completar.**

Fizemos uma viagem.
  We took a trip.
O senhor já fêz a conta?
  Have you calculated the bill?

d. Of completing any specific age or having a birthday.

Êle faz anos hoje.
  He has a birthday tomorrow.
Fêz trinta anos no sábado passado.
  He was thirty years old last Saturday.

e. Of acting. The acting may be in a play, etc., or figurative. The word **papel** may be used with the verb, or not.

O Dutra fêz o galã.
  Dutra played the romantic lead.
Você fêz o bobo.
  You acted a fool.
Lourdes vai fazer o papel de Ana.
  Lourdes will play the part of Anna.

f. With the meaning **fingir.** This is similar to the preceding, except that the acting is done with the intent of deceiving.

Êle fêz que não sabia.
  He pretended not to know.
Êle se faz de tolo.
  He pretends to be stupid.

g. As an equivalent of **causar.**

O frio fêz o Edgar ficar doente.
  The cold made Edgar sick.
O adubo faz as plantas crescer.
  Fertilizer makes the plants grow.

h. Impersonally, in describing the weather.

Está fazendo bom tempo hoje.
  The weather is fine today.
Faz frio aqui no inverno.
  It is cold here in winter.

i. Impersonally, in counting past time. It measures the time intervening between a point in past time and another point subsequent to it.

Faz três anos que não vejo você.
I haven't seen you for three years.
Amanhã fará um mês que estou aqui.
Tomorrow I will have been here a month.

j. To mean "to cause to become." The object may be oneself or another.

O patrão fêz Adauto chefe de seção.
The boss made Adauto head of a section.
O presidente se fêz ditador.
The president made himself a dictator.

k. To refer to a verb previously used. It serves as a pro-verb, so that the verb previously used need not be repeated. This usage is much less frequent than in English.

O bicho ficou bêbado, como costumam fazer os gambás.
The animal got drunk, as opossums are accustomed to doing.
Êle nem consertou o carro, nem tentou fazê-lo.
He neither repaired the car nor tried to do it.

l. In innumerable idiomatic expressions whose meaning often cannot be deduced from the words that compose them.

Fazer gazeta=matar a aula.
To play hooky.
Fazer caso de=prestar atenção a.
To pay attention to.

§339. **Dever.** In the meaning of "to owe," this verb is used in all tenses and moods. But in other uses, which might be termed modal, only the simple tenses are used. In these meanings, it is important to distinguish the role of each tense form. These uses include:

a. Probability. The present tense expresses probability in present or future time, followed by a present infinitive. Probability in past time also is expressed by the present, but followed by a perfect infinitive. The imperfect expresses probability in past time only if used in sequence following a verb in a past tense.

Essa cadeira não deve ser confortável.
That chair must not be comfortable.
Êle deve estar sòzinho.
He must be alone.
Devem ser três horas.
It must be three o'clock.

Amanhã deve chover.
Tomorrow it will probably rain.
Vou te dar uma coisa que te deve agradar.
I am going to give you something which should please you.
Êle deve ter-se atrasado.
He must have been delayed.
Êle achava que devia ser o amigo.
He thought it must be his friend.

The expression **dever de**, which expresses probability, is not used in BF.

b. Obligation. The obligation can vary greatly in force, from a weak one which may or may not be heeded, to one which amounts almost to compulsion. The force of the obligation depends upon the situation rather than on the form of this verb.

Obligation in the future may be expressed by the future of **dever**, but more often the present is used.

Isso deverá ser contado a todos.
That should be told to everyone.
Êste documento não deve sair do arquivo.
This document should not leave the files.

For obligation in the present, the present of **dever** is used.

Devo ir trabalhar agora.
I must go to work now.
Todo mundo deve votar.
Everybody should vote.

The imperfect and the conditional are used for obligation in the past which might still be carried out.

Êle já estava comprometido, e devia continuar.
He was already obligated, and should continue.

They are also used of a present obligation which is not being carried out:

Você devia (deveria) estar trabalhando.
You ought to be working.

The imperfect or conditional is used with a perfect infinitive to express a past obligation which was not carried out.

Eu devia lhe ter dado alguma coisa.
I should have given him something.

Você deveria ter feito a mudança já antes.
 You should have moved before now.
A senhora devia ter sido mais boazinha para êle.
 You should have been nicer to him.

§340. **Ficar.** This verb has such a wide range of meanings and uses that it seems worthwhile to clarify them. It assumes the meanings of various other verbs on occasion, including some very different from the others. It may be equivalent to:

a. **Permanecer.**

Eu vou ficar em casa.
 I am going to stay at home.

b. **Continuar.**

A gente fica lembrando por muito tempo.
 One keeps remembering for a long time.
Ela ficou andando.
 She kept walking.
Vocês não ficarão impunes.
 You won't remain unpunished.

c. **Estar.**

Irina fica presa.
 Irene is arrested.
Êle fica fora de perigo.
 He is out of danger.

d. **Ser.**

Ela fica bonita de luto.
 She is pretty in mourning.
Êste jardim fica bonito.
 This garden is pretty.
Não faz! Isso fica feio.
 Don't do it! That's ugly.

e. **Começar** or **chegar a ser** or **estar.**

Êle ficou sendo prefeito da cidade.
 He became mayor of the city.
Fique sabendo.
 Know this.
Isto está ficando cacête.
 This is getting boring.

f. **Estar localizado, estar situado.**

A casa fica na esquina.
   The house is on the corner.
Onde fica o correio?
   Where is the post office?

g. **Ser,** as the auxiliary of the passive.

Eu cai e fiquei ferido.
   I fell down and got hurt.

ADVERBS

Formation of adverbs

§341. Formation by suffix. Adverbs are formed regularly from adjectives by the addition of **-mente** to the feminine form of the adjective, or to the common form of those adjectives which do not have a special feminine form. While the adverb is considered to be one word, clear vestiges remain of the time when the two parts were separate words.

a. Stress. The stress of the adjective remains, even though it may violate the rule that the secondary accent of a word occurs on the second syllable preceding the main stress. As a matter of fact, either of the two stresses of the adverb form may be the stronger, depending on the rhythm and intonation of the sentence.

Êle entrou devagar, mas saiu ràpidamente.
He entered slowly, but left rapidly.

b. Separation of the suffix. When two or more adverbs of this type are used in series, the adverbial suffix is ordinarily used only with the last. All adjectives take the feminine form required by the adverbial ending.

O trabalho foi feito rápida e completamente.
The work was done rapidly and completely.

§342. The masculine singular adjective as adverb. This use is widespread, although much less frequent than the use of the special adverb form in **-mente**. It is often difficult to be certain whether a given form is to be considered an adverb or an adjective. The only sure test is the absence or presence of agreement.

Elas correram rápido como um raio.
They ran quick as a flash.

Cf. **Elas correram rápidas como um raio.**

237

§343. Original adverbs. There are very numerous adverbs not formed on the roots of adjectives. The classification of these words is complex and often uncertain. Many of them serve, or may be modified to serve, as other parts of speech. The relationships among adverbs, prepositions, and conjunctions are especially complex. For convenience in discussing them, they will be considered in the classifications given below.

Usage of the adverbs

§344. The demonstrative adverbs of place. Roughly, these correspond to the three persons of the personal pronouns and to the three positions of the demonstrative pronouns.

To **eu, êste**	**aqui, cá.**
To **você, êsse**	**aí.**
To **êle, aquêle**	**ali, lá acolá.**

They have naturally been extended to other uses, in which the idea of physical position is vague or lost. They are used:

a. To express location in space. The words **aí, ali, aqui** generally refer to a rather specific and limited space, while **cá, lá,** and **acolá** may be used in the same situations, or they may refer to a larger and less clearly defined area. **Acolá** is used almost entirely along with one or more of the other demonstrative adverbs, in order to refer to yet another position.

> **Chega para cá; aí, não; aqui mesmo.**
> Come over here; not there, right here.
> **Cá no Brasil há muita serra.**
> Here in Brazil there are many mountains.
> **Põe a mala ali.**
> Put the bag right there.
> **Eu gosto da vida lá na fazenda.**
> I like life out on the farm.
> **Êle correu de lá para cá, e de cá para acolá.**
> He ran hither and thither and away over yonder.
> **Me dá cá isso.**
> Give that here.

b. To express movement in space. All of the demonstrative adverbs may be used to express movement toward the place indicated by each word, but such usage is not frequent. **Cá** and **lá** are so used more than the others, especially with common verbs of motion. In the great majority of cases, the word **para** is used with all of them to indicate movement. For examples, see §356b.

> **Vem cá. Vai lá. Chega aqui.**
> Come here. Go there. Come closer.
> **Êle foi lá e ficou.**
> He went there and stayed.

c. To express a moment in time. In this usage, **aqui** and **cá** refer to the present moment, **aí** to a moment previously referred to, or to a point not very far distant in the past or the future. **Ali** is hardly distinguishable from **aí** in reference to time. **Lá** may refer to any moment in the past or the future.

> **De uns dias para cá, êle tem andado macambúzio.**
> For the last few days he has been downcast.
> **Lá por uma vez, era um lavrador.**
> Once upon a time there was a farmer.
> **Espera para lá.**
> Wait until then.
> **Até lá, as coisas mudam.**
> By then, things will change.
> **De aqui em diante não como mais camarão.**
> From now on I won't eat any more shrimp.
> **Até ali êle tinha trabalhado.**
> Up to then he had worked.
> **Daí por diante, o menino sempre se comportou.**
> From then on the boy always behaved well.

d. Without demonstrative meaning. The words **cá** and **lá**, especially the latter, are often used to give a certain color and connotation to a phrase, without any reference to place or time. The exact force of the adverbs varies from one expression to another, without its being possible to deduce any general sense from their usage.

> **Eu entendo cá disso? (Eu não entendo.)**
> What do I know about that?
> **Eu sei lá. (Eu não sei.)**
> I don't know.
> **Sou lá capaz disso? (Não sou.)**
> Would I be capable of that?
> **De mal, lá isso nunca estiveram. (Não chegaram a tanto.)**
> They never really were at odds.

Conta lá isso como é. (Vamos, conta de uma vez.)
Come on and tell us how it is.
Os da casa 13 não são lá essas coisas. (Não valem muito.)
Those who live in house 13 don't really amount to much.
Como lá diz o outro. (Como a gente diz.)
As people say.
Que é lá isso? (Que diabo é isso?)
What in the world is that?

§345. Other adverbs of place. In addition to the demonstratives, the principal adverbs of place are **adiante, diante, atrás, trás, detrás, adentro, dentro, fora, afora, longe, perto, cêrca, além, aquém, avante, embora, abaixo, debaixo**, and **acima**. Their usage differs greatly from one to another, so that few, if any, general indications can be made.

a. **Diante, trás, detrás, debaixo** are almost never used alone. They occur frequently in combination with prepositions, forming either compound adverbs, compound prepositions, or adjectival phrases.

Não vou lá de agora em diante.
I am not going there from now on.
Ela parou diante do espelho.
She stopped in front of the mirror.
O cachorro sujou as patas de diante.
The dog got his forepaws dirty.
Êle voltou para trás.
He turned back.
O carro precisa de pneus novos nas rodas de trás.
The car needs new tires on its back wheels.
Êle chegou debaixo de chuva.
He arrived in the rain.
Cf. Ela está no andar de baixo.
She is on the lower floor.
O pai ficou detrás. (*Rare in* BF.)
The father remained behind.
Está detrás da porta.
It is behind the door.

b. **Além, aquém, avante, cêrca,** as adverbs, are literary and obsolescent. Only **além** is used in combination with any frequency.

Além do embrulho, o carteiro trouxe uma carta.
Besides the package, the mailman brought a letter.

c. **Adiante, atrás, longe, avante** (Lit) are used to indicate either place or direction.

> **Continuamos adiante três quilômetros.**
> We went on forward three kilometers.
> **A casa é lá adiante.**
> The house is on ahead.
> **Êle voltou atrás sôbre os passos.**
> He retraced his steps.
> **Viajamos longe no mês passado.**
> We traveled a long way last month.

d. **Atrás** is also used of expressions of time. Only this adverb and **diante** of this group have real temporal meaning. They specify points in the present or the past, from which time is counted.

> **Eu cheguei aqui por primeira vez vinte anos atrás.**
> I came here for the first time twenty years ago.

e. **Dentro** and **fora.** These generally refer to location in space but can, in some cases, be used to indicate movement.

> **As crianças estão lá dentro.**
> The children are in there.
> **Eu era do grupo, mas caí fora.**
> I was in the group, but I got out.

f. **Adentro, afora, abaixo, acima,** and **além** are mostly limited to use after **mais,** in BF, except in the postpositional use of the first four. See §358.

> **Mais adentro no mato há uma cacimba.**
> Farther on into the woods there is a waterhole.
> **A primeira aldeia fica nas margens do rio, a segunda mais além.**
> The first village is on the banks of the river, the second one farther on.

g. **Embora.** As an adverb, this word is used of movement only, and is mostly confined to use with **ir, vir, mandar,** and a few other verbs.

> **Eu vou-me embora.**
> I am going away.
> **Não demora mais! Vem embora.**
> Don't wait longer! Come away.

h. **Perto** and **cêrca** (Lit) generally refer to place, and are only occasionally used of movement.

> **Êle está perto de aqui.**
> He is near here.
> **Será que êle vem para perto?**
> Do you think he will come close?

i. **Algures, alhures,** and **nenhures,** indicating either place or direction, are now archaic, replaced by phrases such as **nalguma parte,** etc. They are sometimes used humorously, because they are archaic.

> **O Paulo sumiu; está alhures.**
> Paul is gone; he is elsewhere.

§346. Adverbs of time. These include **hoje, ontem, amanhã, agora, ora, já, cedo, tarde, antes, depois, então, logo, ainda, outrora** (Arc), **sempre, nunca.** There is no special problem in their use.

§347. Adverbs of manner. These include **bem, mal, assim, rápido, devagar,** and most adverbs derived from adjectives. There are no special problems in their use as adverbs of manner, but the first two have other uses as well. See §349.

§348. Adverbs of doubt. These include **talvez, acaso** (SLit), **quiçá** (Lit), **porventura** (Lit). For use of the subjunctive with them, see §241.

§349. Adverbs of quantity and intensity. These include **bem, mal, muito, pouco, bastante, assaz** (Lit), **demais, algo** (Lit), **tão.** They may modify an adjective or another adverb, except that **mal** modifies adjectives only. All of them regularly precede the word modified, except **demais,** which follows it.

> **Tenho um carro bem bom.**
> I have a very good car.
> **Êle respondeu bastante depressa.**
> He answered quite rapidly.
> **Vi uma porta mal fechada.**
> I saw a door that was not quite closed.
> **Êle chegou tarde demais.**
> He arrived too late.
> *Cf.* **Um homem por demais violento.**
> A man who is too violent.

§350. **Sim** and affirmation.

a. Answer to a question with verb. An affirmative answer to a question may be given with **sim**, but it is seldom done in BF. One answers by repeating the verb or the auxiliary only, if there was one, of the question. The same tense and number are used as in the question, but the person varies to fit the logical situation. The verb is not accompanied by either subject or object.

> **Vocês compreendem a lição? Compreendemos.**
> Do you understand the lesson? Yes.
> **Esta casa foi feita por seu pai? Foi.**
> Was this house built by your father? Yes.
> **Êles estão comendo? Estão.**
> Are they eating? Yes.
> **Você vai tomar banho de mar? Vou.**
> Are you going swimming? Yes.
> **Hei de esperar aqui? Há.**
> Am I to wait here? Yes.

b. Question does not include a verb. If the question is an implied one or otherwise does not contain a verb, the affirmative answer is usually **é**.

> **Frio hoje, hein? É.**
> Cold today, huh? Yes.
> **Bonita moça, aquela. É.**
> A pretty girl over there. Yes.

c. **Sim** in emphatic agreement. If the second speaker wishes to emphasize his affirmative answer, he may add the word **sim** after the verb form which constitues his affirmation.

> **Você fêz isso? Fiz, sim.**
> Did you do that? Yes, I did.
> **Êsse é seu irmão? É, sim senhor.**
> Is that your brother? Yes, sir, it is.

d. **Sim** for emphasis in statements. When placed before the verb in statements, **sim** makes the statement strongly emphatic. Often this construction is used for contrast with a preceding negative statement.

> **A mulher dêle, esta sim era muito feia.**
> As for his wife, she really is very ugly.
> **Paulo não tem filhos, mas Martinho sim tem.**
> Paul doesn't have any children, but Martin does.

e. **Sim** to request assent. One may request the assent of another person by placing an interrogative **sim** at the end of the statement.

Vou saltar do ônibus aqui, sim? (Está bem?)
I am going to get off the bus here, O. K.?
Pára de bobagens, sim? (Quer?)
Stop the nonsense, will you?

f. Affirmation in elliptical sentences. **Sim** expresses affirmation or agreement in elliptical sentences, following certain verbs and **que**.

Eu acho que sim.
I think so.
João diz que sim.
John says so.
Creio que sim.
I believe so.

g. Ironical assent. The expression **pois sim** is ironical assent, in effect a negative.

Comprei um carro novo. —Pois sim! (Não acredito.)
I bought a new car. Really?

§351. Negative adverbs. **Não, nunca, jamais.** For these and negation in general, see §477 ff.

§352. Interrogative and relative adverbs. The same words are used as interrogative and relative adverbs. As interrogatives, they are treated in §477. The relatives are:

a. **Quando**, of time. There are no special problems connected with it, except that it must express time, and may not become a relative pronoun, even though its antecedent is a noun of time.

Era domingo quando fui à igreja.
It was Sunday when I went to church.
Irei no próximo aniversário, quando farei 21 anos.
I will go on my next birthday, when I will be 21.
Fui no domingo em que estivemos no Rio. (*Not* quando.)
I went on the Sunday when we were in Rio.

b. **Onde**, of place. Referring to a noun of place, it may become a relative pronoun, without expressing place.

Vamos ao Rio, onde há belas praias. (=lugar em que)
We are going to Rio, where there are beautiful beaches.
Fui ver a casa onde nasci. (=em que)
I went to see the house where I was born.

c. **Donde, de onde.** BF usually employs the sceond form when it refers to place. **Donde** is used frequently to refer to an idea previously expressed, the consequences of which are to follow.

> **Vamos a Vassouras, de onde vem um bom queijo.**
> We are going to Vassouras, where a good cheese comes from.
> **Vocês ouviram os argumentos, donde concluimos que é preciso melhorar a situação dos camponeses.**
> You have heard the arguments, from which we conclude that it is necessary to improve the situation of the peasants.

d. **Aonde, para onde.** These are used to express movement toward the place mentioned by the antecedent, with the differences in meaning described under the prepositions **a** and **para**. **Aonde** and **onde** are frequently confused.

e. **Como.** In addition to its uses as an interrogative and relative adverb, it may be used in exclamations. See §482. **Como** is not much used as a relative, being replaced usually by **que**.

> **Vou preparar esta galinha desta maneira, como fazia minha mãe.**
> I am going to prepare this chicken this way, as my mother used to do.
> **Vou tentar fazer como êle fêz.**
> I am going to try to do as he did.
> **Agora você faz do mesmo jeito que êle.**
> Now you do exactly what he did.

f. **Quanto** expresses quantity or degree. It may also be used in exclamations. An example of use as a relative adverb:

> **Só então êle compreendeu quanto gostavam dêle.**
> Only then did he understand how much they loved him.

§353. Other simple (one-word) adverbs. The following are adverbs which do not fall into the preceding classifications, but which present some problems.

a. **Aliás.** This word is used to correct immediately an erroneous statement made by the speaker.

> **Eu tenho dois, aliás três, bons amigos.**
> I have two, or rather three, good friends.

b. **Assim** expresses manner. It may be equivalent to **desta maneira, dessa maneira,** or **de tal maneira.**

> **A gente chega e diz assim: A senhora dá licença?**
> One comes up and speaks thus "May I be excused?"

> **Usa o garfo, assim como fazem os outros.**
> Use your fork, just as the others do.

After a noun it is equivalent to **dêsse tipo.**

> **Êle tinha pena de criaturas assim.**
> He was sorry for creatures like that.

Assim como assim=em qualquer caso, de todos modos.

> **Não via mais nenhuma casa habitada; assim como assim, estava mesmo perdido.**
> He didn't see another inhabited house; in any case, he was really lost.

c. **Até.** As an adverb, this word expresses a somewhat surprising degree or extent of a condition, quality, action, etc., sometimes also with the connotation that the contrary was believed or had been stated.

> **O homem estava até com cara de riso.**
> The man even showed signs of laughter.
> **Até parecia que o sujeito tinha parte com o capeta.**
> It even seemed that the fellow had a pact with the devil.
> **Eu até me divirto.**
> On the contrary, I have a good time.
> **Era pouco até o que êle fazia.**
> What he was doing was actually very little.
> **Farei isso até com grande satisfação.**
> Why, I will be very happy to do that.

d. **Mesmo** as an adverb may express:
Insistence on the factualness of a statement.

> **O quarto só dava mesmo para a cama.**
> The room was really only big enough for the bed.
> **Esta canja é mesmo boa.**
> This chicken soup is really good.

A surprising degree of a condition, action, etc. It may be combined with **até** in this case, to strengthen the effect.

> **Mas, mesmo assim, não se achou satisfeito.**
> But, even so, he wasn't satisfied.
> **Temos filmes até mesmo do Japão.**
> We have films even from Japan.

A strengthened and more exact meaning of an adverb of place or time which it follows.

Êle caiu ali mesmo.
He fell down right there.
Vamos sair agora mesmo.
Let's leave right now.

That the exact cause is the statement which follows.

Não vão nos adjudar, mesmo por serem nossos rivais.
They are not going to help us, for the very reason that they are
our rivals.

e. **Só, sòmente, apenas.** These are synonyms, nearly always interchangeable, with the meaning **ùnicamente, meramente.** But the word
só is also used in situations in which **tudo** might be expected.

Êle só (sòmente, apenas) ouviu a voz de um homem no escuro.
He merely heard the voice of a man in the dark.
O senhor quer mais alguma coisa? —Não, é só.
Do you wish something else? No, that's all.

f. **Todavia, porém.** These words are synonyms. The meaning is
intermediate between **mas** and **a pesar disso.**

É um homem que não presta; todavia, não seria capaz de um crime.
The man is no good; however, he wouldn't be capable of a crime.

§354. Combinations of adverbs. The adverbs of place, and to a
limited extent of time, combine with each other to form what
amounts to compound adverbs. The first of the two is usually a
demonstrative, most frequently **lá** or **cá**, less often **ali, aí,** or **aqui.**
These phrases may also express direction, although this is usually
made more specific by the use of a preposition. See §356, below.

Quem está aí fora?
Who is out there?
Êles ficam lá fora, e nós cá dentro.
They stay out there, and we in here.
Vejo um cavalo lá longe.
I see a horse away out there.
Senta aqui perto.
Sit close here.
Lá então morávamos na fazenda.
At that time we lived on a farm.
Olha ali em baixo.
Look down there.

§355. Formation of compound adverbial expressions with a preposition. Many adverbial expressions, consisting of an original preposition and an adverb—sometimes a noun or an adjective—have become welded into one word. Often this is a mere convention of writing, and other combinations could be considered one word with equal or even greater justice. In general, this has no importance for the spoken language; the expression is felt as a unit in most cases, as long as the expression is adverbial. However, an adjectival expression as in **o andar de baixo** is, in fact as well as in writing, two separate words.

Compare		*with*
diante	**de + ante**	**em diante**
adiante	**a+ de+ ante**	**para diante**
atrás	**a + trás**	**para trás**
acima	**a + cima**	**em cima**
debaixo	**de + baixo**	**em baixo**
devagar	**de + vagar**	**com vagar**
depressa	**de + pressa**	**com pressa**
deveras	**de + veras**	**de verdade**

De aqui and **de repente** are pronounced as one-word adverbs, respectively **daqui** and **derrepente**. The unity of this last word is revealed by the fact that the first vowel is pronounced **e**, not with the vowel **i** of the preposition.

§356. Compound adverbs formed with prepositions and adverbs. A very large number of compound adverbs are in common use which consist of combinations of one or more prepositions with one or more adverbs of place or time. The possible combinations are too numerous to list. General types are discussed below.

a. Formed with **por**. This prepositon with an adverb of space or time may indicate a vague and indefinite area of space or time throughout which, or within which, a thing or event is located. With adverbs of place only, it may express movement through the area.

Não há disso por cá.
There is none of that around here.
Êle deve estar por aí.
He must be around there.
Seu irmão ficou por lá.
Your brother stayed around there.

Como vai aquilo lá por baixo?
How are things down there?
Que é que você fazia por então?
What were you doing along about then?
Por agora não fazemos mais isso.
Nowdays we don't do that any more.
Daí por diante não viram mais gente conhecida.
From then on they saw no more familiar people.
O cachorro passou por baixo. (*Or* **por debaixo.**)
The dog ran underneath.
Haroldo chegou por trás e falou.
Harold came up behind and spoke.

b. Formed with **para.** **Para** in combinations of this type indicates movement toward the place named by the adverb. **Para** may be omitted at times, but is usually expressed to make specific the idea of movement.

Pode ir lá para dentro. (*Also* **lá dentro.**)
You may go in.
Fala para aí.
Speak in that direction.
Espera para lá. (=**Até então.**)
Wait until then.
Sobe para lá.
Go up that way.
Vou aí para fora.
I'm going out there.
Vem para cá. (*Also* **vem cá.**)
Come here.
Tem sido assim de uns dias para cá.
It has been that way for the last few days.
Êle tocou para trás.
He went back where he came from.
Helena chorou para dentro.
Helen cried inwardly.
Ela cose para frente e para trás.
She sews backwards and forwards.
Êle empurrou a cadeira para bem longe.
He pushed the chair away off.

c. With **de.** This indicates direction from which, in space or time.

Por que não fizeram lá de cima esta sua obra? (começando lá em cima, progredindo para baixo.)
Why didn't they do the job from the top down?

O chefe falou lá de dentro.
The boss spoke from inside (the house).
Ouvi passos vindos lá de baixo. (*Also* de lá em baixo.)
I heard steps resounding from below.
Vou gritar cá de fora.
I am going to shout in from out here.
A casa, vista cá de fora, era feia.
The house, seen from out here, was ugly.
Eu conheci ela de longe.
I recognized her from afar.
De aqui em diante, não vou mais lá.
From here on in, I go there no more.
Daí até hoje, não vi mais nem a sombra dêle.
From then until this day, I have never seen even his shadow.

De may also express origin or cause of events, ideas, with one of the demonstrative adverbs.

Esta criança é órfã—daí a timidez.
This child is an orphan—hence its timidity.
Sofreram muito durante a guerra; de lá (daí) vem a amargura que se nota na conversa dêles.
They suffered much during the war; from that arises the bitterness that is noticed in their talk.

d. With **em**. **Em** generally indicates location, when followed by **cima** or **baixo**, occasionally by **fora**.

Deixei a mala lá em cima.
I left my bag up there.
Vê aquela terra lá em baixo.
Look at that land down there.
Saiu por êste mundo em fora.
He went out into the world.

With adverbs of time, sometimes space, it indicates direction.

Daí em diante.
From then on.
De longe em longe.
At long intervals.

§357. Order of words in compound adverbs. It should be noted that in adverbial phrases consisting of two adverbs of place and a preposition, the preposition is generally placed between the two adverbs.

Isso caiu lá de cima.
That fell from up there.
Vem cá para fora.
Come out here.
Existem onças lá por perto.
There are jaguars around near there.

§358. Postpositions. Four adverbs may act as postpositions, being placed always after the noun, which then has no article.

O carro desce montanha abaixo.
The car comes down the mountain.
Subiram rio acima.
They went up the river.
Os bandeirantes penetraram terras adentro.
The pioneers penetrated inland.
O barco estava águas afora da costa do Atlântico.
The boat was some distance out from the Atlantic coast.

However, a much more frequent construction uses a preposition (and the definite article, if required by sense), followed by the noun and these adverbs.

Êle correu pela escada abaixo.
He ran down the stairs.
Trepou pelo cipó acima.
It climbed up the vine.
Viram gente de janela adentro.
They saw people inside the window.

§359. Adverbs in adjectival phrases. The adverbs of place and time form adjectival phrases with the preposition **de**, modifying a noun or pronoun. The usual meaning of the adverb, "at that place," etc., has been modified to "that place," etc. The demonstrative adverbs may precede the phrase.

Está no andar de cima.
He is on the upper floor.
Como eram as môças de então?
What were the girls of those days like?
Põe os biscoitos no tabuleiro de fora.
Put the cookies on the outside tray.
A gente lá de dentro quer saber.
The people who are inside want to know.
O melhor será um juiz lá de fora.
The best will be a judge from outside.

PREPOSITIONS

General considerations

§360. Development of the prepositions. The loss of the cases of Latin—total in Portuguese except in the personal pronoun—necessitated a greatly expanded use of prepositions. The number existing in Latin was insufficient for the required uses and has tended to increase as the language developed. New prepositions were formed in various ways—combining old ones, transferring words from other uses, and forming phrases which act as prepositions. In some of these phrases, the meaning of the noun has been lost, for all practical purposes, so that the phrase amounts to a new preposition. In most, however, the noun is still felt as an autonomous word.

§361. Case of the object of a preposition. Most of the traditional prepositions surviving from Latin, and many newly formed ones, require that the words they govern be in the accusative case. However, only the first person singular pronoun, the relatively little used old second person singular, and the third person reflexive reveal any distinction of case after a preposition. Several words which are definitely prepositions in function are regularly followed by the nominative, and less cultured speakers sometimes employ it after some others.

> **Era um homem gordo feito eu.**
> He was a fat man like me.
> **Houve dez convidados, afora eu.**
> There were ten guests, besides me.
> **Vão todos, menos eu.**
> All are going, except me.
> **Fala igual a eu.**   **Inc**
> Speak like me.

When a preposition is followed by two or more objects joined by e, all but the first are nominative. There is vacillation in the case of the first, since the situation occurs so infrequently, the tendency being to make it nominative only if an identifiable nominative follows.

Estão tramando uma conspiração contra você e eu.
They are plotting a conspiracy against you and me.
Não há nada entre ela e eu.
There is nothing between her and me.
Não podem fazer nada sem mim e êle.
They can't do anything without me and him.
Isso fica entre tu e eu.
This must be kept between you and me.

§362. The basic historical prepositions. The following words are the basic stock of prepositions. They are mostly used solely as such, although some may combine with **que** to form conjunctions. They are: **a, além, ante, até, após, com, contra, de, desde, em, entre, para, por, perante, sem, sob, sôbre,** and **trás. Além** and **até** are also used as adverbs.

Other words have come to be used as prepositions, sometimes clearly felt as such, at other times retaining little or much of their earlier function. Several of these are discussed below. In some cases, the prepositional use is clearly shown by the fact that these words no longer express agreement. E.g., **exceto, segundo, salvo, feito.**

Below are listed the common prepositions, simple and compound, with the principal uses of each. The compound ones are listed under the principal word of each, whether the words are now written separately or together. This matter is, of course, purely arbitrary. The compound prepositions given are those which act as single prepositions. Many other phrases exist in which the meaning of the noun is still intact, so that we have a preposition + noun + another preposition. The line between these two is, of course, very vague, and can only be drawn arbitrarily.

Usage of prepositions

§363. Use of **a.** Because of the great preponderance of the letter *a* in Portuguese, and to avoid long strings of vowels, Brazilians have replaced **a** in very many expressions with **em, para, com, de, por,** etc. It is used to express:

a. Direction up to a place. It implies that the subject arrives at the destination, but that this is not his permanent nor habitual location. In the latter case, **para** is used. In borderline cases, **para** is preferred. If, on the other hand, the subject is going to the place with the intention of leaving immediately for another place, **em** is often used.

> **Eu vou à cidade.**
> I am going downtown.
> **Vários americanos foram ao Brasil passar o verão.**
> Several Americans went to Brazil to spend the summer.
> **Mamãe e Maria já foram à missa.**
> Mother and Mary have gone to mass.
> **Vamos para casa.**
> We are going home.
> **Todos os brasileiros já voltaram para o Brasil.**
> All the Brazilians have returned to Brazil.
> **Vamos em casa antes de ir à cidade.**
> Let's go by the house before going downtown.

b. Position in space. For the most part, this meaning is expressed by **em** in BF. One hears occasional use of **a**, in most cases carry-overs from Lusitanian and literary constructions. In some cases a real difference in meaning is expressed by the two prepositions, so that **a** has been kept in use.

> **Êle está à porta. (BF=Êle está na porta.)**
> He is at the door.
> **Estamos sentados à mesa; põe os pratos na mesa.**
> We are seated at the table; put the plates on the table.
> **Ela tinha uma criança ao pé; eu pisei no pé dela.**
> She had a child beside her; I stepped on her foot.
> **Fazia um calor de 40° à sombra; por isso, eu fiquei na sombra.**
> It was forty degrees in the shade; for that reason I remained in the shade.

c. Position at a distance from a place.

> **A vila fica a duas horas de viagem.**
> The town is two hours away.
> **A estrada acaba a trinta quilômetros de aqui.**
> The road ends thirty kilometers from here.

d. Position in time. Here **a** is the usual preposition. Cf., however, usage of **de** and **em** in expressions of time. See §§505a,b; 389j,k.

> **José chegou em casa à noite.**
> Joe got home at nightfall.

Levantei às oito horas.
I got up at eight o'clock.
Como quiabo às vezes.
I eat okra at times.

With the days of the week, expressing habitual action on those days, **a** is more usual with masculine days, **em** with feminine ones. However, either preposition may be used with either.

Aos (nos) domingos.
On Sundays.
O avião sai nas (às) sextas-feiras.
The plane leaves on Fridays.

e. Limit of time toward the future. But compare use of **em** §389r.

Daí a instantes, o trem se pôs em movimento.
Instants later, the train started up.
De hoje a um ano estarei de volta.
A year from today I will be back.

f. The indirect object. But **para** is more frequent and may replace **a** in practically all cases.

Êle deu um presente ao João. (*Or* para o João.)
He gave a present to John.
Délia não disse nada disso a mim. (*Or* para mim.)
Delia didn't say anything about that to me.

g. Means of locomotion. It is limited to the examples given below.

Você sabe andar a bicicleta?
Do you know how to ride a bicycle?
Êle viajou a cavalo.
He traveled on horseback.
Terei que ir a pé.
I'll have to go on foot.

h. Dative of ownership. This usage is literary. BF uses **de**.

Ela tomava o pulso ao doente.   Lit (BF=do doente.)
She took the patient's pulse.

i. Dative of separation. This usage is archaic. BF uses **de**.

Roubaram um cavalo ao fazendeiro.   Arc
They stole a horse from the farmer.

j. The objective genitive. It is used only where **de** would be ambiguous. Even then, BF often does not make the distinction, using **de** in spite of the resulting ambiguity.

> **Contou-nos uma história sôbre a caça ao tigre.**
> He told us a story about jaguar-hunting.
> *Cf.* **A caça do tigre foi um fracasso; não matou nada.**
> The jaguar's hunt was unsuccessful; he didn't kill anything.
> **Aquela tribo pratica o culto ao macaco.**
> That tribe practices monkey-worship.

k. A personal direct object. It is heard with nouns which refer to God, and very infrequently with personal pronouns.

> **Devemos amar a Deus.**
> We should love God.
> **Incomoda alguém se abro a janela? —A mim não incomoda.** Rare
> Will it bother anyone if I open the window? It won't bother me.
> **A êle não levavam na onda. Era sabido demais.** Rare
> They didn't fool him. He was too clever.
> **Era tão ruim que dasafiava a Deus e ao mundo.**
> He was so wicked that he defied God and the world.

It is also used in the expression **um ao outro**, whether it is dative or accusative.

> **Os dois são primos, mas odeiam um ao outro.**
> The two are cousins, but they hate each other.

l. It is used after many verbs before a dependent infinitive. Usage of this preposition, another one, or of no preposition is determined entirely by the conjugated verb. With verbs of motion, except **ir** and **vir**, it may express purpose. Otherwise it is only a formal requirement, adding nothing to the meaning.

> **Começou a chover.**
> It began to rain.
> **Fui convidado a falar.**
> I was invited to speak.
> **Êle saiu a comprar pão.**
> He went out to buy bread.

m. Following certain adjectives, before a noun, pronoun, or infinitive. The adjectives are usually related to verbs which require **a**.

> **Vimos uma pedra semelhante a uma vaca.**
> We saw a stone that looked like a cow.

Ceder agora seria equivalente a perder.
To yield now would be equivalent to losing.

n. It is used after certain nouns before another noun or pronoun.

Há uma grande falta de estímulos à agricultura.
There is a great lack of encouragement of agriculture.
Devemos obediência aos pais.
We owe obedience to our parents.

o. With the masculine definite article, before an infinitive. The resulting expression is equivalent to a clause, the meaning varying with the situation.

Ao entrarmos em casa, tiramos os sapatos.   **SLit**
When we went into the house, we took off our shoes.

p. In innumerable adverbial phrases, to express a wide range of meaning.

by means of:
    Levar à fôrça; escrever a lápis.
    To take by force; to write with pencil.
manner:
    Andar às cegas; vestir à francesa; escolher ao acaso; falar aos trancos
    e barrancos.
    To go blindly; to dress in French style; to choose at random; to speak in jerks and starts.
distribution:
    Duas vezes ao dia.
    Twice a day.
grouping:
    Homens aos milhares; andar dois a dois; comprar pão aos quilos.
    Men by the thousand; to walk two by two; to buy bread by the kilogram.
according to:
    Ao meu ver, você está enganada.
    As I see it, you are mistaken.

§364. **Além.** This word is used alone as a preposition only in a few fixed expressions, such as **além-mar.** It has been replaced otherwise by **além de, para lá de, do outro lado de,** etc.

§365. **Além de** is used to express:

a. Location in space.

Isso aconteceu além do Amazonas.
That happened beyond the Amazon.

b. Movement to a destination in space.

Êle foi além das fronteiras. (*Also* **para além das fronteiras.**)
He went beyond the borders.

c. In addition to.

Além da banca de advogado, êle tem um negócio.
Besides his lawyer work, he has a business.
Não vou nêsse carro velho. Além do mais, você não sabe guiar.
I am not going in that old car. Besides, you can't drive.
Além de reclamar do preço, êle não me paga.
In addition to complaining of the price, he doesn't pay me.

§366. **Ante** and **perante** are usually interchangeable. They are used to express:

a. Position in the presence of persons, usually suggesting judgment.

Êle compareceu ante (*or* **perante**) **o juiz.**
He appeared before the judge.
O artista se apresentou ante o público.
The artist presented himself to the public.

b. Situation in the face of events.

Ante esta situação, os políticos se acovardaram.
Faced with this situation, the politicians turned coward.

c. The use of **ante** in expressions of time is archaic, except in compound words, such as **anteontem**.

§367. **Antes de** expresses earlier time.

Chegamos antes das seis.
We arrived before six.

§368. **Após** and **após a** are literary and archaic except in certain compound words.

Após a vitória.   Lit and Arc
After the victory.
A literatura de após-guerra.
Post-war literature.
Após a uma missa.   Arc
After a mass.

§369. **Até** and **até a.** No difference in meaning is observable between the two expressions. BF uses **até** alone. It expresses:

a. Movement up to a point in space.

> **Ela chegou até a porta.**
> She came up to the door.

b. The end of the period of time of an action.

> **A monarquia durou até 1889.**
> The monarchy lasted until 1889.

c. Final limit of time for performing an action.

> **Você tem que acabar a lição até quarta.**
> You must finish the lesson by Wednesday.

d. Limit of extent, degree, etc.

> **Lutaram até o último homem.**
> They fought to the last man.
> **Êle levou a esquisitice até a loucura.**
> He carried eccentricity to the point of madness.

§370. **Através de** expresses:

a. Passage through a division of space or through a material object.

> **Estou vendo êle através da janela.**
> I see him through the window.

b. Passage through an immaterial thing.

> **Esta palavra chegou até nós através do latim.**
> This word came to us through Latin.

c. Means.

> **Muitos conseguem levantar-se a uma clase superior através dos estudos.**
> Many manage to rise to a superior class through study.

§371. **Baixo.** From this adjective are formed several phrases which are used as prepositions. In some a preposition is combined with **baixo** into one word; in other cases all parts are written separately. The manner of writing is purely traditional and arbitrary. All refer to physical position below. For figurative meanings, see **sob**, §436.

a. **Debaixo de** indicates a position in space lower than that of its object. It is SLit, replaced in BF by **embaixo de.**

Viajamos debaixo de um céu azul.
We traveled under a blue sky.
Chegamos debaixo de chuva.
We arrived in the rain.

b. **Embaixo de** has the same meaning as the preceding and is the usual form in BF.

Escondeu-se embaixo da cama.
He hid under the bed.

c. **Abaixo de** indicates usually an inferior degree or extent.

Venderam-lhe um chapéu abaixo de sua medida.
They sold him a hat smaller than his size.

It may indicate an inferior status.

Abaixo de Deus, foi você que me ajudou.
Under God, it was you who helped me.

Indicating physical position, it is archaic.

Abaixo da superfície de Goiaz, há muito minério.   Lit and Arc
Under the surface of Goiaz there are many minerals.

d. **Para baixo de** indicates movement toward a lower position in space.

O pássaro passou para baixo de um carro.
The bird ran under a car.

e. **Por baixo de** indicates movement through space underneath.

O cachorro passou por baixo da mesa.
The dog passed under the table.

§372. **Cêrca de** indicates approximate quantity or number.

O Gomes plantou cêrca de mil pés de café.
Gomes planted about a thousand coffee trees.

Less frequently, it indicates proximity in space. BF uses **perto de.**

Há uma árvore cêrca da casa.   Lit
There is a tree near the house.

a. **Acêrca de** indicates that its object is the subject of conversation, writing, etc.

Estou lendo uma crônica acêrca da juventude transviada.
I am reading an article about juvenile delinquents.

§373. Cima is a noun which enters into several prepositions to which it contributes the general meaning of "above."

a. **Acima de** may indicate a greater degree or extent.

Temos trinta graus acima de zero.
We have thirty degrees above zero.
Seja honesto, acima de tudo.
Be honest, above all.

It may indicate a position in space, literal, or more usually figurative.

Levanta a bola acima da cabeça.
Raise the ball above your head.
Êste assunto está acima da minha cabeça.
This subject is over my head.

b. **Em cima de** indicates position on the upper surface of, or above an object. The sense may, at times, be figurative.

O prato está em cima da mesa.
The plate is on top of the table.
O céu fica em cima de nós.
The sky is over us.
Não quero botar os olhos em cima dêle.
I don't want to lay my eyes on her.

c. **Para cima de** indicates movement onto the top of.

O gato levou o pão para cima da casa.
The cat took the bread on top of the house.

d. **Por cima de** indicates passage over the top of.

Olhou-me por cima dos ombros.
He looked at me over his shoulders.
O avião passou por cima da cidade.
The plane passed over the city.

It may indicate addition to what has already happened, to a degree that becomes excessive or outrageous.

Ainda por cima de me xingar, roubou meu casaco.
On top of calling me names, he stole my coat.

§374. Com is used to express:

a. Accompaniment.

Eu fui com êle.
I went with him.
Êle está com dois dólars.
He has two dollars.

b. Accompanying circumstances.

O carteiro chegou com escuro.
The mailman came after dark.
Êle vivia com o nariz no céu.
He lived with his nose turned up.
Você está com medo?
Are you afraid?

c. Means.

Êle fechou a porta com chave.
He closed the door with a key.
A carta foi escrita com pena.
The letter was written with a pen.
A rua será coberta com asfalto.
The street will be covered with asphalt.

d. In relations with.

Mamãe tem freguesia com ela.
Mother is a customer of hers.
Não tenho compromisso com êle.
I have no obligations to him.

e. Opposition.

Tenho briga com êle.
I have a quarrel with him.
O campeão vai lutar com três.
The champion is going to fight with three.

§375. **Como** is really a conjunction, not a preposition. Since it often takes the place of a preposition in the sentence, it is included here. It is followed always by the nominative case. The meaning is "similar to."

Faz como eu.
Do as I do (like me).
Nunca vi ninguém como ela.
I never saw anyone like her.

§376. **Conforme** expresses exact correlation to another situation.

Êle cumpriu conforme o prometido.
He carried out as promised.
Me comportarei conforme o caso.
I'll behave according to the situation.

§377. **Contra** expresses:

a. Physical opposition.

Êle lutou contra os três.
He fought against the three.

b. Intellectual opposition.

Eu sou contra a ditadura.
I am against the dictatorship.

c. Location touching. It often has the connotation of pressure.

Deixou-se cair contra o ombro do pai.
He let himself fall against his father's shoulder.

§378. **De** forms several contractions, in addition to those given under the articles and demonstratives: **daqui** (not written), **daí, dali, donde.** It is used:

a. To express ownership.

Esta casa é do João.
This house is John's.

b. To express origin, by birth, manufacture, etc.

Êle é de Roma.
He is from Rome.
Temos melões de Portugal.
We have melons from Portugal.

c. To express origin of progress in space.

Visto de aqui, de perto, é bonito.
Seen from here, nearby, it is beautiful.
Êle saiu da cidade.
He came out of the city.

d. To express origin of progress in time.

Isso durou de então a hoje.
That has lasted from then until today.

De há muito, êle vem se queixando.
He has been complaining since long ago.

e. Before means of transportation, especially of persons.

Êle viajou de trem, de carro, de avião, de barco, etc.
He traveled by train, by car, by plane, by boat, etc.

f. To connect two nouns, the second of which modifies the first. No article is used.

Uma lâmpada de mesa.
A table lamp.
Uma noite de verão.
A summer night.

g. To express means. This use is limited to relatively few expressions.

Tudo estava coberto de neve.
Everything was covered with snow.
De faca não se briga.
On doesn't fight with a knife.

h. To express agency, usually not of a person. The usage is limited.

Êle foi atacado da doença.
He was attacked by the disease.

i. To express cause of a condition.

Estou morto de tão cansado.
I am dead from weariness.
Ela chorou de pura manha.
She cried from sheer stubbornness.

j. With the meaning "concerning, on the subject of."

O que o senhor acha do Pedro?
What do you think of Peter?
Vamos falar dos ausentes.
Let's talk about the absent.

k. In partitive expressions.

Quero um chope do bom.
I want a draft beer of the good kind.
Eu sou das lourinhas.
I am one of the little blondes.

Um pouco de açúcar.
A bit of sugar.
Não há nada de novo.
There is nothing new.

l. To express extent of change of quantity.

A temperatura baixou de dez graus.
The temperature went down ten degrees.
O preço aumentou de pouco.
The price went up a little.

m. After certain exclamations. These are primarily of pity, but sometimes of congratulation. A following noun or pronoun indicates the person to whom it applies.

Coitado de mim!
Poor me!
Olha o felizardo do Soares.
Look at that lucky fellow Soares.

n. With nouns and adjectives, to form adverbial phrases. These express attendant circumstances, quality, manner, etc.

De propósito, de vez, de esguelha, de repente.
Purposely, for keeps, askance, suddenly.
Êle caiu de nariz no chão.
He fell on his nose on the ground.
Os dois andavam de mal.
The two were at odds.
O coitado chegou aqui de fazer pena.
The poor fellow came here in a pitiful state.
Ela vem vindo de mansinho.
She comes creeping softly.
A porca enferrujou de vez.
The nut has rusted for keeps.

o. With adverbs of time and place, to form adjective phrases.

As moças de então.
The girls of those days.
O lado de fora.
The outside.

p. To express position in space. It is heard mostly with the noun **lado.**

Está do outro lado do rio.
It is on the other side of the river.

Caiu do lado de fora.
It fell from the outside.

q. To express the occasion. It is used with a demonstrative and vez.

Desta vez você não me escapa.
This time you won't escape me.
Daquela vez não vimos mais o Barbosa.
That time we saw Barbosa no more.

r. Following numerous verbs before an infinitive.

Acabou de fazê-lo.
He has just done it.
Esqueceu-se de voltar.
He forgot to return.

s. To connect most nouns with a following infinitive.

Eu tenho vontade de rir.
I have an urge to laugh.
Êle está com medo de falar.
He is afraid to talk.

t. Following numerous adjectives, before a noun, pronoun, or infinitive.

Êle é capaz de fazê-lo.
He is capable of doing it.
Estou seguro disso.
I am sure of that.

§379. **Dentre** indicates that one or more individuals mentioned form part of the group defined by its object. The preposition is literary.

Dentre os vereadores eleitos é o Sr. Sampaio.   **Lit**
Among the councilmen elected is Mr. Sampaio.

§380. **Dentro** is an adverb of place which enters into several prepositional phrases.

§381. **Dentro de** expresses:

a. Interior position in space.

Há um pátio dentro do edifício.
There is a patio inside the building.

b. Position within nonphysical limits.

Dentro dos limites da possibilidade, farei tudo para ajudar você.
Within the limits of possibility, I will do anything to help you.

c. Position within limits in time.

Dentro de um mês estarei com você.
Within a month I will be with you.

§382. **Dentro em** expresses position within limits in time. It is used only in certain expressions.

Êle deve chegar dentro em breve.
He should arrive soon.
Veremos uma mudança real dentro em pouco.
We will see a change in a short time.

§383. **Para dentro de** indicates movement toward the interior.

Vem cá para dentro de casa.
Come here inside the house.

§384. **Por dentro de** expresses:

a. Movement through the interior.

Passei por dentro do parque.
I passed through the inside of the park.

b. Position throughout the interior.

Por dentro de mim parecia que havia um bloco de gêlo.
It seemed there was a block of ice inside me.

§385. **Depois de** expresses posterior time.

Depois da meia-noite.
After midnight.

§386. **Desde** focuses attention not only on the point of origin, but also on the line of movement to the point of destination.

a. In space.

Desde o telhado, pode-se ver o rio.
From the roof, one can see the river.

b. In time.

Desde aí, dedicou-se à política.
From then on, he devoted himself to politics.

§387. **Diante de** expresses:

a. Position preceding in space.

Senta aqui na fila diante de mim.
Sit here in the row in front of me.

b. In the presence of. It does not give the sense of being judged, as in the case of **ante** and **perante**.

O novo cantor vai aparecer diante dêste auditório.
The new singer is going to appear before this audience.

c. Confrontation with a state of affairs.

Diante desta situação, Teles recuou.
Faced with this situation, Teles drew back.

§388. **Durante** refers to the extent of time between limits, or to an action thought of as requiring the passing of time.

Choveu durante a noite.
It rained during the night.
O povo se escondeu durante a batalha.
The people hid during the battle.

§389. **Em** forms several contractions in addition to those given under the articles and demonstrative pronouns: **noutro, n(a) água, nalgum.** It expresses:

a. Location in the interior.

Êle está no Rio.
He is in Rio.
Ela morou na França.
She lived in France.

b. Location not necessarily in the interior. The rather indefinite area includes the interior but may apply to the general vicinity as well. This preposition has largely replaced **a** in this meaning in BF.

As crianças estão na escola.
The children are at school.
Papai está em casa.
Daddy is at home.

c. Location on top of anything.

O prato está na mesa.
The plate is on the table.

d. Position on the surface, not necessarily the top.

O quadro está na parede.
The picture is on the wall.

e. Position with relation to, not exactly specified.

No outro lado, há um atalho. (*More often,* **do outro lado.**)
On the other side, there is a shortcut.

f. Movement to the interior.

Ela entrou na casa.
She entered the house.

g. Movement onto the top.

O gato pulou na mesa.
The cat jumped onto the table.

h. Movement to the surface, from the outside.

O carro jogou lama nêle.
The car threw mud on him.

i. Movement or extension around, in a few expressions.

A varanda dá volta na casa. (*More often,* à casa.)
The porch goes all around the house.

j. Position in time. (*But cf.* **a,** *in this use.*)

Nas segundas, têrças e quartas.
On Mondays, Tuesdays, and Wednesdays.
No dia cinco de junho.
On the fifth of June.
De hora em hora nas meias horas.
Every hour on the half-hour.
Na semana próxima.
Next week.

k. Extent of time within limits.

Eu faço isso em pouco tempo.
I will do this in a short time.
Isso não se faz num dia só.
That isn't done in a single day.

l. More or less vague limits of time of a state or condition.

Em criança, eu brincava com êle.
As a child, I played with him.

Tôda a cidade está em movimento.
The whole city is in movement.

m. Change or transformation. It is used after an expression of changing, especially a verb.

Quer mudar isto em trôco miudo?
Will you put this in small change?
Ela se viu transformada em dama da sociedade.
She saw herself transformed into a lady of society.

The verb **virar** does not require the preposition.

Aí ela virou onça.
Then she turned into a tiger.

n. Measure of quantity, especially increase or decrease.

O banco foi roubado em seis milhões.
The bank was robbed of six million.

o. Before the present participle. This usage is limited, relatively rare in literature, more so in BF. See §3890.

O camarada, em lá chegando, ficou aflito.   Lit
The fellow, on arriving there, became worried.
Em Deus me ajudando, vou melhorar de vida.   Lit
If God helps me, I am going to improve my behavior.

p. The language used. It may be omitted, if the language may be the direct object of the verb.

Tenho vários livros em português.
I have several books in Portuguese.
Falavam (em) bom brasileiro.
They were speaking (in) good Brazilian.

q. Passage to a place which is to be left at once.

Vamos em casa antes de ir à estação.
Let's pass by the house before going to the station.

r. Before the second member of an expression denoting series.

De hora em hora Deus melhora.
God improves things by the hour.
Isso acontece de vez em quando.
This happens from time to time.
Os ciganos andam de cidade em cidade.
The gypsies go from city to city.

s. Before an infinitive. It follows relatively few verbs, and some nouns and adjectives, mostly derived from them.

Êle hesitou em aceitar.
He hesitated to accept.
O toque consiste em manter a temperatura exata.
The important thing is to keep the exact temperature.

§390. **Entre** expresses:

a. A position in space intermediate between two others.

Entre a porta e a janela há um sofá.
Between the door and the window there is a sofa.

b. An intermediate position in time.

Tudo isso passou entre as duas e as três.
All this happened between two and three.

c. Position within a group.

A casebre fica entre árvores.
The hut is among trees.

d. Movement between or among.

Passamos entre (*also* **por entre**) **os pés de mandioca.**
We passed among manioc plants.

e. A conflict of two qualities, each of which is partly revealed.

Ela ficou na dúvida, entre furiosa e divertida.
She was in doubt, half furious, half amused.
Era um homem estranho, entre faquir e profeta.
He was a strange man, half fakir, half prophet.

§391. **Exceto,** originally a past participle used absolutely, is revealed as a preposition by the fact that it no longer expresses agreement. However, it is still followed by the nominative.

Todos foram exceto eu.
Everybody went except me.

§392. **À exceção de** has the same meaning as the preceding. The object is in the accusative.

Todos foram à exceção dêle.
All went with the exception of him.

§393. **Com a exceção de** is used as the preceding but is more frequent.

Todos foram com a exceção dêle.
All went with the exception of him.

§394. **Exclusive** is equivalent in meaning to **excluindo.** It is followed by nouns, and is SLit.

Recebeu uma quantia bem grande pelos direitos autorais, exclusive os direitos de cinema.   SLit
He received a very large quantity in royalties, not including the movie rights.

§395. **Frente a** expresses confrontation, physical or figurative.

O promotor, frente ao acusado, expôs o caso.   SLit
The prosecutor, facing the accused, explained the situation.
Frente à crise econômica, o govêrno não reagiu.   SLit
In the face of the economic crisis, the government did nothing.

§396. **À frente de** expresses:

a. Position facing.

À frente do hotel, havia um chafariz.
In front of the hotel there was a fountain.

b. Leadership.

O general foi despachado, à frente de um exército.
The general was sent at the head of an army.

c. Position in advance of.

Alguém me espera à frente do caminho.
Someone is waiting for me at the end of the road.
Miss Mato Grosso parecia estar à frente das concorrentes.
Miss Mato Grosso seemed to be ahead of her competitors.

§397. **Em frente de** expresses position before the face or front of.

O carro parou em frente da casa.
The car stopped in front of the house.

§398. **Na frente de** is interchangeable with **à frente de.**

Uma menina ia na frente da parada.
A girl was going at the head of the parade.

§399. **Para a frente de** indicates movement to the front of.

Deixaram a môça passar para a frente de fila.
They let the girl pass to the head of the line.

§400. **Pela frente de** indicates movement across the front, or across a line of vision.

Passamos pela frente de uma coisa triste—um desastre de carro.
We passed in front of a sad thing—a car wreck.

§401. **Defronte de** is a more literary variant of **em frente de.**

João chegou defronte do espelho.   **Lit**
John came in front of the mirror.
Pus os dois um defronte do outro.   **Lit**
I put the two facing each other.

§402. **Fronteiro a** is another literary equivalent of **em frente de.** The adjective expresses agreement.

Há uma colchoaria fronteira ao hotel.   **Lit**
There is a furniture store in front of the hotel.

§403. **Igual a** expresses more or less exact similarity. In substandard speech it often is heard followed by the nominative case.

Êste sapato não é igual ao par.
This shoe is not like its mate.
Fala igual a eu.   **Subst**
Speak like me.

§404. **Incluído** is usually treated as an adjective, with agreement, but sometimes as a preposition, without agreement.

Éramos sete, incluídas as crianças.
There were seven of us, including the children.
São acusados de atividades ofensivas, incluído também tentativas de rebelião. —Jornal.
They are accused of offensive activities, including attempts at rebellion.

§405. **Inclusive** is equivalent in meaning to the present participle **incluindo.**

Foram todos à festa, inclusive as crianças.
Everybody went to the party, including the children.

§406. **Ao invés de** expresses the exact contrary of another proposition.

Ao invés de estudar, ela passa o tempo namorando.
Instead of studying, she spends her time flirting.

§407. **Junto a** may express:

a. Proximity.

Havia uma cabana junto a um fio de água.
There was a cabin near a small stream of water.

b. Relationship with.

Querem pedir, junto ao govêrno, escolas para os filhos.
They want to ask the government for schools for their children.

§408. **Junto de** expresses proximity.

A cadeira está junto da porta.
The chair is beside the door.

§409. **Junto com** expresses accompaniment.

Êle foi junto com o pai, num dia de feira.
He went along with his father on a market day.

§410. **Ao lado de** expresses location, literal or figurative. In this and other phrases containing **lado,** the noun nearly always retains something of its primitive meaning.

Êle lutou na Itália, ao lado dos americanos.
He fought in Italy, at the side of the Americans.

§411. **Do lado de** is usually followed by an adverb of place, and indicates the position specified by that adverb in relation to another object.

Fica do lado de cá da casa.
It is on this side of the house.

§412. **Longe de** expresses a distant location.

Longe dos olhos, longe do coração.
Far from the eyes, far from the heart.

§413. **Ao longo de** expresses a parallel position.

Há palmeiras ao longo da praia.
There are palm trees along the beach.

§414. **Menos** expresses an exception. It is followed by the nominative.

Todos foram menos eu.
All went except me.

§415. **De modo a** expresses both manner and purpose.

Arranja seus negócios de modo a não ficar muito tempo na cidade.
Arrange your business so as not to stay long in town.

§416. **Para** is always pronounced **pra**, except in expressions of the type given in (i), where it always has two full syllables. It expresses:

a.   Direction toward a place, without presuming arrival.

Vamos para frente.
Let's go forward.
Saíram para o Rio.
The left for Rio.

b.   Movement to a place, including arrival and more or less permanent stay.

Eu vou para casa.
I am going home.
Mudou-se para a cidade.
He moved to town.

c.   Purpose, in a wide range of situations.

Eu fico para jogar.
I am staying to play.
Os russos têm-se esforçado para estabelecer a paz.
The Russians have made an effort to establish peace.

d.   The limit of future time. It is more or less equivalent to **até** in the same circumstances.

Adiei a partida para o trem da tarde.
I put off the departure until the afternoon train.
Espera para lá, eu te pago essa!
Just wait (till then), I'll pay you back.
Para quando devemos entregar esta compra?
When should we deliver this purchase?

e.   A period of future time, implying intention.

Êle vai a Copacabana para quinze dias.
He is going to Copacabana for two weeks.

f. The indirect object of a verb. It has largely replaced **a** in this use in BF. The latter is, however, still used.

Ela falou para mim.
She spoke to me.
Dá isso para aquêle cavalheiro.
Give this to that gentleman.

g. Comparison, especially after certain adverbs and adjectives.

Isso é muito caro para comprar.
This is too expensive to buy.
Êle tem bastante gasolina para a viagem.
He has enough gasoline for the trip.

h. The intended recipient of an article, the benefits of labor, etc.

Há uma carta para você.
There is a letter for you.
Eu trabalho para o patrão.
I work for the boss.

i. An undefined moment in time within the next future unit. In this case, it is pronounced in two syllables.

Êle vem só para o ano.
He isn't coming until next year.
Você vem à cidade para a semana?
Are you coming downtown next week?

j. Before an infinitive. It follows certain verbs as a general connective or may be used after any verb, to express purpose.

Êle pediu para ficarmos.
He asked us to stay.
Diga-lhes para trazerem o violão.
Tell them to bring their guitar.
Êle foi convidado para jantar.
He was invited to eat.

k. It is used following a clause and introducing an infinitive, which expresses an action succeeding the other. The infinitive expresses a consequence or continuation of the other, but not purpose.

Ela chegou de noite, para sair no dia seguinte.
She arrived at night, to leave on the following day.

l. It is used between the terms of a proportion.

A está para B como X para Y.
A is to B as X is to Y.

m. After **estar,** it indicates that the action of the infinitive is about to begin.

Êle está para partir.
He is about to leave.

§417. **Para com** expresses relationship to or treatment of a person or group. **Com** may be omitted.

Êles eram muito maus para com os fracos.
They were very bad to the weak.
Você é ruim para mim.
You are mean to me.

§418. **Para lá de** expresses:

a. Position beyond.

A casa é para lá do rio.
The house is beyond the river.

b. A greater degree.

Êste bolo é para lá de bom.
This cake is more than good.

§419. **Para cá de** expresses position nearer the speaker.

Fica um pouco para cá da cidade.
It is a little on this side of town.

§420. **Per** is an archaic survival, used only in literature, in a very few expressions:

Per si, de per si, de permeio.
By itself, each for itself, in the middle.

Todos têm que achar, cada um de per si, o caminho da vida. Lit
We all have to find, each for himself, the road of life.

§421. **Perto de** expresses proximity.
a. Literal.

Põe o guarda-chuva aí perto da porta.
Put the umbrella there by the door.

b. Figurative, i.e., approximation.

Tenho perto de duzentas páginas escritas.
I have nearly two hundred pages written.

§422. **Para perto de** expresses movement into the vicinity.

Chega aqui para perto de mim.
Come here near me.

§423. **Por perto de** expresses movement through the vicinity. **Por** may be omitted.

Ela passava sempre por perto de mim.
She always passed close by me.

§424. **Apesar de** expresses unsuccessful opposition. The noun has lost all force in this expression, so that it is purely prepositional.

Apesar de tudo, ainda gosto dêle.
In spite of everything, I still like him.
Apesar de ainda estarmos ali, começaram a brigar.
In spite of our still being there, they began to quarrel.

In the expression **com pesar de**, the noun has its full force, so that the entire phrase does not serve as a preposition.

§425. **Por.** This preposition has a vast area of usage, often over-lapping other prepositions, frequently difficult to define, often result-ing in fixed expressions who sense varies considerably. It is used to express:

a. Movement through space.

O marujo subiu pelo mastro acima.
The sailor went up the mast.
O passarinho saiu pela janela.
The bird went out through the window.
Viajamos por mar, por terra e pelo ar.
We travel by sea, by land, and through the air.
Alguma coisa passou pela nossa frente.
Something passed in front of us.
Êle jogou os ossos pelo ombro.
He threw the bones over his shoulder.

b. Location in a more or less vague area, without movement.

Não há gente por aqui?
Aren't there any people around here?

Estou ouvindo alguém aqui por perto.
I hear someone around near here.
Ali por dentro, pode ouvir o som de violões.
There on the inside you can hear the sound of guitars.

c. Location in the general vicinity of a point in time.

Por então, o irmão dela aparece.
Along about then, her brother appears.
Almoçamos lá pelas duas da tarde.
We have lunch at about two o'clock.
Pela manhã, íamos pescar.
During the morning, we went fishing.

d. Distribution by units of time.

O carro ia a sessenta quilômetros por hora.
The car was going sixty kilometers per hour.
Êle vem uma vez por semana.
He comes once a week.

e. Agent of an action.

Êste livro foi escrito por Campos.
This book was written by Campos.

f. Means.

Pela côr da luz, sabiam o que se queimava.
By the color of the light, they knew what was being burned.
Êle foi ferido por uma pedra.
He was wounded by a stone.

g. Cause, through concern or interest.

Amanhã vou à cidade por você.
Tomorrow I am going downtown because of you.

h. Exchange for.

Paguei pela comida.
I paid for the food.
Recebemos três cruzeiros pelo dólar.
We receive three cruzeiros for a dollar.

i. Substitution.

Você quer trabalhar por mim? (=no meu lugar.)
Do you want to work in my place?

Substituiram uísque nacional pelo legítimo.
They replaced domestic whisky with the real kind.

j. Cause or motive.

Talvez por isso mesmo, êle não voltou.
Perhaps for that reason, he did not return.
O comércio está estrangulado por falta de transportes.
Business is strangled for lack of transportation.
Sofremos muito pelo calor do verão. (*Or* por causa do calor.)
We suffered a lot because of the heat of summer.

k. Mode of address.

Eu trato êle por você. (=Dirijo-me a êle dizendo "você.")
I address him as *você*.
Trata-se uma moça solteira por "senhorita."
An unmarried lady is addressed as *senhorita*.

l. Identification of a noun with the subject of certain passive verbs.

Êle é tido por ladrão.
He is held to be a thief.
Alceu Amoroso Lima, mais conhecido por Tristão de Athayde.
Alceu Amoroso Lima, better known as Tristão de Athayde.

m. Duration of time. **Por** can nearly always be omitted, except when the prepositional phrase precedes the verb.

Eu esperei lá (por) muito tempo.
I waited there (for) a long time.
Por muitos anos êle serviu como delegado federal.
For many years he served as a federal congressman.

n. Purpose, following expressions of strong effort. It is now almost always replaced by **para** in this usage.

Esforçou-se por levantar a pesada tampa.   (BF=para levantar)
He made an effort to raise the heavy lid.

o. Limitless extent of a quality expressed by an adjective or adverb, followed by a verb in the subjunctive.

Por pobrezinha que seja, não vai morrer de fome.
No matter how poor she may be, she isn't going to die of hunger.

p. The origin of a quality. More often, **de** is used.

Êle é sovina por natureza.
He is a miser by nature.

q. After numerous verbs, before a noun or infinitive.

Êle acabou por deitar-se.
He finished by going to bed.
Estou esperando por José.
I am waiting for Joe.

r. In many adverbial phrases, in which the exact meaning of the preposition is not easily analyzed, but which serve to create an adverbial form of the noun or adjective.

Êle é surdo por total.
He is totally deaf.
Essas conferências são por demais longas.
These speeches are too long.
Por sua vez, o deputado falou.
In his turn, the congressman spoke.
Por fim, deixou o jôgo.
Finally, he quite gambling.
Por último se deita em cama.
At last he goes to bed.
O senhor tem carne hoje, por acaso?
Do you have any meat today, by chance?

§426. **Em prol de.** The word **prol** is used only in two expressions —this prepositional phrase and the adjective phrase **de prol.** The preposition indicates that the action is performed on someone's behalf. It is literary.

Lutaram em prol da liberdade.   **Lit**
They fought on the side of liberty.

§427. **Próximo de** is equivalent to **perto de,** but less frequently used.

a. It expresses proximity.

Vi uma latada próximo da entrada.
I saw an arbor near the entrance.

b. It may express approximation in quantity.

Convidei próximo de vinte pessoas.
I invited nearly twenty people.

§428. **Quanto a** (*also* **em quanto a**) only refers to its object, without any added meaning.

(Em) quanto aos demais, não diremos nada.
As for the others, we won't say anything.

§429. **Ao redor de** expresses physical location, encircling.

Constroem muros ao redor das casas.
They build walls around the houses.

§430. **Em redor de** is interchangeable with the preceding, but less used.

Há vários subúrbios em redor da cidade.
There are several suburbs around the city.

§431. **Em riba de** is equivalent to **em cima de**, but is substandard and regional.

O ladrão se escondeu em riba do telhado.   **Subst and Reg**
The thief hid on top of the roof.

§432. **Salvo** is equivalent to **exceto**, and like it does not take an object in the accusative.

Todos se perderam salvo o guia.
All were lost except the guide.

§433. **Segundo** cites its object as authority. It takes a pronoun object only in the third person, or in the new second, and this only rarely. Thus, no case can be established for the object.

Papai deve chegar amanhã, segundo Mamãe.
Daddy is to arrive tomorrow, according to Mother.

§434. **Sem** is a negative preposition. It expresses:

a. Lack of accompaniment.

Ela foi à igreja sem o marido.
She went to church without her husband.

b. Lack of possession.

Estou sem dinheiro.
I am without money.

c. With the infinitive, simple negation.

Entramos sem saber quem estava lá. (=não sabendo.)
We entered without knowing who was there.

d. With the infinitive, and referring to a noun, the equivalent of the negative of the past participle.

As paredes ficaram sem caiar. (=não caiadas.)
The walls remained unwhitewashed.

§435. **Senão** expresses exception. It is literary, probably driven from the spoken language by the combination **se não**.

Não teve outro remédio senão deixá-lo ficar. **Lit**
There was nothing to do but let it remain.

§436. **Sob** is used with figurative meanings, while **em baixo de** and related expressions are used with literal meanings.

Compra roupa feita sob medida.
He buys clothes made to measure.
Esta cidade fica sob o controle do exército.
This city remains under the control of the army.

§437. **Sôbre** expresses:

a. Position higher than, either on or above the upper surface.

Vimos um balão sôbre a cidade.
We saw a balloon over the city.
Põe o prato sôbre a mesa.
Put the plate on the table.

b. Movement on or over the upper surface.

O avião passou sôbre a casa.
The plane passed over the city.
A lagartixa correu sôbre a mesa.
The lizard ran over the table.

c. An equivalent of **contra**, in military usage.

O exército avançou sôbre a cidade.
The army advanced upon the city.

d. The subject of a discussion or treatise.

O conferencista falou sôbre a juventude transviada.
The lecturer spoke on juvenile delinquents.

§438. **Em tôrno de** expresses:

a. Location encircling a point.

Ainda existem florestas em tôrno da cidade.
There still exist forests around the city.

b. Movement encircling a point.

Os cães corriam em tôrno da casa.
The dogs ran around the house.

§439. **Em tôrno a** is used figuratively, with the literal meaning reserved for the preceding.

Tem havido discussões em tôrno a uma nova constituição.
There have been discussions concerning a new constitution.

§440. **Trás** expresses:

a. Position behind. It is archaic and poetic in this usage.

Trás as nuvens, o sol está brilhando.   Poetic
Behind the clouds, the sun is shining.

b. In addition to, with the connotation that the addition is excessive.

Trás haver trabalhado o dia inteiro, ainda teve que andar a pé para casa.
In addition to working all day, he still had to walk home.

§441. **Atrás de** expresses:

a. Position behind.

A cadeira está atrás da porta.
The chair is behind the door.

b. The purpose of acquiring. The usage is relatively infrequent, but colloquial.

Ela entrou no concurso atrás de publicidade.
She entered the contest in pursuit of publicity.
Ela foi para a cidade atrás de um marido.
She went to the city after a husband.

§442. **Detrás de** has the literal meaning of **atrás de** (441a), but is comparatively little used.

Está detrás da porta.
It is behind the door.

§443. **De trás de** expresses movement from a position behind and is more used than the preceding.

Êle saiu de trás da mesa.
He came out from behind the table.

§444. **Por trás de** and **por detrás de** express:

a. Movement performed in a position toward the rear.

Chegou por trás de mim e me deu um susto.
He came up behind me and gave me a fright.

b. Position within an indefinite area to the rear.

Um grupo de homens estava reunido por trás do prédio.
A group of men is gathered behind the building.

A lua surgiu por detrás da serra.
The moon rose behind the mountain.

§445. **Em volta de** expresses:

a. Position encircling a point.

Mandei fazer uma cêrca em volta do jardim.
I ordered a fence built around the garden.

b. Movement encircling a point.

O lobo corria em volta da casa.
The wolf was running around the house.

§446. Variant usages. As can readily be seen from the preceding paragraphs, the usage of prepositions frequently overlaps. Often two, three, or even four constructions are possible, sometimes used with more or less equal frequency. If one were to make a list of all possible alternatives, it would be very long. Often some of the variants are largely literary in Brazil, sometimes they represent the usage of Portugal, sometimes all are more or less current in BF. One strong tendency may be noted in BF—the steady erosion of the use of the preposition a. The following list gives a few of the alternative constructions which illustrate the range of variation.

Está à venda.	**Está em venda.**	It is on sale.
Está a salvo.	**Está em salvo.**	He is safe.
Sair a campo.	**Sair em campo.**	To enter the lists.
Pela vida afora.	**Pela vida em fora.**	Throughout life.
Primeiro a sair.	**Primeiro em sair.**	First to go out.
Chegar à cidade.	**Chegar na cidade.**	To arrive in the city.
A casa ao lado.	**A casa do lado.**	The house next door.
Às vezes.	**Por vezes.**	⎱ At times.
	Algumas vezes.	⎰
Ao redor.	**Em redor.**	Around.
Ao fim de.	**No fim de.**	At the end of.

À frente do hotel.	Em frente do hotel. Na frente do hotel.	⎫ ⎬ In front of the ⎭ hotel.
Duas vezes ao dia.	Duas vezes por dia.	Twice a day.
Andamos à noite.	Andamos de noite.	We walk at night.
Êle puxa ao pai.	Êle puxa pelo pai.	He takes after his father.
Vai aos domingos.	Vai nos domingos.	He goes on Sundays.
De janela para janela.	De janela em janela.	From window to window.
Visto de frente.	Visto pela frente.	Seen from the front.
Deu parte na polícia.	Deu parte à polícia.	He reported to the police.
Êle segurou na enxada.	Êle segurou a enxada.	He held the hoe.
Vamos em frente.	Vamos para frente.	Let's go forward.
Em três de maio.	A três de maio. No dia três de maio.	⎫ On the third of ⎭ May.
Habito na casa.	Habito a casa.	I live in the house.
Falou a mim.	Falou para mim.	He spoke to me.
Espera até lá.	Espera para lá.	Wait until then.
Ontem de manhã.	Ontem pela manhã. Ontem à manhã. Na manhã de ontem. Pela manhã de ontem.	⎫ ⎬ Yesterday ⎭ morning.

NEGATION

General rules of negation

§447. Negation before the verb. The most general rule in the use of negative expressions in Portuguese is that in any negative clause containing a verb, a negative word must precede the verb.

Não vou.
I am not going.
Êle não tinha visto o gato.
He had not seen the cat.
Nunca encontrei com êle.
I never met him.

§448. The negative and object pronouns. If there is a personal pronoun object of the verb, it precedes the verb immediately, separating it from the negative word. Nothing else may separate **não** from the verb, but other negatives may often be separated from it by several words.

João não me viu.
John did not see me.
Ninguém, fôsse quem fôsse, podia fazer as pazes entre aquêles dois.
No one, no matter who it was, could make peace between those two.

§449. Negatives which precede the verb. If the negative serves as the subject of the clause, it logically precedes the verb, and no further negation is necessary.

Ninguém sabia que eu estava aqui.
No one knew that I was here.
Nenhum dos dois chegou antes das seis.
Neither of the two came before six.

§450. Negatives which follow the verb. If the negative serves as the object or nominative complement of the verb, it logically follows. If no other negative precedes the verb, **não** must be used.

Não é ninguém.
It isn't anyone.
Não vi nenhuma criança em casa dêle.
I didn't see any child in his house.

§451. *Negatives which may precede or follow.* The negative adverbs may either precede or follow the verb. A prepositional phrase containing a negative may also be placed in either position. In unusual cases, an object may precede or a subject follow. In all cases, if no other negative precedes the verb, **não** must be used before it.

Nunca estive lá.
I have never been there.
Não estive lá nunca.
I have never been there.
Em caso algum farei o que você quer.
In no case will I do what you wish.

§452. *Negative adjectives and nouns.* The negative which precedes the verb may be an adjective, or even a noun.

Com você é impossível discutir nada.
With you it is impossible to discuss anything.
Na completa impossibilidade de fazer nada, vou desistir.
In the complete impossibility of doing anything, I'm giving up.

However, a better construction, and much more used, is to say **qualquer coisa, qualquer pessoa,** for **nada, ninguém.**

Com você é impossível discutir qualquer coisa.
With you it is impossible to discuss anything.

§453. *Use of two or more negatives.* The addition of more negatives to an expression does not change its negative character. There must be one negative before the verb, but the others may be placed wherever the logic of the sentence permits.

Nunca esperei que ninguém fizesse nada para mim.
I never expected that anyone would do anything for me.
Não encontramos nunca nenhuma caça que ninguém quisesse matar.
We never ran across any game that anyone wished to kill.

§454. *The negative after comparisons.* In comparisons in which the second element includes all others of a class, the negative is used.

Êle sabe nadar melhor do que ninguém.
He knows how to swim better than anyone else.
Êle nada melhor do que alguém. (=certa pessoa.)
He swims better than someone.
Agora ela chora mais do que nunca.
Now she cries more than ever.
Êle sabe fazer um discurso como ninguém.
He knows how to make a speech like nobody else.

Usage of the various negative words

§455. **Não.** This is the general adverb of negation. In speech, when unstressed, it weakens in pronunciation to **nõu, nõ, num,** or may have its full orthographic value.

a. It may be used alone.

Você vai comigo? —Não.
Are you going with me? No.
Não! Menino, não faz isso!
No, child, don't do that!

b. It may be followed by the verb of the question. A negative answer to a question containing a verb often includes the verb, along with the negative. The verb is used in the same tense and number as in the question, but the person is the one required by logic. If the verb is made up of more than one word, the first auxiliary only is used. This type of answer carries no greater emphasis than the simple negative.

Você abriu a porta dos fundos? —Não abri.
Did you open the back door? No.

c. **Não** before and after the verb. To express emphasis, a second **não** is used, after the verb.

O senhor gosta daquela môça? —Não gosto, não.
Do you like that girl? No, I don't.

d. **Não** after the verb only. In BF, this second negative is often used following the verb of reply, with the first negative omitted. The word used may be emphatic or not. The first negative is most often omitted in short clauses, such as short answers to questions and in exclamations.

Tem fósforos aqui? —Tem, não.
Are there matches here? No, there aren't.

Você foi à festa? —Fui, não.
Did you go to the party? No, I didn't.

e. Position of object pronouns with **não**. The object pronoun is placed between the word **não** and the verb. It is not placed before the negative in subordinate clauses, as is often done in Lusitanian Portuguese.

O caixeiro falou com um homem que não me conhece. (*Not . . . que me não conhece.*)
The cashier spoke to a man who doesn't know me.

f. Position of **não** with words other than verbs. When **não** is used with an adverb, pronoun, or noun, without a verb, it follows such words, separated by a slight pause.

Agora, não.
Not now.
O senador é político, o Dr. Viegas, não.
The senator is a politician, Dr. Viegas is not.
Ela não quer, e eu também não.
She doesn't want to, and I don't either.

g. Position of **não** with verb understood. However, if a verb has been previously expressed and its meaning is assumed in a second expression, the negative precedes other words in such phrases as the following.

Êle entrou no prédio escuro, mas não sem medo.
He entered the dark building, but not without fear.
Ela usava o chapéu preto, não o azul.
She was wearing the black hat, not the blue one.
Somos brasileiros, não americanos.
We are Brazilians, not Americans.
Êle chega na quarta, se não antes.
He arrives on Wednesday, if not before.

h. Pleonastic **não**. There is a very limited use of a redundant, or pleonastic, **não** following certain verbs, such as "fear," "imagine," etc., although the meaningless negative is usually omitted there.

Imagina o susto que não levei.
Imagine the fright that I got.
Eu temo que êle não faça uma tolice.
I am afraid he will commit some foolishness.

i. **Já não.** This expression is rare in BF. Its meaning is usually expressed by **não ... mais.**

> **O Pedro já não mora aqui.**
> Peter no longer lives here.
> **O Pedro não mora mais aqui.**
> Peter doesn't live here any more.

The two words usually retain their separate meanings in BF, even when used together.

> **Já não lhe contei? (=Não lhe contei já?)**
> Haven't I already told you?

j. **Não é.** The expression **não é** is used following a statement, to request the agreement of the hearer. In BF, in a conversation of normal speed, and when there is no emphasis on the expression, it is pronounced **né.** Except for the pronunciation, it generally does not vary. It may be used after any tense of a verb. However, after a preterite tense **não foi?** is also possible. The word **assim,** sometimes added to the expression in Portugal, is not used in Brazil.

> **Êsse carro é novo, não é?**
> That car is new, isn't it?
> **Wilmar conseguiu um emprego, né?**
> Wilmer got a job, didn't he?
> **Houve um incêndio, não é?**
> There was a fire, wasn't there?
> **Você se escondeu, não foi?**
> You hid, didn't you?

A few other common verbs may be used in the question instead of é, following a statement in which they have been used.

> **Você está ainda naquela casa, não está?**
> You are still in that house, aren't you?
> **Houve uma greve, não houve?**
> There was a strike, wasn't there?

k. **Pois não.** This expression is affirmative, equivalent to **claro, naturalmente,** in answer to a suggestion or request.

> **O senhor quer me dar um auxìliozinho? —Pois não.**
> Will you give me a little help? Of course.
> **Vamos comer? —Pois não, estou com fome.**
> Shall we eat? Sure, I'm hungry.

§456. **Algum** is a negative adjective only when it follows a noun. It may be used in the negative in the singular only.

De modo algum. (=De nenhum modo.)
    By no means.

§457. **Jamais** is a negative adverb. It may be placed before the verb or after it if a negative precedes. It is comparatively rare in BF, much less used than **nunca.**

Jamais fiz uma coisa dessas.
    I never did a thing like that.
Não vi tal coisa jamais.
    I never saw such a thing.

a. **Jamais** may follow a verb which is not preceded by a negative, but it does not have a negative meaning in this case.

Você deve me visitar, se fôr jamais ao Recife.
    You should visit me, if you ever go to Recife.

b. It is used without negative force in questions, even preceding the verb. The situation is such that it does not matter appreciably whether the word is negative or not.

Jamais conheceu o Sr. Pontes?
    Did you ever meet Mr. Pontes?

c. In BF, this usage of **jamais** is also rare. It is replaced by **já** with past tenses, by **alguma vez** with the present, and with the future by the latter or **algum dia.**

Você já foi à Bahia?
    Have you ever been to Bahia?
Se fôr alguma vez, vai gostar.
    If you ever go, you will like it.
Você passa alguma vez pelo Méier?
    Do you ever pass through Meier?
Você vem outra vez ao Brasil algum dia?
    Are you ever coming back to Brazil?

§458. **Nada.** This is a neuter pronoun, invariable in form, equal in meaning to **nenhuma coisa.**

Não quero nada.
    I don't want anything.
Nada fará com que o Gilberto fique aqui.
    Nothing will make Gilbert stay here.

a. **Nada** followed by a partitive. It is often followed by **de** before a noun, pronoun, or adjective, with a partitive meaning.

Não há nada de novo.
There is nothing new.
Não estou de acôrdo com nada disto.
I'm not in agreement with any of that.
Nada de violência, por favor.
No violence, please.
Êsse homem não tem nada de santo. (=Ele não é santo.)
This man doesn't have any characteristics of a saint.

b. **Nada** modified by an adjective. However, if the adjective actually modifies **nada**, it follows without a preposition.

Êsse homem não tem nada santo. (=Não possui nenhum objeto santo.)
That man doesn't have anything holy.
Aqui não se encontra nada bom.
Here you don't find anything good.

c. **Nada** as an adverb. This word may be used adverbially, with the meaning **em nenhum grau.**

Isso não nos ajuda nada.
That doesn't help us a bit.
Ela não é nada feia.
She is not a bit ugly.

d. **Nada** as a noun. This word may be used as a masculine noun, with a definite article.

Devemos respeitar um homem que saiu do nada e pôde subir até a posição dêle.
We must respect a man who rose from nothing and could rise to his position.

e. Emphatic pronunciation. In very emphatic usage, this word is often pronounced with two *d*'s, the second slightly fricative. It may be repeated once or twice.

Não vou te dar nad-da, nad-da, nad-da.
I am not going to give you anything at all.

f. **Qual nada.** This expression is used for emphatic dissent and is equivalent to **de modo nenhum.**

Eu vou lhe pagar o trabalho que fêz. —Qual nada!
I am going to pay you for the work you did. By no means.

§459. **Nem.** This word is most often a conjunction, the negative of **ou.**

a. Use following **não** and a verb. It follows the negative verb, with or without intervening words, connecting a second element which is also negative. This second element may be a noun, a pronoun, a verb, an adverb, or a phrase.

> **Não vi Paulo nem Pedro.**
> I did not see Paul nor Peter.
> **Não conheço nem êle nem ela.**
> I don't know him nor her.
> **Não fumo nem bebo.**
> I don't smoke nor drink.
> **Não vou cedo nem tarde.**
> I am not going, either early or late.

Before a verb, it may be replaced by **e não.**

> **Não fumo e não bebo.**
> I don't smoke and I don't drink.

b. Repetition of **nem.** It may be repeated as many times as necessary. It may be used immediately after the negative verb and repeated before each following term, or it may be used only before the last one.

> **Não gosto nem de peixe, nem de polvo, nem de lula.**
> I don't like either fish, octopus, or squid.
> **Não gosto de peixe, de polvo, nem de lula.**
> I don't like fish, octopus, nor squid.

c. **Nem** after **sem.** Nem is used to connect two words after **sem,** or two clauses after **sem que.**

> **Ficou sem comer nem beber.**
> He neither ate nor drank.
> **É uma criança sem pai nem mãe.**
> It is a child without father or mother.
> **Fizemos o serviço sem que ninguém se queixasse nem reclamasse.**
> We did the work without anyone's complaining nor protesting.

d. **Nem** used instead of **não.** Before **muito, tanto, todo,** and **sempre, nem** is used instead of **não. Não** may be used following these words, but only in the answer to a statement or question which contains one of these words.

Você tem muita sorte. —Nem muita, *or* **muita, não.**
You have a lot of luck. Not much.
Todos vão à igreja. —Nem todos, *or* **todos, não.**
All go to church. Not all.
É bom ser rico. —Nem sempre.
It is good to be rich. Not always.

e. **Nem . . . nem.** The use of two (or more) examples of this word makes a correlative conjunction. The first occurrence may be before the main verb, replacing **não.** Whether used here or elsewhere, the two or more elements which are joined together must be of the same grammatical type.

Êle nem nada nem mergulha.
He neither swims nor dives.
Nem você nem eu devia estar aqui.
Neither you nor I ought to be here.
Não vou nem cedo nem tarde.
I am not going either early or late.

f. **Nem** as an adverb. When used before a verb, noun, pronoun, adverb, or phrase, and not serving as a connective with a preceding negative element, **nem** is adverbial, with the meaning "not even."

Wenceslau estava tão triste que nem comia.
Wenceslaus was so sad that he didn't even eat.
Nem Hitler faria uma dessas.
Not even Hitler would do a thing like that.
Nem eu sou tão ruim como êle.
Not even I am as bad as he.
Não vou nem de noite.
I am not going, even at night.
Se você não reagir, amanhã nem avisar êle manda.
If you don't protest, tomorrow he won't even let you know.
Não me deu nem uma palavra.
He didn't say a single word to me.

g. Adverbial use after a negative expression. If **nem** connects a negative verb or other word or expression with a following one, if can only be a conjunction. If the meaning desired is adverbial, it must be expressed by **nem ao menos, nem mesmo,** or **nem sequer.** This last is little used in BF. Its second word may be separated from **nem** by one or more words.

O rapaz não servia nem ao menos para entregar roupa nem carregar água.
The boy was no good even to deliver clothes or carry water.

The second **nem** in this case may be replaced by **ou**.

These longer expressions may be used, even where **nem** alone would have this meaning, to give more emphasis.

Nem (mesmo) o presidente pode revogar a lei.
Not even the president can revoke the law.
Andamos o dia inteiro e não vimos nem uma paca (sequer).
We walked all day and we didn't see even a paca.

h. **Que nem.** This expression, following a verb or in a situation where a verb is understood, is equivalent to **tanto como** or **mais que**.

Êle apanhava que nem cachorro.
He was beaten worse than a dog.
O covarde corria que nem um gamo.
The coward ran faster than a deer.

i. **Nem que.** This is a conjunction, the negative of **mesmo se**. It is followed regularly by the subjunctive.

Eu não queria ser velho, nem que fôsse também rico.
I wouldn't want to be old, not even if I were also rich.

§460. **Nenhum.** Either an adjective or a pronoun, this word is the negative of **algum** and might be considered in its use as an adjective as an emphatic negative article.

Não tenho nenhum chapéu. (*Emphatic.*)
I don't have any hat.
Não tenho chapéu. (*Unemphatic.*)
I have no hat.

a. **Nenhum** in the plural. The use of this word in the plural is infrequent, since no real difference exists between the singular and the plural.

Não tenho nenhuns conhecimentos nêste campo. (*Or* **nenhum conhecimento.**)
I have no knowledge in this field.

b. **Nenhum** after the noun. If this word follows the noun, it becomes more emphatically negative. Only the singular may be so used.

Não estou vendo homem nenhum.
I don't see any man.

c. **Nenhum** as a pronoun. As a pronoun, this word refers to an individual or a group previously mentioned, or understood from context. Or, perhaps more accurately, it causes the verb to deny that a statement is true of any individual of a group. It is generally singular.

> **Não posso casar com nenhum dos dois.**
> I can't marry either of the two.
> **Estou a nenhum. (=nenhum dinheiro.)**   **Gir**
> I am broke.

d. Difference between **nenhum** and **nem um**. These two expressions are often indistinguishable, and in most cases the meaning would be exactly the same. However, when the word **nem** is stressed, **nem um** has a different meaning.

> **Não tenho nem um pão. (Não tenho nem ao menos um pão, muito menos carne, etc.)**
> I haven't even a loaf of bread.
> **Não tenho nenhum pão. (Estou na completa falta de pão, embora possa ter carne, etc.)**
> I haven't any bread.

§461. **Ninguém** is a pronoun referring only to persons, always singular in form, and negative. The meaning is **nenhuma pessoa**.

> **Com o govêrno ninguém pode.**
> Nobody can fight the government.

Ninguém is ordinarily treated as masculine but is construed as feminine if the reference is clearly to a female person.

> **Estive na praia a manhã tôda, mas não vi ninguém que fôsse bonita.**
> I was at the beach all morning, but I didn't see anyone who was pretty.

§462. **Nunca.** This is a negative adverb, a synonym of **jamais** in the negative uses of the latter. The two are interchangeable in the negative usages, but **nunca** is much more frequent.

a. Position in the clause. It may be placed before the verb or, if **não** or another negative precedes, after it.

> **Nunca fui a Brasília.**
> **Não fui nunca a Brasília.**
> I have never gone to Brasilia.

For still more emphasis, **nunca** may be shifted to the very end of any relatively simple clause.

Não fui a Brasília nunca.

b. **Nunca** preceding for balance. If other negative words are to follow the verb, **nunca** tends to precede it, to give better balance to the clause.

Nunca encontrei ninguém lá.
I never met anyone there.

c. Use of both **nunca** and **jamais**. For especially strong emphasis, one may use both **nunca** and **jamais**.

Nunca jamais nesta vida quero ver aquela cara outra vez.
Never, never in my life do I want to see that face again.

§463. **Sem** is a negative preposition. It requires negative words following it but does not require a negation before the verb which precedes it.

Eu vou sem esperar por ninguém.
I am going without waiting for anyone.

a. **Sem** before a verb. If **sem** precedes an infinitive, or **sem que** a conjugated verb, no other negative is required before the verb when other negatives follow.

Passamos pela sala sem ver ninguém.
We passed through the living room without seeing anyone.
Fizemos o serviço sem que o freguês se queixasse de nada.
We did the work without the customer's complaining of anything.

b. The conjunction **sem que**. This conjunction is invariably followed by the subjunctive of the verb.

§464. **Senão**. The preposition and conjunction **senão** is almost unused in BF. One sometimes hears the word used as a noun, in the sense of **defeito**.

a. As a preposition. Usage is rare.

Não teve outro remédio, senão deixar o homem ficar lá.
There was nothing to do but let the man remain there.
Não teve mais remédio do que deixar o homem ficar lá.   **BF**

b. As a conjunction. It is archaic, if not obsolete, as a conjunction introducing an affirmative clause which rejects the proposition stated in the previous clause. It is here replaced by **mas**, occasionally emphasized by a following **sim**.

> **Não travou relações com os intelectuais, mas (sim) com os grandes financeiros.**
> He didn't establish relations with the intellectuals, but with the great financiers.

§465. **Tampouco** is an adverb, the negative of **também**. It is obsolescent in BF, being usually replaced by **também não**.

a. **Tampouco** used with a verb. Like other negative adverbs, **tampouco** requires a negative preceding the verb, if it follows.

> **Eu tampouco quero ir.**
> I don't want to go either.
> **Eu não quero ir, tampouco.**
> I don't want to go either.

b. Without a verb. It does not require another negative.

> **Carlos não quer. —Eu tampouco.** *Or* **Tampouco eu.**
> Charles doesn't want to. I don't either.

c. Use of **também não**. In this expression, now generally used for **tampouco**, each word takes its normal place in the clause.

> **Carlos não quer. —Eu também não.**
> Charles doesn't want to. I don't either.
> **Êle também não estava aqui.**
> He wasn't here either.
> **Aníbal não foi também.**
> Anibal didn't go either.

§466. Negative slang words. There are a number of words used in slang as equivalents of regular negative words. Among these are **neca** and **neres**, used either singly or together, to mean **nada**.

> **Êsse sujeito não sabe neca de neres do assunto.**
> That guy doesn't know a blasted thing about the matter.

Other expressions show vigorous denial.

> **Ela é bonita. —Bonita, uma ova! (Não é nada bonita.)**
> She is pretty. Pretty, my foot!
> **Você é quem vai fazer isso. —Eu, uma vírgula. (Não vou.)**
> You are the one who is going to do that. Like fun I am.

§467. Negations with no negative words. A number of expressions have acquired negative meaning from the circumstances of their use, although they contain no negative word. Others have probably lost the negative word they once possessed, since they were used in circumstances in which negation was self-evident.

Eu sei lá. (=Eu não sei.)
 I don't know.
Eu tenho lá palacete. (=Eu não tenho, como você bem sabe.)
 I don't have a mansion.
Absolutamente! (De nenhuma maneira.)
 Absolutely not!
Você aceita bombons? —Obrigado. (=Não aceito.)
 Will you have some chocolates? No, thank you.
Perdão, eu lhe pisei o pé. —Tem importância. (=Não tem importância.)
 Pardon me, I stepped on your foot. It doesn't matter.

RELATIVE PRONOUNS

§468. General considerations. A relative pronoun refers to a noun or pronoun previously mentioned and introduces a subordinate clause which modifies the antecedent. The relative pronoun itself may be used as the subject of the subordinate clause, as the object of the verb, or as the object of a preposition. The use of the subjunctive is dealt with in §§242 ff. Some of the relative adverbs may, at times serve as relative pronouns. However, they are considered with the adverbs, §352.

§469. The relative pronoun **que.** This is by far the most frequently used of the relative pronouns. It may be used as subject or object in the relative clause, be singular or plural without change of form, and may refer to persons or things.

Olha o homem que está nadando lá longe.
Look at the man who is swimming away out there.
É o mesmo que eu vi ontem na cidade.
It is the same one that I saw yesterday downtown.
É uma telha que caiu daquela obra.
It is a tile that fell from that construction.

a. Agreement of verb after **que.** The verb agrees in person and number with the antecedent of **que,** when the relative is its subject.

Passaram vários cachorros que perseguiam um gato.
There passed several dogs that were chasing a cat.
Nós, que estudamos tôdas as noites, vamos bem na escola.
We, who study every night, are getting along well in school.
Fui eu que fiz isso.
It was I who did that.

b. Use of a preposition with **que.** Any of the short prepositions may be used before **que.** The preposition must be placed before the relative, not at the end of the clause. After a preposition, **que** does not refer to persons.

A casa a que vou é de meu tio.
The house that I am going to is my uncle's.
Essa é a cidade em que meu tio mora.
That is the city in which my uncle lives.
Esta é a razão por que desisti da idéia.
This is the reason for which I gave up the idea.

c. Not used with long prepositions. With a preposition consisting of more than one word, and even some one-word prepositions, e.g., **segundo**, **que** is not used. One may use **o qual**. See §475, below.

d. Omission of prepositions with **que**. BF shows strong resistance to the use of any preposition with a relative pronoun. The lowest levels of speech do not use them at all. The higher levels tend to avoid them as much as possible without entering into noticeable conflict with the accepted norms of the literary language. There are several means of avoiding their use.

(1) A verb which requires a preposition before a noun or pronoun loses it and treats **que** as a direct object, on all levels of the spoken language.

Eu gosto de você.
I love you.
Você é a pessoa que eu gosto.
You are the person that I love.
Êle precisa de uma chave.
He needs a key.
A coisa que êle precisa é uma chave.
The thing he needs is a key.

(2) If a preposition is required by the sense of the sentence, it cannot be omitted without destroying the clarity of meaning. The lower levels of speech place the preposition at the end of the clause, followed by a pronoun object.

Êsse é o cavalo em que eu vou.   Lit
That is the horse that I am going on.
Êsse é o cavalo que vou nêle.   Inc
That is the horse that I am going on.
Era essa a faca que o cangaceiro não se apartava dela.   Inc
That is the knife from which the bandit was never separated.

(3) If the sense remains reasonably clear without the preposition, it is simply omitted.

Aquela é a môça em que falam tanto na cidade.   Lit
That is the girl that they talk about so much in the city.
Aquela é a môça que falam tanto.   BF
That is the girl they talk about so much.

(4) More careful speakers tend to avoid such prepositions by a different construction of the sentence.

Êsse é o cavalo que eu vou montar.   BF
That is the horse that I am going to ride.
Aquela é a môça que é tão falada na cidade.
That is the girl who is talked about so much in the city.
A casa onde eu vou é de meu tio.
The house where I am going is my uncle's.
Essa é a cidade onde meu tio mora.
That is the city where my uncle lives.
Esta é a razão de eu desistir da idéia.
This is the reason for my giving up the idea.

e. **Que** not omitted. The relative pronoun **que** is never omitted when it refers to a noun or pronoun.

É o homem que eu vi.
It is the man (that) I saw.

f. Omission of the antecedent. In certain expressions the antecedent of **que**, when it would be the object of the preceding verb, may be omitted. **Que** is followed by the infinitive in such cases.

Não há [nada] que fazer.
There is nothing to be done.
Vamos ver se temos [alguma coisa] que comer.
Let's see if we have something to eat.

g. Use of **é que.** This expression is at times added after the subject, with no additional meaning, but simply to call attention to the subject.

Nós é que erramos.
It was we who made a mistake.
Vocês é que apanharam.
It was you who were beaten.

§470. **O que** as a neuter relative. This relative is invariable in form. It refers to the previous expression, idea, etc., but never to a noun.

Ouvi duas velhas falando mal de meu irmão, o que não gostei nada.
I heard two old women speaking ill of my brother, which I didn't
like at all.

§471. **O que**, demonstrative plus relative. This should not be confused with the preceding. It consists of the demonstrative pronoun
o, which may vary for gender and take plural forms in the masculine
and feminine, followed by the relative pronoun **que**. **O** may be either
the subject or the object of another verb.

Escuta o que estou lhe dizendo.
Listen to what I am telling you.
Olha as que estão atravessando a rua.
Look at the ones who are crossing the street.
O que eu vi foi uma ferradura.
What I saw was a horseshoe.

When the demonstrative is a subject, both it and the relative
are often omitted in BF.

[O que] eu queria era ver a cara dêle.
What I wanted was to see his face.
Eu vi foi uma ferradura.
What I saw was a horseshoe.

§472. Use of **só** as a relative pronoun. This word is often used in
expressions of the type given in the preceding section. It is equivalent
in meaning to **tudo o que** in this construction.

Eu só queria era ver a cara dêle.
All I wanted was to see his face.

The word is used pronominally, but without relative use, in
another very common expression. The meaning is simply **tudo**.

Que mais o senhor queria? —É só.
What else did you want? That is all.

§473. **Quem** as a relative pronoun. This relative is either singular
or plural without change of form. It refers to persons only.

a. As a simple relative, it is used in BF only after short prepositions, but is generally avoided even in this situation.

O homem para quem eu dei a chave, fugiu.
The man to whom I gave the key ran away.
É aquêle o rapaz em quem você confia?
Is that the boy whom you trust?

Without a preposition, **que** is used.

É aquêle o rapaz que inspira confiança em você?
Is that the boy who inspires confidence in you?

b. **Quem** with antecedent included. This usage is very frequent in BF. Its verb is always in the third person, usually singular, but the plural is also heard.

Quem fêz isso fui eu.
The one who did that was I.
Não sou eu quem puxa o saco.
I am not the one who flatters.
Quem fizeram bem foram os músicos.
The ones who performed well were the musicians.

The presumed antecedent included in the word may be negative.

Não haverá quem me ajude?
Isn't there anyone who will help me?

§474. The relative possessive **cujo**. This word is not used in BF. The construction of sentences in BF is such that no need is felt of a possessive relative.

O Sr. Pires é o homem cuja casa eu comprei.   Lit
Mr. Pires is the man whose house I bought.
O Sr. Pires era o dono da casa que comprei.   Lit and BF
Mr. Pires was the owner of the house I bought.
O Sr. Pires é o homem que eu comprei a casa dêle.   Subst
Mr. Pires is the man that I bought his house.

§475. The relative **o qual**. This relative is literary, or at the least, semi-literary. It is seldom heard in conversation, but is used somewhat in writing. It is used principally following long prepositions, where **que** and **quem** are not used. It changes for gender and number (**a qual, os quais, as quais**), but can hardly be said to be used to clarify an antecedent through agreement. It is used in writing:

a. After a long preposition.

São estas as regras, segundo as quais não podemos adiar o concurso.
Lit
These are the rules, according to which we cannot put off the contest.
Chegamos ao hotel, enfrente do qual estava o carro do delegado.
Lit
We arrived at the hotel in front of which was the police chief's car.

b. In parenthetical expressions. The usual situation is that the parenthetical expression refers to a part of the individuals mentioned by the noun previously used.

> **O exame foi administrado a todos os rapazes, alguns dos quais não puderam acabar.**
> The examination was administered to all the boys, some of whom were unable to finish.

c. Replacement of **o qual**. Elsewhere, **que** generally replaces **o qual**, practically always in BF, usually even in writing.

§476. **Quanto.** This relative includes its antecedent and is equivalent to **todo o que.** It may be used as a neuter, or masculine or feminine in either number.

> **Você pode tomar quanto quiser.**
> You may take as much as you wish.
> **Vou contar a notícia a quantos encontrar na rua.**
> I am going to tell the news to everybody I meet on the street.

§477. The interrogative words. These include **que** (and **o que**), **quanto, quem, qual, onde** (**donde, aonde**), **quando, como, por que, cadê,** and **hein.** Some of these are easily used and present no difficulty. A few of them require some explanation.

a. **Que** is either a pronoun or an adverb. It becomes **quê** when stressed.

> **Que é isso?**
> What is that?
> **Que carro é seu?**
> Which car is yours?

b. **O que** is a pronoun only. It may replace **que** at any time as a pronoun. It is more often used when the speaker wishes to give emphasis to the interrogative. At other times, the rhythm of the phrase is the decisive factor. It becomes **o quê** when stressed.

> **O que foi?**
> What was it?
> **Você fêz o quê?**
> You did what?

c. **Quem** is a pronoun referring to persons. The same form is used for singular and plural.

> **Quem fêz isso?**
> Who did that?
> **De quem são as luvas?**
> Whose gloves are they?
> **Quem foram que fizeram isso?**
> Who were they that did that?

d. **Qual** is a pronoun referring to things. In BF it is sometimes used as an adjective also. It has a plural **quais.**

> **Qual é seu nome?**
> What is your name?

Quais são as cidades principais do Brasil?
What are the principal cities of Brazil?
Qual casa é sua?   Subst
Which house is yours?

e. **Cadê** (with some regional variants in pronunciation) is a popular substandard interrogative equivalent to **onde está**, frequently heard among educated persons. Grammarians prefer **que é de**, an artificial correction.

Cadê o João?   Subst
Where is John?

f. **Hein** is pronounced with a nasal form of the diphthong **éi**, otherwise unknown in the speech of Rio de Janeiro. It is used to ask for a repetition of what was said and in similar requests for an answer. It is occasionally a substitute for **não é**.

Hein? Que foi que você disse?
Huh? What did you say?
Quer me trazer êsse brinquedo, hein?
Will you bring me that toy, huh?
Você ia fugir, hein?
You were going to run away, were you?

§478. Question order. The order of an interrogative sentence varies considerably with the type of question.

a. Without an interrogative word. Such a question is nearly always expressed in the same order as a declarative sentence in BF. Only the intonation indicates interrogation.

Eu não lhe disse?
Didn't I tell you?
O senhor falou com meu amigo?
Did you speak to my friend?
Aquêle português que é dono do açougue é do Minho?
Is that Portuguese who is the owner of the butcher shop from Minho?

b. With an interrogative word as the subject. When an interrogative pronoun is the subject of the verb, or the noun subject is modified by an interrogative adjective, the order is also that of a declarative sentence.

Quem fêz isso?
Who did that?

Quantas pessoas foram à festa?
How many people went to the party?

c. With an interrogative word as the object. There are several possibilities in this case. If the subject is a pronoun, it may precede or follow the verb if there is no likelihood of confusion.

Que acha você?
What do you think?
O que você acha?
What do you think?

But if both subject and object are persons, the subject must precede the verb.

Quem você viu?
Whom did you see?

For emphasis on the subject, it may be placed before the interrogative.

Você o que acha?
What do you think?

The subject is more likely to follow the verb if it is a noun, especially if it is modified.

Quantos comprou o farmacêutico?
How many did the druggist buy?

d. With an interrogative adverb. In general, the situation is the same as the preceding. However, there is a somewhat greater probability of placing the subject after the verb.

Para onde você vai?
Where are you going?
Para onde vai você?
Where are you going?
Onde fica a Avenida Copacabana?
Where is Copacabana Avenue?
Como você quebrou a janela?
How did you break the window?
Quando êle viu você?
When did he see you?

e. Subject precedes the predicate. There is no tendency to place the subject after a predicate complement in questions, even when the subject follows the verb. Such a question as **É bonita a moça?** would indicate only that the subject was an afterthought.

f.   Order with compound verbs. In questions in which the verb is in a perfect tense, or in the progressive form of any tense, or in the passive voice, the subject nearly always precedes the verb. It may not follow the auxiliary, nor the entire verb phrase, in BF, except in cases in which a declarative sentence might be expressed in a different order.

> **Você já tinha feito a barba?**
>   Had you already shaved?
> **Aquela casa velha e estragada que vimos no ano passado está caindo já?**
>   Is that old ruined house we saw last year falling down by now?

§479.   Use of **é que** in questions. Any interrogative word may be followed by **é que**, after which the question takes the order of a declarative sentence. Long questions, and those whose subjects are long, are especially likely to use this construction, but it is also the most usual one even in short questions.

> **De quem é que você está falando?**
>   Of whom are you speaking?
> **Como é que uma mulher de respeito pôde fazer uma coisa dessas?**
>   How could a respectable woman do a thing like that?
> **Quando é que as eleições vêm de novo?**
>   When do the elections come again?

a.   Tense of **é que**. This expression may be used in the present tense, no matter what the tense of the main verb is. However, when the question is in the preterite, this expression very often is also put in the preterite.

> **Que foi que o Saci fêz?**
>   What did the Saci do?
> **Como foi que a luta terminou?**
>   How did the wrestling come out?
> **Quando é que êle foi embora?**
>   When did he go away?
> **Que é que você tem feito?**
>   What have you been doing?
> **Que é que êle estava fazendo?**
>   What was he doing?

b. **É que** without an interrogative word. This expression may be used to begin a question which does not have an interrogative. The meaning is, in this case, **é verdade que.** The expression is less frequent here than after an interrogative.

> **Por que você não nada? É que não sabe?**
> Why don't you swim? Is it because you don't know how?

§480. **Questions of conjecture.** Several of the commoner verbs and auxiliaries are used directly in the future tense at times in questions of conjecture, but for the most part such questions begin with **será que.** This tense form is the usual one, but occasionally the conditional is used before a past tense.

> **As mulheres estarão prontas?**
> Do you suppose the women are ready?
> **Haverá alguma visita em casa dêles?**
> Do you suppose there is a visitor at their house?
> **Será que os operários vão fazer greve?**
> Do you think the workers will go on strike?
> **Será (*or* seria) que êles já sabiam isso de antemão?**
> Could they know that beforehand?

§481. **Question requesting agreement.** As in other languages, a speaker may, instead of asking a question, make a statement, followed by an expression asking for confirmation of its accuracy. This form in BF is **não é,** in rapid speech pronounced **né.**

> **Você vai tomar o avião, não é?**
> You are going to take the plane, aren't you?

INTERJECTIONS AND EXCLAMATORY EXPRESSIONS

§482. Use of exclamations. The Portuguese language is particularly rich in interjections and has a strong tendency to use a fragment of a sentence as an exclamation, instead of a complete sentence. Naturally, the more colloquial levels of speech are the richest in exclamations.

§483. The interjections. There are a considerable number of interjections which serve no other purpose and are not used as words except in exclamations. The following list is by no means complete, but will give an idea of the richness of the vocabulary of interjections.

Ah, oh, olá, ué (*also* **uê**), **zás, pum, ói** (*also* **ôi**), **uh, ai, ui, uf, ó, psiu, ora, eh, ih, puxa, arre, hein, eia, eita** (*also* **êta**), **oba, upa, hei.**

§484. Special phonetic features. Interjections in any language are likely to show special phonetic features, including sounds not a part of the regular phonemic system of the language.

a. The glottal stop consonant, which does not occur in Portuguese elsewhere, even to separate long series of vowels, is frequently heard in interjections. It may occur at the beginning of an interjection which begins with a vowel.

      Eh! eh!   **Ih!**   **Uf!**

It may occur at the end, if the interjection ends in a vowel.

      Ué!   **Ih!**

It may separate two or more interjections used one after the other.

      Oh! oh!

b. Pronunciation of **psiu**. This word has two unusual phonetic features. First, the consonant group at the beginning is never broken up by the intrusion of a vowel, as happens habitually in other words. Cf. **p(i)sicologia**. Second, the vowels are unvoiced.

c. **hein**. This word is pronounced with a nasalized version of the diphthong **éi**. In other situations, in the pronunciation of Rio, we always find only the close e (**ê**) nasalized, although in some regions the open vowel is frequent.

§485. Use of **ai**. In addition to its more common use as an inter-jection of pain, physical or mental, **ai** may express pity for a specific person. It is followed by **de** before the noun or pronoun which iden-tifies the person.

Ai de mim.
Poor me!

§486. Interrogatives used in exclamations. The interrogative pro-nouns and adjectives are also used as exclamations, or to introduce an exclamatory phrase or sentence. Since each has certain peculiari-ties, they are discussed individually below.

a. **Que**. When used as a pronoun, this word may occur alone as an exclamation, or it may occur at the end of a longer expression. In either case, it becomes **quê** if strongly stressed.

Êle é quê!?
He is a what?

Que may be used adverbially, modifying an adverb or an adjective.

Que bonita ela é!
How pretty she is!
Que bem o homem falou!
How well the man spoke!

When used with a noun modified by an adjective, the adjective may precede or follow, as in other cases. Formerly, when the adjec-tive followed, the use of **mais** or **tão** was frequent before it. It is still sometimes met with in literature but is very rare in BF.

Que môça bonita!
What a pretty girl!
Que coisa chata, concurso de beleza sem mulata. —Cançao de Jack-son do Pandeiro.
What a boring thing, a beauty contest without a mulatto girl!

When **que** modifies the object of the verb or the predicate nomina-tive, it precedes with its noun or adjective, followed by the subject, then the verb.

Que barulho êle fêz!
What a noise he made!
Que grande você está!
How big you have gotten!
Que cara o João mostrou!
What a face John revealed!

However, the subject sometimes follows the verb, especially if it is longer.

Que caras estão as casas!
How expensive houses are!

b. **O que** may be used instead of **que** as a pronoun and is much the more usual of the two. If it is used alone, or at the end of the exclamation, it becomes **o quê**.

Você é feio. —O quê?
You are ugly. What?
Você vai fazer o quê?
You are going to do what?

c. **Qual** as an exclamation indicates sharp disagreement with a statement made by another. It may be further strengthened by the addition of **o quê**.

Você é responsável desta situação. —Qual! or **Qual o quê!**
You are responsible for this situation. What?

d. **Como.** Used alone, **como** may indicate that the statement is difficult to accept or that it is considered improper or even insulting. It may also introduce an exclamatory sentence. In this case, it is followed by normal declarative order.

Isso é mentira! —Como?
That's a lie! What?
Como ela é bonita!
How pretty she is!
Como eu queria ir com você!
How I would like to go with you!

The subject may be placed after the verb in a few cases difficult to define. A longer subject tends to follow.

Como é bonita aquela môça!
How pretty that girl is!
Como fazem barulho êsses moleques.
How those kids do make noise!

e. **Quanto.** As an exclamatory word, **quanto** may be an adverb, an adjective, or a pronoun. As an adjective, it is usually singular, as a pronoun, more often plural.

Quanta mulher bonita a gente vê por aqui!
　How many pretty women one sees around here!
Quantos existem que não têm meta na vida!
　How many exist who have no goal in life!
Quanto me surpreende essa notícia!
　How this piece of news surprises me!

§487. Exclamations with other words. Almost any appropriate word or phrase may be used as an exclamation. Some of these are not used as such in other languages. Words frequently used as exclamations include:

a. The various personages of Christian religion. Those referring to God, the Virgin, etc., are considered perfectly normal and are not offensive.

Meu Deus do céu!
Minha Nossa Senhora!
Ai, Jesus!

However, diabo! is considered quite strong and somewhat improper.

b. Other special words and expressions include:

Puxa!	expressing astonishment.
Pudera!	expressing the fact that the situation is not at all astonishing.
Não diga!	indicating surprise at a statement heard.
Essa é boa!	indicating disbelief, or a reaction that the statement is absurd.
Mentira!	indicating, not that the statement is a lie, but that it is difficult to accept at once.
Ora essa!	indicating that the statement is absurd.
Ora bolas!	indicating that the speaker is furious.
Papagaio!	indicating exultation.

c. Almost any expression may be introduced by an interjection and treated as an exclamation.

Oh mulher cruel!
　Oh, cruel woman!
Êta riacho grande!
　Wow, what a big creek!
Ah homem tratante!
　You double-crosser!
Ih coisa chata!
　What a boring thing!

Oh gente sem educação!
    What bad-mannered people!

d. When the subject is a demonstrative pronoun. Both the introductory word and the verb (usually **ser**) may be omitted. The subject is placed at the end of the sentence.

Bela potranca, aquela.
    That's a pretty filly.
Gordo, êsse menino.
    That's a fat boy.

The subject may be replaced by a demonstrative adverb.

Negócio sujo, aí.
    That's a dirty business.

CONJUNCTIONS

§488. The co-ordinating conjunctions. The conjunctions **e** and **ou** require no explanation. For **nem**, see negation, §459. The principal one remaining is **mas**.

This conjunction (pronounced in Brazil in the etymologically correct form **mais**, in Rio sometimes **mães**) expresses either a contrast or an exception. It may be used in all cases, including following a negative statement, before a contrasting affirmative one, in which **senão** was formerly used.

> **Êle estava cansado, mas trabalhou sempre até a hora de parar.**
> He was tired, but kept on working until quitting time.
> **Não quero água, mas cerveja.**
> I don't want water, but beer.

When **mas** indicates an exception to the rule, it may be replaced by either of the two more emphatic words **todavia** and **porém**.

> **Esta é a regra, mas (porém, todavia) há várias exceções.**
> This is the rule, but (however) there are several exceptions.

§489. The subordinating conjunction **que**. This is the most universal of the subordinating conjunctions. It is identical in form with the relative pronoun **que**. It is used:

a. To form compound conjunctions. Added to various types of words and phrases, **que** transforms them into compound conjunctions. These conjunctions are very numerous and for the most part are treated elsewhere, under the uses of the subjunctive, §237 ff.

> **Logo que, de modo que, sem que, no caso que, dado que, etc.**
> As soon as, so that, without, in case, granted that, etc.

b. After a word requiring a preposition. When a verb, adjective, or noun requires a preposition before a word or expression which follows, **que** must be added if the following expression contains a finite verb.

Êle se opõe a que eu ganhe o pôsto.
He opposes my getting the position.
Obrigaram os jogadores a que deixassem de fumar.
They obliged the players to stop smoking.

Prepositions other than **a** may be, and usually are, omitted before **que**.

Estou seguro (de) que é êle.
I am sure that it is he.
Êle consentiu (em) que eu ficasse.
He consented to my remaining.
Eu gostaria (de) que você me acompanhasse.
I would like for you to accompany me.
Êle saiu antes que eu pudesse falar com êle.
He left before I could speak to him.

c. To introduce a noun clause. The clause may be used as subject or object of the verb. Indirect statement is included.

Creio que é êle.
I believe it is he.
Parece que vai chover.
It seems that it is going to rain.
É provável que nos tenham visto.
It is likely that they have seen us.
Êle disse que ia conosco.
He said that he was going with us.

d. Before **sim** and **não**. When **sim** and **não** are used instead of a clause, after such verbs as **dizer, pensar, crer, achar, acreditar, esperar, parecer**, they are preceded by **que**.

Êle disse que sim.
He said so.
Eu acho que não.
I think not.
Esperamos que sim.
We hope so.

e. To introduce an optative subjunctive. Such constructions assume some such verb as **querer** or **mandar**. **Que** is often omitted and may always be. It is used mostly when the expression is a reply to another person.

Que é que o João vai fazer? —Que fique aqui.
What is John going to do? Let him stay here.

f. To introduce an indicative statement. These statements are usually short and exclamatory.

Socorro! Que me batem!
Help! They are beating me!

g. As a weaker synonym of **porque**.

Deixa isso, que eu faço.
Leave that; I'll do it.
Não fala nêle, que aí vem.
Don't speak of him. There he comes.

h. As an equivalent of **tal que**.

Êle ganhou uma surra, que teve que guardar cama.
He got a beating, so hard that he had to stay in bed.
A situação está que arde.
The situation is such that it is boiling.

§490. The subordinating conjunction **se**. This word is used:

a. To introduce a condition. See §237.

b. To introduce an alternative situation. In this case it is followed by the indicative.

Não sei se vou ou fico.
I don't know whether I'll go or stay.

c. To introduce an exclamatory clause. This use is not frequent. It usually expresses surprise, sometimes vague disagreement.

José está em casa. —Pois, se eu acabo de sair de lá, e não vi!
Joe is at home. Why, I just left there, and I didn't see him!

§491. **Segundo, conforme.** These may be used either as prepositions or as conjunctions. In the latter usage, the meaning is "in accordance with that which."

Segundo me dizem, as estradas lá não são boas.
According to what they tell me, the roads aren't good there.
Você deve fazer conforme fizerem os outros.
You should behave according as the others do.

§492. **Desde que, visto que, uma vez que, dado que, já que.** All of these allege the expression that follows as the reason for the statement of the main clause.

Desde que estamos aqui, vamos parar para ver a cidade.
Since we are here, let's stop to see the city.
Está boa até demais; já que está, deixa ficar. —Canção.
It's too good to be true; since it is, let it be.

§493. For other compound conjunctions, with the constructions which they introduce, see §240 ff.

COMPARISON OF ADJECTIVES AND ADVERBS

§494. The comparison of equality. This is usually made with **tanto . . . como**. The word **tanto** may be a pronoun, an adjective, or an adverb.

Êle tem tantos como eu.
  He has as many as I.
Êle viu tantas cidades como eu.
  He saw as many cities as I did.
Êle viajou tanto como eu.
  He traveled as much as I did.

a. Comparison in terms of an adjective or adverb. Before an adjective or adverb, **tanto** is shortened to **tão**. It may frequently be omitted entirely.

Ela é tão alta como eu.
  She is as tall as I.
O bicho escorreu tão rápido como um raio.
  The animal ran quick as a flash.
Êle é pobre como um cachorro.
  He is as poor as a dog.

Tão is also used before a noun in similar expressions.

Êle é tão homem como o outro.
  He is as much of a man as the other.

b. **Tanto . . . quanto**. This is a more literary expression which may be used instead of **tanto . . . como**. It is comparatively rare in BF.

Êle tem tanto quanto quer.
  He has as much as he wants.
Eu farei tanto quanto estiver ao meu alcance.
  I will do as much as may be in my power.
Quantas línguas falas, tantos homens vales.   **Lit**
  You are worth as many men as you speak languages.

c. Other expressions of comparison. The following also may express equality or near equality.

Êle apanhava que só cachorro.
He was beaten like a dog.
Ela é ruim que nem você.
She is as bad as you.
Homem tão bonito feito êle não existe.
Such a handsome man as he does not exist.

§495. The comparative degree of adjectives and adverbs.

a. Regular comparison. Regular comparison is made by placing **mais**, for the comparative of superiority, or **menos** for the comparison of inferiority, before the positive form.

Mais alto, mais cedo, menos feio, menos tarde.
Taller, earlier, less ugly, less late.

b. Irregular comparison. The following adjectives and abverbs have irregular forms of the comparison of superiority:

bom, bem	melhor
good, well	better
mau, mal	**pior**
bad, badly	worse
pequeno,	**menor**
little	little
pouco	**menos**
few, little	less
grande	**maior**
great, large	greater, larger
muito	**mais**
much	more

Pequeno may also be compared regularly.
Ruim may take either **pior** or **mais ruim**.
If the word **bem** modifies a participle, it is compared by placing **mais** before it, rather than changing to **melhor**.

A mulher mais bem vestida do grupo.
The best-dressed woman of the group.

The irregular comparatives are sometimes reinforced by a redundant **mais**, in substandard speech.

Em casa tenho outro mais melhor ainda.   Subst
At home I have another still better.

c. Extent of difference in comparison. The comparative form may be modified by various expressions which indicate the extent of difference. These include indefinite expressions such as:

Isto é um tanto melhor que aquilo.
This is a bit better than that.
Êle é bem mais velho.
He is quite a bit older.
É bastante mais frio.
It is quite a lot colder.
Êle é ainda mais feio que ela.
He is even uglier than she.

A definite extent may be expressed by nouns of measure, etc., with numbers.

Sou dois pés mais alto do que êle.
I am two feet taller than he.
Isso é cem vezes maior.
That is a hundred times bigger.
Êle é mais jovem que ela treze anos.
He is thirteen years younger than she.
Êle é treze anos mais jovem que ela.
He is thirteen years younger than she.

§496. Connective between the two terms of the comparative.

a. General connectives. In most cases, the comparative may be followed by **que** or **do que**, with no difference in meaning.

A lagoa é mais funda do que (or que) a poça.
The lake is deeper than the puddle.

b. When the second term is a verb. Only **do que** can be used.

É mais fundo do que o senhor se imagina.
It is deeper than you imagine.

c. After **mais** or **menos**. Either **que** or **do que** may be used, except when one of these is used alone, followed by a number. In this case, **de** is used.

Eu quero mais biscoitos; tenho menos que (or do que) êle.
I want more cookies; I have fewer than he.
Não quero menos de três.
I don't want less than three.

§497. Forms of the comparative superlative of adjectives. The superlative has the same form as the comparative, regular or irregular. It is distinguished from the comparative by the fact that it has the definite article.

O melhor, o mais alto, o menos confortável.
The best, the tallest, the least comfortable.

The irregular superlatives **máximo** and **mínimo** are sometimes used instead of **maior** and **menor** when the noun is otherwise modified.

Vou fazer o máximo esfôrço possível.
I am going to make the greatest possible effort.

a. Use of the definite article. The article precedes the noun, whether or not the adjective precedes. It is not repeated after the noun, if the adjective follows.

É o melhor carro fabricado no Brasil.
It is the best car made in Brazil.
Êle é o homem mais feio que conheço.
He is the ugliest man I know.

Even though only two individuals are being compared, the article is used.

Décio é o mais alto dos dois.
Decio is the taller of the two.

When the adjective is used as a predicate nominative, the article is used to distinguish which individual is concerned; it may be omitted if only the quality is indicated.

Os quatro são fortes, mas João é mais alto. (*Or* o mais alto.)
The four of them are strong, but John is tallest. (the tallest.)

b. Use of the possessive adjective. The possessive adjective may take the place of the article with the superlative. Of course, the article may be used or omitted with the possessive.

Êle é meu amigo mais íntimo.
He is my most intimate friend.

c. Use of the demonstratives. These may be used instead of the article but do not clarify the difference between the comparative and the superlative.

Vamos alugar êste apartamento mais bonito. (=Mais bonito de todos *or* mais bonito que aquêle.)
Let's rent this prettier (or prettiest) apartment.

498. The comparative superlative of adverbs.

a. The form. The superlative is not generally distinguished from the comparative.

b. Use of the definite article. It is not used in most cases with the superlative of adverbs. But when the superlative is followed by an expression which defines, or otherwise describes, the group to which it is compared, the article is used.

De todos os rapazes, Roberto nada melhor.
Of all the boys, Robert swims best.
Êle se levanta o mais tarde de todos.
He gets up latest of all.
Levanta mais tarde que todos.
He gets up later than any others.
Vem o mais cedo que puder.
Come the earliest you can.

c. Comparison of adverbial phrases. **Mais** may be placed before an entire phrase, if it is felt as adverbial.

O balão ia embora, levado cada vez mais para cima.
The balloon was going away, carried ever more upward.
Procura conhecê-lo mais de perto.
Try to know him more intimately.
A casa fica mais para cá.
The house is farther in this direction.
Anda mais devagar.
Walk more slowly.

But if the phrase is felt as based on a noun with independent meaning, **mais** is placed before the noun.

Temos que agir com mais vagar.
We have to act with more deliberation.

§499. The absolute superlative. This form indicates a very large degree of a quality, without directly comparing it to those of other individuals.

a. The regular forms. It is formed regularly by the addition of the suffix **-íssimo** to the stem of an adjective or of a simple adverb. For the adverbs in **-mente**, the superlative suffix is added to the adjective stem, with the adverb suffix following.

Grandíssimo, cedíssimo, rapidìssimamente.
Extremely large, very early, very rapidly.

b. Latinized forms. A considerable number of adjectives of various types have superlatives derived directly from their Latin forms. Most of these are learned borrowings and are used only by some writers. BF tends to create regular superlative forms from these adjectives. Only a few adjectives revert to their Latin forms before the superlative ending in BF, the most important group being those which end in **-vel** in Portuguese.

Notável—notabilíssimo; provável—probabilíssimo; simples—simplicíssimo; antigo—antiqüíssimo.
Notable—extremely notable; probable—most probable; simple—very simple; ancient—very ancient.

Most of the others have been regularized in BF.

Difícil—dificilíssimo; nobre—nobríssimo.
Difficult—very difficult; noble—most noble.

But the Latin form in **-érrimo** has struck the popular fancy, perhaps because of its very absurdity, and in colloquial speech it is often applied to words whose origins do not conform to this pattern. The intention of the speaker is often humorous.

A sogra ficou bravérrima.   Subst
The mother-in-law got extremely furious.

c. Superlatives taken from Latin irregular forms. A few irregular absolute superlatives taken directly from Latin irregular forms are in common use.

Bom.	**Êste café é ótimo. (*In* Minas Gerais, boníssimo.)**
	This coffee is excellent.
Mau.	**Seu gôsto é péssimo.**
	Your taste is very bad.
Grande.	**Os lucros foram máximos.**
	The profits were extremely large.
Pequeno.	**Trabalhou com resultados mínimos.**
	He worked with very small results.

In practice, **lindo** is used as an absolute superlative of **bonito**.

d. Superlative formed with adverbs. An equivalent to the absolute superlative can be formed by placing any one of several adverbs before the adjective or adverb.

Êle está livre e muito livre.
He is free and quite free.
Isto é terrìvelmente doce.
This is terribly sweet.
Esta carne é para lá de boa.
This meat is more than good.

e. Superlative by mode of pronouncing. An intensive form of the adjective, sometimes also of the adverb, which is similar in effect to the absolute superlative, is produced by prolonging the stressed vowel of the positive form and giving the word a special intonation.

O Buarque tem um carro novo gra-a-ande.
Buarque has an enormous new car.
Você é rui-im.
You are very bad.

§500. Prepositions following the superlative. To connect the superlative to the group with which it is compared, the preposition **de** is used.

Êste é o maior do mundo.
This is the largest in the world.
Dos males o menor.
[Let's take] the least of the evils.

De may be replaced by **entre**, although it is not frequent in BF.

Êle é o mais sábio entre os estadistas de hoje.   SLit
He is the most learned among today's statesmen.

In comparisons with all past time, one may use **jamais**, or **já**.

É o maior programa de obras jamais visto.
It is the greatest program of public works ever seen.

§501. Comparison of nouns. As certain nouns can be used as predicate nominatives or as appositives, in the character of a modifier of a noun or pronoun, they can be compared also.

O Roberto é mais velho do que êle, mas é mais criança.
Robert is older than he, but he is more of a child.
Paulo, mais homem que o outro, não tomou susto.
Paul, more manly than the other, did not take fright.
Ela é mulher, e muito mulher.
She is a woman, and every bit a woman.

§502. Excessive degree. To express an excessive degree of an adjective or adverb, the usual construction is to place **demais** after it.

Êste carro é grande demais.
This car is too big.
Meia-noite é tarde demais.
Midnight is too late.

If the situation is clear from context, **muito** may be used with the same effect.

Êste é muito grande para caber na mala.
This is too big to go into the suitcase.

Some other expressions are also used.

A fita é por demais longa.   **SLit**
The film is too long.

§503. Connective after excessive degree. Following **demais** or an equivalent, the preposition **para** is used before the purpose for which it is excessive, or the person who finds it excessive.

Isto é pesado demais para mim.
This is too heavy for me.
Êste é muito grande para caber na mala.
This one is too big to go into the suitcase.

EXPRESSIONS OF TIME

§504. The hour. Time in the sense of "hour of the day" is regularly **hora**, not only in telling time by the clock, but in other and more vague expressions as well. The time of day is given with numbers up to twenty-four in all official uses—train schedules, television programs, etc., but not in ordinary conversation.

a. Inquiring time of day. The plural is used in questions.

Que horas são?
   What time is it?
A que horas você chega?
   At what time will you arrive?
Já deram as horas?
   Has the clock struck?

b. Giving the time. One uses the verb **ser**, followed by a cardinal number in the feminine form, but without an article. The verb is singular only when followed by **uma**.

São duas (horas).
   It is two (o'clock).
É uma.
   It is one.

Minutes beyond the hour are added.

São três e vinte.
   It is three twenty.
É uma e quinze.
   It is one fifteen.

The half-hour is expressed by **meia**, an adjective agreeing with **hora**.

São quatro e meia.
   It is four thirty.

The quarters can be expressed either by minutes or as **quarto**, a masculine noun.

São cinco e um quarto.
It is a quarter after five.
São cinco e quinze.
It is five fifteen.

Minutes before the hour are expressed in various ways.

São dez menos cinco.
It is five to ten.
Faltam cinco para as dez.
It is five to ten.
São quinze para as dez.
It is fifteen to ten.
Falta um quarto para as dez.
It is a quarter to ten.

Outside of schedules, etc, the number twelve is seldom used. One says **meio-dia** and **meia-noite**.

c. Assigning the time. The time is assigned by using the preposition **a**, combined with the feminine form of the definite article.

Isso aconteceu à uma.
This happened at one.
Vamos às duas.
We are going at two.
Às três e vinte.
At three twenty.
Às quatro e meia.
At four thirty.
Às cinco e um quarto.
At five fifteen.
Às dez menos cinco.
At five minutes to ten.
Às cinco para as dez.
At five minutes to ten.
Ao meio-dia e meia.
At twelve thirty P.M.
À meia-noite.
At midnight.

d. To approximate the time. One may say:

Êle deve estar aqui lá pelas duas horas.
He should be here around two.
Serão três horas já.
It must be three o'clock already.

e. Other uses of **hora**. This word is used in numerous other expressions in which no definite hour by the clock is mentioned.

> **Está na hora de sair.**
> It is time to leave.
> **Nós chegamos encima da hora, mas o trem veio fora de hora.**
> We arrived on the hour, but the train came off schedule.
> **Isso veio na hora H (agá).**
> That came in the nick of time.
> **O avião sai na hora certa?**
> Does the plan leave exactly on time?
> **São horas de comer.**
> It is time to eat.
> **Os trens chegam de hora em hora nas meias horas.**
> The trains arrive every hour on the half hours.
> **De hora em hora Deus melhora.**
> From one hour to another God betters things.

f. Striking the hour. The normal verb used is **dar**, sometimes **bater**. The hour struck is considered to be the subject, unless "clock" is mentioned, and the verb agrees wtih the number of the hour struck. With the number, either the definite article precedes or the word **hora** follows.

> **Estão dando as quatro.**
> Four o'clock is striking.
> **A Gata Borralheira devia sair quando desse meia-noite.**
> Cinderella was to leave when it struck midnight.
> **Vão bater quatro horas agora.**
> It is going to strike four now.
> **O relógio bateu cinco horas.**
> The clock struck five o'clock.

Referring to the dial, rather than the sound, one can say:

> **O relógio está marcando as quatro e meia.**
> The clock is pointing to four thirty.

§505. The parts of the day. The day is divided into four parts—**manhã**, **tarde**, **noite**, and **madrugada**, each of which may regard as six hours. **Madrugada** is the least used of the four, and usually calls attention to either a late hour at night or an unusually early hour in the morning. In conversation, time of day is given in terms of twelve hours, and the part of the day follows to explain it.

São dez horas da noite.
It is ten o'clock at night.
Às nove da manhã.
At nine A.M.
Êle chegou só às três e meia da madrugada.
He didn't arrive until three thirty in the morning.
Às quinze para as quatro da tarde.
At a quarter to four in the afternoon.

To specify the part of a day, a variety of expressions exist, of which the most used is the following:

Hoje de tarde.
This afternoon.
Sábado de noite.
Saturday night.
Ante-ontem de madrugada.
Day before yesterday in the morning.
Amanhã de manhã.
Tomorrow morning.

One can use **à**, but with **tarde** and **noite** only.

Hoje à tarde.
This afternoon.
Sexta-feira à noite.
Friday night.

The following expressions mean either "sometime during" or "all during":

Hoje pela tarde vamos jogar.
This afternoon we are going to play.
Ontem pela noite choveu.
It rained last night during the night.
Pela tarde de hoje vão remar na Lagoa.
Sometime this afternoon they are going to row on the Lagoon.
Na manhã de hoje.   Rare
This morning.
Na parte da tarde fomos nadar.
During the afternoon we went swimming.
Durante a noite de ontem choveu.
During the night last night it rained.
Tôdas as noites as mulheres jogavam cartas.
Every night the women played cards.

These expressions may identify only the part of the day, without referring to the day itself.

Êle acordou bem de manhãzinha.
    He woke up quite early in the morning.
De tarde fui dar minha lição.
    In the afternoon I went to teach.
De noite faz um frio danado.
    At night it gets awfully cold.
À noite as ruas estão desertas.
    At night the streets are deserted.
Gostamos de passear pela manhã.
    We like to stroll during the morning.
Pela côr da lua, podia dizer se na manhã seguinte o mar era manso
    ou bravo.
    By the color of the moon, he could tell whether the sea would
    be calm or rough on the following morning.
Em uma tarde treinava e na outra descansava.
    On one afternoon he trained and on the next he rested.

§506. The day. There are various ways of counting the days—in relation to the present day (today), as days of the week, as days of the month, etc.

a. With relation to the present. The days may be counted back or forward from today. The words used are: trasanteontem, anteontem, ontem, hoje, manhã, depois de amanhã. Before trasanteontem, one says quatro dias atrás, faz quatro dias, or há quatro dias. After depois de amanhã, one says de aqui a três dias.

The word hoje includes the entire period of twenty-four hours. It is not necessary to express "tonight" separately, if the meaning is clear.

Vamos ao teatro hoje às nove.
    We are going to the theater tonight at nine.
Hoje à noite (or hoje de noite) vamos à cidade.
    Tonight we are going downtown.
Vamos ao cinema esta noite.
    Let's go to the movies tonight.

For the present day in general, "nowadays," we may say:

Hoje em dia.
    Nowadays.
No dia de hoje.
    Today (nowadays).
Na atualidade.
    At the present time.

b. The days of the week. Of the days of the week, **domingo** and **sábado** are masculine. The others are femine compound nouns which form their plurals by adding **s** to both parts. The second part is very often omitted.

> **Hoje é sexta.**
> Today is Friday.
> **Temos aula segundas, quartas e sextas.**
> We have classes Mondays, Wednesdays, and Fridays.

To identify the day on which something happens, we may use **em** and the definite article, or omit both.

> **Eu fui lá domingo.**
> I went there Sunday.
> **Êle vai falar na sexta.**
> He is going to speak on Friday.

If the day is modified by an adjective, both preposition and article are used. However, the expressions **que vem, vindouro, passado** may be used without either preposition or article.

> **Vou lá (no) sábado vindouro.**
> I am going there next Saturday.
> **Ela vai casar (no) domingo que vem.**
> She is going to get married next Sunday.
> **Isso aconteceu (no) sábado passado.**
> That happened last Saturday.
> **Êle vem no último domingo do mês.**
> He is coming on the last Sunday of the month.

With the indefinite article, **em** is usual, but occasionally omitted.

> **Isso aconteceu num sábado.**
> That happened one Saturday.
> **Vamos à churrascaria numa quinta-feira.**
> We are going to the barbecue place on a Thursday.

In the plural, referring to habitual events on those days, the most usual practice is to use **aos** with the masculine days, **nas** with the feminine ones. However, the reverse is also acceptable.

> **Vamos à igreja aos domingos. (***Or*** nos domingos).**
> We go to church on Sundays.
> **Temos aulas nas têrças e quintas. (***Or*** às têrças e quintas.)**
> We have classes on Tuesdays and Thursdays.

In many expressions, the article is optional.

Até (o) domingo.
Until Sunday.
O programa para (o) sábado.
The program for Saturday.

In others, it is practically always omitted.

Não choveu antes de quarta-feira.
It did not rain before Wednesday.
Segunda vem depois de domingo.
Monday comes after Sunday.
O jôgo de sábado último.
Last Saturday's game.

c. The days of the month.

One inquires the day of the month by asking:

Qual é a data de hoje?
What is the date of today?
Que dia do mês é hoje?
What day of the month is today?

In answer, cardinal numbers are used, except for first.

Hoje é o primeiro.
Today is the first.
Hoje é o dia primeiro.
Today is the first.
Amanhã será (o) dia dois.
Tomorrow will be the second.
Foi sábado, três de junho, de 1966.
It was Saturday, June 3, 1966.

d. For identifying the date on which something happens, there are three constructions. The first is used almost always in BF.

Vamos ter eleições no dia cinco de novembro.
We are going to have an election on the fifth of November.
Em cinco de novembro, a estrada foi aberta.
On the fifth of November, the road was opened.
A três de julho haverá um queima em "A Exposição."
On the third of July there will be a sale at "The Exposition."
Eu te encontro lá no dia onze.
I'll meet you there on the eleventh.

e. For locating a date approximately during the month or year, the following expressions may be used:

Em fins do mês corrente.
Toward the end of this month.
Em meados de março.
About the middle of March.
Em princípios de janeiro.
In the first part of January.
Em fins do ano vindouro.
Toward the end of next year.

The preposition **a** may be substituted for **em** in these expressions.

A meados de novembro.
Toward the middle of November.

For locating an event within the month, **em** only is used.

Estivemos em Iguassu em abril.
We were at Iguassu in April.
Isso foi no mês de outubro.
That was in the month of October.
Tudo isto aconteceu em 1930 (mil novecentos e trinta).
All this happened in 1930.

When the word **mês** is not accompanied by the name of the month, em may be used or omitted.

Estivemos lá êste (*or* neste) mês.
We were there this month.

§507.   The seasons. With the names of the seasons, the preposition em and the article are used. If the name of the season is modified, the preposition may be omitted.

Vamos lá êste (*or* neste) verão.
We are going there this summer.
Nevou muito o (no) inverno passado.
It snowed a lot last winter.
Faz calor aqui no verão.
It is hot here in summer.
As flores brotam na primavera.
The flowers come forth in the spring.

§508.   General expressions of time.

a. Extent of time. The prepositions **durante** and **por** may be used, or no preposition at all.

Eu estive no Brasil oito meses.
I was in Brazil eight months.

A exposição fica aberta durante oito dias.
The show is open for eight days.
Seu irmão fica por lá durante um ano.
Your brother will remain there for a year.
Por muito tempo teremos que viver com esta situação.
For a long time we will have to live with this situation.

In this last example, the preposition is required because of the position in the sentence of the time expression. The preposition may be omitted if the expression is placed later in the sentence.

Teremos que viver muito tempo com esta situação.
We will have to live a long time with this situation.

b. Terminal point in time. To express the final point in time by which something is to be done, the preposition **até** is used.

O tintureiro diz que entrega a roupa até quarta.
The cleaner says that he will deliver the clothes by Wednesday.
Preciso entregar êste livro até o fim do ano.
I must hand in this book by the end of the year.

c. Future periods of time. To express a future division of time, the following expressions are used:

O mês vindouro.
Next month.
O próximo mês.
Next (the next) month.
O mês próximo vindouro.
Next month.
O mês que vem.
The coming month.
Vou lá para o ano. (=No ano que vem.)
I am going there next year.
Vamos à Europa, sem ser neste ano, no outro. (=De aqui a dois anos.)
We are going to Europe year after next.

d. Future time without expressed divisions.

De aqui a três meses.
Three months from now.
De hoje em diante.
From today on.
De aqui em diante.
From now on.
De aqui por diante.
From now on.

e. Time following any period.

No ano seguinte, êle fêz um sucesso.
In the following year, he was a success.
No próximo mês, eu ia viajar.
In the following month I was going to travel.
Saimos no dia imediato ao aniversário dêle.
We left on the day after his birthday.

f. Past divisions of time.

A semana passada.
Last week.
O mês próximo passado.
Last week.
No último mês.
In the last month. (During the past month.)
O ano próximo findo.
The year just past.

g. A point in past time, as measured from the present. There are three ways—the verb **fazer**, used impersonally; the verb **haver**, used impersonally; and the adverb **atrás**. The verbs are used in the present tense. The word **há**, in spite of its verbal origin, is unstressed and indistinguishable from the preposition **a**. The adverb **atrás** follows the expression of time.

Faz dois anos que êle aceitou o emprego.
He accepted the job two years ago.
Êle comprou um carro faz um mês.
He bought a car, a month ago.
Isso aconteceu já faz tempo.
That happened some time ago.
Há dois anos que a ponte caiu.
The bridge fell down two years ago.
Êle passou aqui em casa há uma semana.
He came by our house a week ago.
Chegou aqui há muito tempo.
He arrived here a long time ago.
Êle começou a exercer a profissão dois anos atrás.
He began to practice his profession two years ago.
Dois dias atrás os preços subiram.
Two days ago prices went up.

h. Length of time gone by up to the present. Several expressions are used to mark the passage of time. The verbs are in the present, if the situation described is still true.

Faz	**Faz um ano que êle está aqui.**
	He has been here for a year.
	Êle está trabalhando faz um mês.
	He has been working for a month.
Há	**Há tempos que a chuva não pára.**
	The rain has not stopped for quite a while.
	Moro nesta cidade há muitos anos.
	I have lived in this city for many years.
Desde	**Sou funcionário público desde o ano passado.**
	I have been a civil servant since last year.
Others	**Esta peça está no palco de uns dias para cá.**
	This play has been on the stage for several days.

Note verbs in the preterite, when the situation has passed.

De então a hoje, ninguém mais viu êste mendigo.
From then up to now, no one has seen this beggar again.
Daí em diante, sempre foi um menino comportado.
From then on, he has always been a well-behaved boy.

i. Length of time gone by up to the past. The same expressions may be used, but all verbs are in the imperfect (or in the pluperfect, if the situation had ceased to be true).

Fazia um ano que êle estava aqui.
He had been here for a year.
Eu morava nesta cidade havia muitos anos.
I had been living in this city for many years.
Eu era funcionário público desde o ano anterior.
I had been a civil servant since the preceding year.
Esta peça estava no palco de uns dias para lá.
This play had been on the stage for several days.
Havia um ano que êle tinha se demitido.
He had resigned a year before.

j. To express alternation of days, etc. One may say:

Temos aula dia sim, dia não.
We have classes every other day.
Êle passa o verão na França, ano sim, ano não.
He spends the summer in France every other year.
Or
Vou lá de dois em dois dias.
I go there every other day.

Êle vai à igreja de oito em oito dias.
He goes to church at weekly intervals.

Irregular periods:

De vez em quando oferecemos uma festa.
From time to time we give a party.
De tempos a tempos êle se lembra de nós. (*Also* de tempos em tempos.)
From time to time he remembers us.

k. Distribution within a period.

Comemos três vezes por dia.
We eat three times a day.
Pagam uma vez por mês.
They pay once a month.

§509. The weather. In describing the weather, two constructions may be used.

a. The verb **estar** may be used, followed by an adjective. The verb is not used in the progressive form.

Hoje o tempo está quente.
Today the weather is hot.
Está frio para o verão.
It is cold for summertime.

By analogy with the use with **frio**, estar is sometimes used with **calor**. The usage is neither recent nor substandard, having been used by Machado de Assis.

Hoje está calor.
Today it is hot.

b. The verb **fazer** is used impersonally, with a noun object. It does not have an expressed subject. If one is speaking of the weather at a given moment, the progressive form is used. The simple form of **fazer** refers to the usual state of the weather.

Hoje está fazendo calor.
Today it is hot.
Que tempo faz no Rio no verão?
How is the weather in Rio in summer?
Ontem fêz um tempo ótimo.
Yesterday the weather was excellent.

§510. Use of **tempo**. Other than in its use with the meaning "weather," **tempo** refers to time in a quantitative sense.

> **Estou aqui há muito tempo.**
> I have been here a long time.
> **Não podemos ir; não dá mais tempo.**
> We can't go; there isn't enough time left.
> **Isso foi no tempo do imperador.**
> That was in the time of the emperor.

§511. Age. This is expressed in Portuguese by using the verb **ter**, and the number of years, months, etc., as the object of it. In a question, one may use the word **idade**, or inquire the number of years. **Idade** is also used along with the number, when one wishes.

> **Quantos anos você tem? —Tenho quarenta.**
> How old are you? Forty.
> **Que idade você tem? —Tenho quarenta anos.**
> How old are you? I am forty years old.
> **Está com quarenta anos de idade.**
> He is forty years old.
> **Aos vinte anos de idade, ela se casou.**
> At twenty, she got married.
> **Um homem fica maior de idade aos vinte e um.**
> A man comes of age at twenty-one.

a. The completion of a number of years of age is expressed with **fazer**.

> **Eu vou fazer quarenta e um anos no mês que vem.**
> I will be forty-one next month.
> **Ela fêz anos ontem, que foi o aniversário dela.**
> She had a birthday yesterday.

b. **Aniversário** refers specifically to birthday. Other types of anniversary are explained explicitly.

> **O nosso aniversário de casamento é no dia 21 de agosto.**
> Our wedding anniversary is the twenty-first of August.

c. **Aos** followed by a number refers specifically to the age of a person.

> **Êle entrou na escola aos treze.**
> He entered the school at thirteen.

CARDINAL POINTS AND DIRECTIONS

§512. The points of the compass. The four cardinal points are: **norte, sul, este** (more often, **leste**), and **oeste**. Between them are found **nordeste, noroeste, sudeste** or **sueste** (and popularly **suleste**), **sudoeste** (and popularly **suloeste**).

§513. Use of the definite article. The words take the masculine definite article, except that **leste** and **oeste** do not do so after the preposition **a**, and often omit it after **para**.

> **Vamos rumo a oeste.**
>   Let's go to the west.
> **A leste de São Paulo.**
>   East of São Paulo.
> **Essa cidade fica mais para oeste.**
>   That city is farther west.
> **Rumo ao norte.**
>   Northward.
> **Ao sul do Paraíba.**
>   South of the Paraiba.
> **Eu vou para o norte.**
>   I am going to the North.

§514. Location with use of the directions. Location in relation to another place is expressed by the preposition **a** before the word of direction, and **de** after it.

> **Mato Grosso fica a oeste de São Paulo.**
>   Mato Grosso is west of São Paulo.
> **Há pouca gente ao norte do Amazonas.**
>   There are few people north of the Amazon.

§515. Use of the words of direction as adjectives. The four words which designate the cardinal points may be used as adjectives, but only in the singular and then to a limited extent.

> **Copacabana fica na Zona Sul.**
>   Copacabana is on the South Side.

Vitória é na costa leste do país.
Vitoria is on the east coast of the country.

a. In most cases we must use either the preposition before the word of direction, or the longer adjectives derived from Latin.

Rio Grande do Sul.
Rio Grande of the South.
América do Norte.
North America.
Os estados do Nordeste.
The northeastern states.
As populações meridionais.
The southern populations.
A costa ocidental.
The west coast.
As regiões orientais do estado.
The eastern regions of the state.
Os invernos setentrionais.
Northern winters.

b. Adjectives derived directly from the directions. A few adjectives exist formed from the Portuguese words for the directions. They are: **nortista, nordestino, sulista** (also **sulino** and **suleiro**). They are used mostly of persons, as nouns or adjectives, but may also be used of things.

§516. Other nouns of direction. As nouns, one sometimes uses other words instead of the more familiar cardinal points. However, they are mostly confined to literature, except when used to designate specific geographic areas.

For **oeste—ocidente, poente, ocaso.**
For **sul—meio-dia.**
For **este—oriente, nascente, levante.**

DIMINUTIVES AND AUGMENTATIVES

§517. Frequency of diminutives. The Brazilians are especially given to the use of diminutives. They are used by children more than by adults, but they are in constant use in the language of the latter also. In conversational speech they occur constantly, expressing many subtle shades of meaning. They are formed by the application of suffixes.

§518. Diminutive suffixes no longer freely applied. A large number of diminutive suffixes exist. However, most of these are now found incrusted in words already formed and are seldom applied to new words. Sometimes only a few words exist which are diminutives formed with a given suffix. In other cases, they are very numerous. These words form a part of the standard vocabulary, but the suffixes are not used with much freedom in new formations. The following are examples of several of these suffixes:

-ito	**palito, senhorita, bonito**
	toothpick, miss, pretty
-ola	**rapazola**
	lad
-acho	**riacho**
	creek
-ico	**Antonico**
	Tony
-eta	**banqueta, fiveleta, chaveta**
	bench, little buckle, light switch
-ebre	**casebre**
	hut
-ote	**meninote, velhote**
	little boy, little old man
-ejo	**lugarejo**
	hamlet
-ete	**diabrete**
	little demon
-ucho	**gorducho**
	fatty

344

These diminutives have in a great many cases become separate words, with meanings of their own. Often the meaning is suggestive of the diminutive but still refers to a different and easily distinguishable idea. Thus **bonito** no longer suggests a meaning similar to **bom**, but its own diminutive has a somewhat similar, although distinct, meaning; **lugarejo** is used as a diminutive of **lugar**, but only in one sense of the latter word; **riacho** is clearly a small example of **rio**, but is felt as a separate word.

§519. The suffix **-inho** (**-zinho**). The principal diminutive suffix which is applied freely today is **-inho**, with its variant form **-zinho**.

a. Choice between **-inho** and **-zinho**. The shorter form is used mostly when the root of the base word ends in an unstressed vowel. This final vowel drops before the suffix.

Livro	livrinho
Book	
Cesta	cestinha
Basket	
Doente	doentinho
Sick person	
Tudo	tudinho
Everything	

It is also used with words which end in **-s** or **-z**.

Lápis	làpisinho
Pencil	
Voz	vozinha
Voice	

The form **-zinho** is added to the entire word, and is used in other cases.

(1) When the base word ends in a diphthong, oral or nasal.

Mãe	mãezinha
Mother	
Boi	boizinho
Ox	

(2) When the base word ends in a stressed vowel, oral or nasal.

Irmã	irmãzinha
Sister	
Sabiá	sabiàzinho
Thrush	

(3) When the base word ends in -l. This sound tends to vocalize, moving toward -u. Thus the last syllable of such words often has a diphthong in current pronunciation.

Animal	**animalzinho**
Animal	
Papel	**papelzinho**
Paper	

(4) When the base word ends in -r, although some words are also made diminutives by adding the shorter form. Since most Brazilians do not pronounce the final -r, in effect, the word ends in a stressed vowel.

Devagar	**devagarinho, devagarzinho**
Slowly	
Par	**parzinho**
Pair	
Dor	**dorzinha**
Pain	
Pomar	**pomarinho, pomarzinho**
Orchard	

(5) Since this suffix is applied freely by all speakers to any word, at any time they wish, these rules are not always followed in practice. In many cases there is free variation between -**inho** and -**zinho**, or the latter is preferred where the former is to be expected.

Árvore	**àrvorezinha**
Tree	
Índio	**ìndiozinho**
Indian	

b. -**inho**, -**zinho** with plural words. These suffixes are applied to plural words in their plural forms, with loss of final -s.

Cestas	**cestinhas**
Baskets	
Livros	**livrinhos**
Books	
Irmãos	**irmãozinhos**
Brothers	
Cães	**cãezinhos**
Dogs	
Corações	**coraçõezinhos**
Hearts	

Animais   animaizinhos
 Animals

c. Retention of stressed vowel of the base word. Although open **o** and open **e** are not normally heard in unstressed syllables in the Portuguese of Rio, these vowels are retained in the base word when the diminutive suffix **-inho** is applied.

Copo (ó)   copinho (ò)
 Glass
Peça (é)   pecinha (è)
 Piece

§520. Use of the suffix **-inho** (**-zinho**).

a. With nouns. This diminutive suffix is applied most frequently to nouns. It refers primarily to size, but may often carry a connotation of affection as well. It is, of course, most frequent in the language of children, but is also used a great deal by adults.

Cachorrinho, gatinho, carrinho, burrinho, pauzinho, um bocadinho, uma porçãozinha, etc.
 Doggy (pup), kitten, little car, little donkey, little stick, a little bit, quite a little bit, etc.

b. With adjectives. It is also used quite freely with adjectives. However, the meaning of the adjective is sometimes intensified and at others diminished when the suffix is applied. Usually the intonation indicates the effect—a higher tone for intensification, a lower one for diminution. The meaning of the base word also affects the influence of the suffix.

É um bebêzinho pequenininho. (Muito pequeno.)
 He is a tiny little baby.
Êle tem uma casa grandinha. (Mais ou menos grande.)
 He has a sort of big house.
Vi um cachorro pretinho. (Completamente preto.)
 I saw a very black dog.
Ela está doentinha. (Um pouco doente.)
 She is a bit sick.
Êle é bonzinho. (É bom, mas não tem outras qualidades.)
 He is rather good.
A sopa está quentinha. (Bastante quente.)
 The soup is good and hot.
Estou prontinho. (Completamente sem dinheiro.)
 I am flat broke.

A brisa é fresquinha. (Agradàvelmente fresca *or* fresca demais.)
The breeze is coolish.

Among the adjectives used with the diminutive suffix are many
past participles.

Vi os dois num banco chegadinhos. (Perto um do outro.)
I saw the two of them on a bench sitting very close.
Estou fritinho da Silva. (Estou completamente arruinado.)   **Gir**
I am completely ruined.
O quarto está arrumadinho. (Bem arrumado.)
The room is neat as a pin.

c.   With adverbs. The diminutives of adverbs of time are used with
great frequency. With several other simple adverbs the form is not
unusual.

Levantei cedinho hoje.   (Muito cedo.)
I got up quite early this morning.
Vou agorinha. (Neste mesmo instante.)
I am going right now.
Até loguinho. (Até muito pouco.)
See you soon.
Êle chegou em casa todinho molhado.
He came home completely wet.
Vamos progredindo devagarzinho.
We are making progress rather slowly.

d.   With pronouns. With the exception of **tudinho**, the diminutives of pronouns are rare except for the language of children. They
sometimes use expressions such as the following:

Eu quero aquêlezinho.
I want that little one.
Estou brincando com elazinha.
I am playing with little her.

e.   With verb forms. These are quite rare and are heard almost
exclusively in the language of children.

Eu estava dormindinho.
I was sleeping tight.
Você estàzinho doente?
Are you a bit sick?

§521.   Use of the suffix -ela. This suffix occurs in a number of
words as a fixed diminutive form. E.g., **magricela, magrela.** It is also

used freely as the usual diminutive suffix with nouns which are identical in form with the feminine form of past participles.

Dá uma chegadela para cá.
Make a little move over this way.
Só tirei da garrafa uma escorropichadela.
In only got the last little drop out of the bottle.
Vai à porta e dá uma olhadela.
Go to the door and take a little look.

§522. Use of **-im**. This suffix is found in some standard words, where it is usually considered a variant of **-inho**. It is heard with considerable frequency applied to nouns, adjectives, and adverbs. It is possibly a shortening of **-inho** in rapid speech.

Eu tenho um gatim pretim.
I have a black kitten.
Você tem que levantar cedim.
You must get up very early.

§523. Frequency of augmentatives. The augmentatives are used almost as frequently as the diminutives in Brazil. There are nearly as many different suffixes, although most of them may not be applied freely to any word one wishes. In addition to the basic idea of increased size, they very often carry a pejorative connotation.

§524. Augmentative suffixes no longer freely applied. Of the large number of suffixes which exist, most are now heard only in certain words. The number of words which may take a given augmentative suffix is in some cases quite large, in others limited to a few.

-orra	**patorra, cabeçorra, beiçorra, manzorra** paw, head, lip, hand
-arra	**bocarra, noitarra** mouth, night
-arrão	**homenzarrão, santarrão, canzarrão, doidarrão, gatarrão** man, saint, dog, madman, cat
-rão	**asneirão, casarão, toleirão** stupidity, house, fool
-aço	**ricaço, gordaço, barcaça** rich man, fat man, barge
-gão	**rapagão, narigão** young man, nose

§525. Forms of the augmentative in -ão (-zão). This is the principal augmentative suffix which is freely applied to a wide variety of nouns.

a. Use of -zão. The use of -z- in these words follows the same rules as in the diminutives. See §519a. However, in many cases in which -zão would be required, this suffix is not used. Many nouns in final -z replace it with -gão.

Livro	livrão
Book	
Carro	carrão
Car	
Boi	boizão
Ox	
Macaco	macacão
Monkey	
Voz	vozeirão
Voice	
Rapaz	rapagão
Young man	

b. -ão (-zão) with plurals. In general, those nouns which modify the last syllable before final -s to form the plural do not take an augmentative form with this suffix. In other nouns, the plural of the augmentative is regular.

Carrão	carrões
Car	
Livrão	livrões
Book	

c. Retention of stressed vowels of base words. As in the diminutive, the stressed vowel of the base word is retained in the augmentative, including open o and e, which are not usually heard in unstressed syllables.

Berro (é)	berrão (è)
Bawl	
Cova (ó)	covão (ò)
Grave	

§526. Use of the suffix -ão (-zão).

a. With nouns. This suffix is applied quite freely to nouns, generally with some meaning of greater size. It very often also gives a connotation of dislike or criticism, either in addition to the other meaning, or instead of it. Occasionally this suffix may express admiration.

Application principally to size:

Esperei aqui um tempão.
I waited here a long time.
Êsse é um gatão.
That is a monstrous cat.

Implying both size and aversion:

A esposa dêle é uma mulherão.
His wife is an Amazon.

Implying largely or entirely aversion:

Êle é um burrão.
He is a great ass.
Aquêle cara é um grosseirão.
That guy is very rude.

Implying admiration:

Puxa! Você tem um carrão!
Whee! You have a huge (fine) car.

b. With adjectives. Augmentatives of adjectives are much less frequent than those of nouns. The suffix -ão is not used as often as -alhão. However, there are many instances of its use.

Esta lagoa tem cada peixe grandão!
This lake has lots of big fish.
Matamos um bacorim gordão.
We killed a very fat pig.

c. With other words. This and other augmentative suffixes are seldom used with words other than nouns and adjectives.

§527. Use of -alhão. The second most frequently used augmentative suffix is really a double suffix, -alhão. It is applied to some nouns, and with considerable freedom to adjectives.

Êsse teatro está levando um dramalhão.
That theater is presenting a melodrama.
O delegado de polícia é um bestalhão.
The police chief is a stupid fool.
Vai lavar as mãos! Não seja porcalhão.
Go wash your hands! Don't be a dirty pig.

Cuidado com o Gomes. Êle é um espertalhão.
Careful with Gomes. He is a clever rascal.
O quitandeiro é um português gordalhão.
The green-grocer is a very fat Portuguese.
No jardim soltam um cachorro grandalhão.
In the yard they turn loose an enormous dog.

§528. Augmentatives of feminine nouns and adjectives. All the suffixes which terminate in **-ão** have feminine forms in **-ona**. This form is applied to feminine nouns which refer to persons and to all feminine adjectives. However, most feminine nouns which do not refer to persons take the masculine form of the augmentative suffix and become masculine.

Ela é uma bobalhona, coitada.
She is a silly goose, poor thing.
A empregada é uma mocetona.
The maid is a big girl.
A filha é uma menina gordalhona.
The daughter is a very fat girl.
Na sala de trás havia um mesão.
In the back room there was a big table.
Êles moram num casarão antigo.
They live in a big old house.
O seringueiro carregava um facão.
The rubber-worker carried a big knife.

INDEX OF SUBJECTS

References are to item (§) not to page; principal reference in italics.

INDEX OF PORTUGUESE WORDS

References are to item (§) not to page; principal reference in italics.

CPSIA information can be obtained
at www.ICGtesting.com
Printed in the USA
LVHW032015130721
692588LV00002B/169

9 780826 512215